T0296740

THE NATURAL LANGUAGE FOR ARTIFICIAL INTELLIGENCE

Cognitive Data Science in Sustainable
Computing
THE NATURAL LANGUAGE
FOR ARTIFICIAL
INTELLIGENCE

Series Editor

ARUN KUMAR SANGAIAH

DIONEIA MOTTA MONTE-SERRAT
CARLO CATTANI

ELSEVIER

ACADEMIC PRESS

An imprint of Elsevier

Academic Press is an imprint of Elsevier
125 London Wall, London EC2Y 5AS, United Kingdom
525 B Street, Suite 1650, San Diego, CA 92101, United States
50 Hampshire Street, 5th Floor, Cambridge, MA 02139, United States
The Boulevard, Langford Lane, Kidlington, Oxford OX5 1GB, United Kingdom

Library of Congress Cataloging-in-Publication Data
A catalog record for this book is available from the Library of Congress

British Library Cataloguing-in-Publication Data
A catalogue record for this book is available from the British Library

ISBN 978-0-12-824118-9

For information on all Academic Press publications
visit our website at https://www.elsevier.com/books-and-journals

Publisher: Mara Conner
Acquisitions Editor: Sonnini R. Yura
Editorial Project Manager: Rafael G. Trombaco
Production Project Manager: Selvaraj Raviraj
Cover Designer: Matthew Limbert

Typeset by SPi Global, India

Working together
to grow libraries in
developing countries

www.elsevier.com • www.bookaid.org

Contents

Authors' biography

Dionéia Motta Monte-Serrat is a Postdoctoral Researcher at the Department of Computation and Mathematics of Faculty of Philosophy, Sciences and Letters of Ribeirao Preto—University of Sao Paulo, FFCLRP-USP, Brazil; Collaborating researcher at Language Institute of University of Campinas, IEL-UNICAMP, Brazil; and Faculty Member at University of Ribeirao Preto, UNAERP, Brazil.

    Prof. Carlo Cattani is a Professor (Habil. Full Professor) of Mathematical Physics and Applied Mathematics at the Engineering School (DEIM) of Tuscia University (VT)-Italy, where he was appointed in 2015. Previously, he has been a Professor at the Department of Mathematics University of Rome "La Sapienza" (1980–2004) and at the Department of Mathematics, University of Salerno (2004–15).

Acknowledgment

We are especially grateful to the colleagues of Academia who contributed directly to the discussions made in this book, interfering with the path of reflections. We highlight them in alphabetical order. We thank Prof. Dr. Antonio Caliri who gave us his time in interviews to discuss the language and its complexity; Prof. Dr. Brenno Caetano Troca Cabella for moments of insightful brainstormings showing his deep and broad interdisciplinary knowledge; Prof. Dr. Evandro Eduardo Ruiz Seron who offered shelter to discussions on computing Mathematics and Artificial Intelligence; Prof. Dr. Girolamo Garreffa (*in memoriam*) in his countless lessons on human cognition with his insightful observations that encouraged reflections on language phenomena in terms of physics and more particularly functional magnetic resonance, fMRI; Dr. Paulo Motta Monte Serrat for his creativity and willingness to transform ideas into figures for this book; and Sidnei Aparecido Agi (*in memoriam*) who contributed to these discussions with his dissertation entitled "Integrative lexical-contextual model for the recognition of textual implication," to obtain the Master of Science degree from the Graduate Program in Applied Computing, Faculty of Philosophy, Sciences and Letters of Ribeirão Preto—USP, Advised by Prof. Dr. Evandro Eduardo Seron Ruiz, 2018. We thank all colleagues and friends who participated in our academic career. Whatever remaining errors are the responsibility of the first author, Dionéia Motta Monte-Serrat.

Acknowledgment

Presentation

The content of this book is based on qualitative research carried out since 2007. There is preference for this perspective of investigation due to the focus on the study of language related to its context. Quantity loses importance to give rise to the quality of the researched object: The natural language. This is a theoretical strategy that transforms a research paper—which, while quantitative, could result in a general list of information—into a comprehensive view about a specific topic, as a qualitative analysis. The content of the subsequent chapters of this book develops a main line of reasoning through a strong analytical ability, reason why it is suggested to study the chapters in the order in which they are organized. We present clear and logical arguments to show the reader something whose existence is admitted, but it is not visible: The underlying structure of natural language.

Support for conducting this new frontier research is found in papers and books that have been published by the authors since 2009. As time goes by a better perspective begins to be shown in new studies about neurocognition and mathematics related to language. Although academically distant from linguistics, it was noticed that a common element, crossing other areas of knowledge, remained unchanged. If an indecipherable structure left clues throughout the study of language in different areas of science, the terrain is well prepared for what we present in this work. Then came the idea of gathering all the knowledge about language acquired over the years and putting into book format, exposing readers, in a concentrated way, to a line of reasoning that runs through various branches of science, so that they are urged to verify for themselves and draw their own conclusions about the enigma of natural language.

We offer the reader a book that, instead of talking about the specific benefits of a discovery, seeks to investigate the subject in a diverse way, organizing the findings and relating them, in a convincing way, to similar discoveries in other branches of science. We believe that this way of working offers the reader the conditions to understand the underlying principles of natural language, providing rewarding results in terms of new revelations.

A discussion of the viability of the behavioralist, pragmatist, or functionalist view to support the extended mind hypothesis is not among the objectives of this book. Based on Saussure's linguistic hypothesis that the meaning is given when the words of a sentence are related to the other words (in relation to), we try to verify what other linguists said about it, to compare our findings with the cognitive phenomena relating the human body and the mind. Some scientific discoveries promoted by neuroimaging help to elucidate several phenomena bringing more security to these findings. As the content of the book progresses, we make inserts on the theory of artificial intelligence (AI). The themes natural intelligence and AI are evolving and gaining importance at the same pace.

The concern of this book is on opinions and motivations about how language works, using this strategy to create insights about what the universal structure of natural language is. We believe that this way of working can help to develop new ideas or hypotheses in the application of this structure to other researches, whether they are about natural language or machine language.

The qualitative perspective helps to discover trends in thoughts or opinions. Although this way of researching has linguistic reasoning, it is accompanied, in this book, by examples and data that prove the findings. Thus we fulfill our goal of finding the root that determines how natural language works; and we go further, showing how this language structure works in scientific data collected by image exams or machine language applications. The reader will realize that this book does not deal with language philosophically. Instead, it reveals the root of natural language that was considered undecipherable until now and shows how it works in natural intelligence and AI.

In some chapters, specific knowledge is required. In this case, we present the theory related to the theme in its due measure. Our goal is not for readers to have a broad understanding of the work of the aforementioned authors but for the former to be guided to learn about the work of a particular author exactly as it pertains to the content of this book. Thus the reason why the historical review is not a strong point of this book is justified. This initiative, in our opinion, prevents readers from getting lost in issues not related to the subject under discussion. We just make them stop to check the findings in experiments and investigations on the behavior of natural language.

During the years 2018 and 2019, several topics around the relationship between natural language and AI were discussed and published, always in search of the theoretical domain capable of endowing this discussion with a scientific character. The interface between neurolinguistics, language, subject, mathematics, logical reasoning, decision-making, subject and time movement in virtual reality, brain injuries, functional neuroimaging lies in the support point for all of them: The universal structure of the language that gives rise to the structure of universal language algorithm. This interface directed this book to a new longer border, combining different types of information, interconnecting biological and logical characteristics of natural language, updating them in the meaning construction. The meaning is the information that is intended to be transmitted; this is the purpose of language: Communication with a recipient. The gathering of those formalized knowledge already published in books, scientific articles, dissertations, and thesis, was transported to this book in a bet that the universal structure of natural language is simple and that this knowledge will reach new demands, going beyond the existing fragmented initiatives. Natural language is exposed from the perspective of the human, natural, and formal sciences, in the hope of contributing to the legitimation and circulation of a new and more comprehensive concept to be worked on by AI.

Natural language is presented as mediating between reality and mind and, at the same time, acting during the mental process of signification. This mediation seeks to transmit information without ambiguity. The latter means confusion about what is transmitted and should be avoided, since it can lead to different interpretations of meaning, making communication ineffective. Ambiguity is considered a defect in communication because it breaks rules of information exchange.

The meaning, to be transmitted, depends on the existence of a set of signals that will be processed by means of an intelligence, be it natural or artificial. Understanding the meaning is not a simple operation, as understanding something can involve the interpretation of facial expressions, body language, tone of pronounced words, punctuation in writing, and so on. The branch of knowledge responsible for the relationship between words and referents in the meaning construction is called semantics, which is divided into subgroups studied in the fields of linguistics, logic, and computing. This subdivision is didactic, focusing to help in understanding the subject.

In this book, we are not concerned with the didactic or scientific division already established. Our argument goes beyond the limits of the scientific division to prove that there is a unique phenomenon that is repeated in the various disciplines. The didactical division disrupts this observation, hence, our choice in investigating natural language from a qualitative perspective, making the relationship between phenomenon and context prevail over the relationship between phenomenon and scientific branch.

It is emphasized in the book content that the sign system of language does not automatically assign meaning. This reality of language functioning makes us consider that the different branches of science construct meaning in different ways. This fact is dealt with in this book to make machine language coders be aware that they must adjust the machine learning functions to the scientific context in which the language will be applied. In this case, it is necessary to contextualize the mathematical rules so that the dynamics of the machine language symbols adapt to each specific scientific field. Chapter 9 of this book contains more details and examples on the construction of meaning in the scientific fields. For now, we limit ourselves to say that there is no absolute way to measure the adequacy of thought to reality. Disciplines are surrounded by methods or criteria for observing reality. Only through the application of a criterion is it possible to know whether a certain image or idea reflects a reality.

Informing the reader that there is no neutral meaning for words and that this meaning is constructed according to the scientific context in which it is being developed, we show how AI can benefit from this knowledge. The strategy to be used to build intelligent systems corresponding to an implemented natural language generation depends on certain requirements linked to knowledge of how the universal structure of natural language behaves in each discipline. A slight generalization of this structure to adapt this new language model to the AI model is also given. In fact, since AI pursues to imitate the process of the human mind, we show that the professional who works with AI cannot ignore the scientific branch in which the application of machine design is intended. It is necessary to overcome the obstacles of the different work criteria imposed by the diverse scientific branches and to dedicate to a more generic and profound structure of language: The axiomatic-logical structure of natural language adjusting the logical-mathematical processes of the machine.

With these considerations in mind, a challenge remains: How to obtain the requirements to transform raw data into resources and how to identify the value of axiomatic elements and logical elements of the language structure, without taking into account the scientific branch from which these data and values are collected? The key to this challenge is the reasoning of the entire content of this book: It covers all chapters in an interconnected manner through an argumentative method. Perelman's argumentative method was chosen to help readers to find a typical pattern that is repeated and, therefore, it is taken as a basis to guide interpretability of all the content exposed here. The course of chapters development focuses on language at work and not static language as result of rules. For this, we work with the logical-axiomatic pattern of the first, which is, in our opinion, the universal form that allows cross-fertilization between natural language and AI. AI will be further enhanced when mastering the combination of technology with its application appropriate to the structure of human language, being aware of the branch of science that sets the tone of meaning formation. Hence the machine can better represent the underlying reality, in some way, addressing the issue of value and contextualization, diminishing ambiguity.

CHAPTER ONE

Introduction

There is a quite large consensus among linguists and cognitivists that language owns a universal structure, and that our brain uses categories of representation when processing information (Pinker, 1994; Jespersen, 1922; Chomsky, 2001; Caramazza and Shapiro, 2004). In particular, these authors have postulated a connection between the natural order of thoughts and the order of words, claiming that a universal structure of language (considered as a set of grammatical categories and relations) is always present in communication (Belletti, 2004).

Until the writing of this book, there is no news of scientific work that specifically demonstrates how universal the human conceptual structure is. There are varied studies concentrating on the way concepts are organized in the human brain and on the reflections of the cultural context on them. These studies do not deny that there are universal properties to human cognition. Semantics, a branch of knowledge dedicated to the study of the construction of meanings expressed by language, provides some information that gives indirect access to an underlying structure of language, which would configure a pattern of conceptual structure. Even with the effort of this branch of linguistics, the meaning is hardly measured and parameterized to the satisfaction. Some researches can be found providing an empirical measure of the semantic proximity between concepts using multilingual dictionaries for translation purposes. Translations based on quantified studies of language sooner or later compete directly with the polysemic characteristic of the language, that is, a word can correspond to more than one meaning, which, in its turn, is represented by different words. There are more sophisticated studies (Youn et al., 2016) that seek to associate the frequency of polysemy linking two concepts as a measure of their semantic proximity and to represent the pattern of these linkages by a weighted network. In short, they intend, through a statistical analysis, reach a subset of a basic vocabulary, showing that there are consistent structural properties in different groups of languages. In our opinion, these quantifying methods can be applied to any semantic domain to a certain extent because there is a limitation imposed by the complexity of natural language. This limitation is revealing in the sense that those studies and quantifying methods are not suitable for circumventing the irregularities of natural language and, for this reason, cannot be considered in the evaluation and observation of the universal attribute of human cognition.

The consensus on the existence of a standard structure of natural language does not mean that this structure is a priori defined by an agreement on some given rules: Mainly because the real essence of language has not yet been defined. The prime strategy of this book putting together some perspectives of language, which are widely used in the fields of Literature, Law, Psychology, Psychoanalysis, Linguistics, Neurolinguistics, Neurophysiology, Neuroimaging, Architecture, Mathematics, and Computational Mathematics, shows the existence of a common structure that remains, no matter how different the language perspectives are in each of these disciplines (see Chapter 9).

This perception may shed some light on the definition of a comprehensive theory of language whose processes organize conceptual information in the mind/brain, going beyond a set of grammatical categories. In this book, we propose a generalization of linguistic theory in the sense of:

(i) recognizing that language has a logical characteristic due to the influence of a grammar containing a finite system of rules that generates infinitely many properly related structures (this is a fragmented view of the language);

(ii) to which we add the axiomatic character of language, encompassing principles that relate those abstract logical structures to the cultural context and to certain mental representations (neurophysiological phenomena) in order to arrive, in the end, at the meaning formation as the result of a comprehensive concept of language.

This broad understanding of language provides a strong foundation on which Artificial Intelligence (AI) can be developed becoming more intuitive and contextualized in the handling of dependent variables, removing its limitations in the semantic representation that usually lead to ambiguous interpretation.

An important utility of this book is to draw readers' attention to language as something alive. The human brain performs several tasks and, when it is articulated within a specific discipline, it suffers interferences in the language production. The result of understanding a living language is the possibility for the researcher to identify how each discipline interferes with the way of thinking and interpreting individuals. Each discipline or scientific field is assumed to be able to show that the universal structure of language is a twofold structure based both on the axiomatic component (living thing) and on the logical component (abstract and related to grammar). This model fits perfectly with the description given by Jespersen (1922, p. 442):

Language is a perpetual song, [...] that rules [in its logical character] a great density of thoughts and forms, which were more meaningless and formless [axiomatic character].

We discuss in detail the two components of the standard language structure as nonstatic elements by focusing on their reciprocal interaction which is strictly compulsory for the generation of a correct value (meaning).

Special attention is paid to the language of social, formal, and natural sciences, prioritizing the relationship of language in these scientific branches in their interaction with AI. To articulate natural and AI, we can understand the latter in a broad sense as a system involving a set of techniques that allow one to automatically discover which representations must be extracted from reality data to classify them. AI allows a machine to learn how resources should be used to perform a specific task. For that, it must learn how to classify tasks mathematically and computationally through the development of specific algorithms. We wager that this task depends on the knowledge of science branch in which AI will be applied and, also, on how the natural language functions. AI is a language specifically designed to computerize some routine work, to single out patterns and regularities such as understanding speech or images, making medical diagnoses, supporting scientific research, and describing a list of mathematical rules (Goodfellow et al., 2016; Nielsen, 2015). There is a big challenge for AI to perform easy tasks when formal description is complicated.

Social Sciences language is understood as something that triggers the symbolic identification of the subject generating value in the formation of meanings, exercising a morphogenic power over him (Lacan, 1966) that, for some reason, is not complete and allows the formation of lapses and ambiguities (Monte-Serrat, 2013, 2014, 2017, 2018). This mode of language operation privileging the subject's historical constitution in his social space should be considered by the AI so that the latter, when classifying input data, should include the set representations of an individual's social character and his individual speech biography.

A contribution from Formal Sciences made it possible to translate linguistic concepts in Mathematics by exploring the logical feature of the language (Levitt, 1996; Monte-Serrat, 2017, 2018; Monte-Serrat and Belgacem, 2017; Monte-Serrat et al., 2017). To make the AI language more comprehensive, we suggest that the spatial dimension is also governed by logic, so that the representation constructed by the machine can interpret data in three dimensions.

The Natural Sciences, in turn, have advanced a lot in the study of language related to the brain functioning. New researches on neurolinguistics bring together a multitude of biological properties to the logical character of language hitherto extensively explored, giving rise to a concept that embodies the harmonious synthesis between mental representations and reality outside the human being (Perlovsky and Kozma, 2007). Understanding language as a phenomenon that unites physical and mental processes, it encompasses the following characteristics: Of a logical-axiomatic mechanism (our bet) and a synchronizer (Belletti, 2004), linking the dynamics of vascular and neuronal networks in a way that functions as a connector of interdependent processes (Perlovsky and Kozma, 2007), mediating the kingdoms real, symbolic, and imaginary (Lacan, 1949). The language presents an intermittent synchronization cycle that configures a central process destined to unite varied and simultaneous functions to compose the mental representation (Perlovsky and Kozma, 2007). These aspects influenced the deep learning algorithm that can take an image of input assigning a value for some objects differentiating one from the other. Although AI has a monumental growth in constructing algorithms that bridge human capabilities and machines there is still much to improve in this sense and we work on ideas that could help to reduce the computational power to process the data.

In addition to analyzing the functioning of language in the fields of science, we make incursions in theories that describe natural intelligence, AI, and in theories of language, to collect, in due measure, different points of view on the concept of language given by varied authors. We believe that the way we present a new and comprehensive concept of natural language answer many issues about how the language works under an axiomatic live feature combined with an abstract logical attribute. We hope to succeed in demonstrating what requirements AI needs to find to achieve the best solution for dealing with natural language.

This book is structured as follows: It has been organized into 11 chapters to best accommodate a variety of readers' interests, showing, in each chapter, a progressive deconstruction of complex elements of language to find, at the end, some basic elements that, compared with "atoms," they can be common to any type of language, whether expressed by speech, writing, drawing, or symbols. This chapter introduces the theme natural language for AI, highlighting both so that the essential characteristics of the former can be replicated in the latter. The content of Chapter 2 is about the need of finding a structure—the universal structure of language—which is the link between natural language and machine language. Chapter 3 describes what is already known about how natural intelligence works. The Chapter 4 focuses on the description of how it came about and what AI is. Chapter 5, on the other hand, focuses on linguistics to describe what natural language is as opposed to conventional language. In Chapter 6 the axiomatic-logical structure of natural language is described to draw a universal model of language, be it natural or artificial. Aspects of natural language that can improve AI are covered in Chapter 7. Chapter 8 draws in detail the universal structure of natural language, which is recognized by linguists, but is not drawn by them in its profound structural details. Chapter 9 warns of the need for a discretionary attitude by computer technicians when designing AI, drawing attention to the fact that natural language behaves differently in distinct branches of Science. Chapter 10 gives an overview of the essence of natural language covered in all chapters of the book. It reminds us that it is language that installs meaning. Before it there is no idea or sense. It is the language that establishes the intermediation of elements of different orders and that is the function of the universal algorithm of language: Determining what is the fundamental relation for the language to be established, forming the meaning. In this chapter the elements of natural language that overlap with elements of machine language are listed, exemplifying through AI how our model of universal artificial language can be applied. Then in Chapter 11, the conclusion in which we explain that this book exposes the natural and artificial language in their structure and it is up to the computational performance experts to better choose which values they will give to the axiomatic and to the logical elements of the natural language universal structure.

References

Belletti, A. (Ed.), 2004. Structures and Beyond: The Cartography of Syntactic Structures. vol. 3. Oxford University Press Inc., New York.
Caramazza, A., Shapiro, K., 2004. Language categories in the brain: evidence from aphasia. In: Belletti, A. (Ed.), Structures and Beyond: The Cartography of Syntactic Structures. vol. 3. Oxford University Press Inc, New York.
Chomsky, N., 2001. Le langage et la pensée. Coll. Petite Bibliothèque Payot. Payot-Rivages, Paris.
Goodfellow, I., Bengio, Y., Courville, A., 2016. Deep Learning. MIT Press, Cambridge, MA.
Jespersen, O., 1922. Language, its Nature, Development and Origin. Henry Holt & Company, New York.
Lacan, J., 1949. Le stade du mirroir comme formateur de la fonction du Je telle qu'elle nous est révélée dans l'experiénce psychanalytique. Revue Française de Psychanalyse, France, pp. 449–455. Octobre 1949.

Lacan, J., 1966. Propos sur causalité psyche. In: Écrits. Tome I. Le Seuil, Paris.

Levitt, N., 1996. Mathematics as stepchild of contemporary culture. In: Gross, P., Levitt, N., Lewis, M. (Eds.), The Flight from Science and Reason. Annals of the New York Academy of Sciences.

Monte-Serrat, D., 2013. Literacy and Juridical Discourse, USP-RP 2013. Thesis guided by Tfouni, L. Retrieved from http://www.teses.usp.br/teses/disponiveis/59/59137/tde-14032013-104350/. (Accessed 28 July 2020).

Monte-Serrat, D., 2014. A questão do sujeito: perspectivas da análise do discurso, do letramento e da psicanálise lacaniana. Ed. Pedro e João, São Carlos.

Monte-Serrat, D., 2017. Neurolinguistics, language, and time: investigating the verbal art in its amplitude. Int. J. Perspect. Public Health 1 (3), 162–171.

Monte-Serrat, D., 2018. Inclusion in linguistic education: neurolinguistics, language, and subject. In: Psycholinguistics and Cognition in Language Processing. IGI-Global.com.

Monte-Serrat, D., Belgacem, F., 2017. Subject and time movement in the virtual reality. Int. J. Res. Methodol. Soc. Sci. 3 (3), 19.

Monte-Serrat, D., Belgacem, F., Maldonato, M., 2017. Decision making: the complexity of choice processes. Int. J. Res. Methodol. Soc. Sci. 3 (4), 22. Oct–Dec 2017.

Nielsen, M., 2015. Neural Networks and Deep Learning. Determination Press.

Perlovsky, L., Kozma, R. (Eds.), 2007. Neurodynamics of Cognition and Consciousness. Springer-Verlag, Berlin Heidelberg.

Pinker, S., 1994. The Language Instinct. Harper-Collins Publishers Inc., New York.

Youn, H., Sutton, L., Smith, E., Moore, C., Wilkins, J., Maddieson, I., Croft, W., Bhattacharya, T., 2016. On the universal structure of human lexical semantics. Proc. Natl. Acad. Sci. U. S. A. 113 (7), 1766–1771.

CHAPTER TWO

Connecting different levels of language reality

2.1 Introduction

To connect realities belonging to different disciplines, a criterion or method is necessary. We make use of the argumentative method to involve all the content of this book, but before we go into it further, it is necessary to explain the basis for the argumentation: The scientific discourse.

First, we need to emphasize that the information carried through scientific texts assumes a different way of explaining events, when compared with an informal transmission of content. The discourse (speech or writing) with scientific characteristics is rooted in a reasoning of cause and effect that differs from our everyday understanding. There are different ways of exposing a subject for everyday understanding or for understanding in the scientific community. The latter, in addition to have a narration, usually comes with cause and effect in terms of objective structures to achieve a conclusion. The reasoning used to expose ideas through a scientific text is syllogistic, which is the most sophisticated in the discursive chain.

The transmission of a scientific finding comes with the following path: The researcher starts from a generic knowledge in which there is a consensus to add a special information and, from that, draw his conclusions. This is the syllogistic reasoning whose model allows an idea to be built from a "known" fact or from a "previously given" text (let us emphasize here that the starting point is "known," we will return to that point later). The conclusion reached integrates special information with existing generic knowledge. This reasoning, to be valid and accepted, depends on its coherence and clarity in the presentation of ideas, so that there is no ambiguity or polysemy. Hence the success of a scientific discourse (speech or writing) depends on this system of cause and effect relationships.

In addition to logical reasoning an argumentative scientific text can be also based on inference, which is crucial for understanding and constructing

The Natural Language for Artificial Intelligence
https://doi.org/10.1016/B978-0-12-824118-9.00012-6

a situation, even when not all details and logical or causal connections are explained. If, on the one hand, we expose the rigidly specified data to clearly lead to a conclusion, on the other, we can make inferences of narrated facts involving the complex world of human beings and reach a conclusion. The gaps in coherence require inference in the last case.

Theoretically the coherence gaps encourage readers to look for the necessary connections and inferences (Otero et al., 2002). There is, then, a specific level at which ideas are clearly stated to be effective in persuading readers; and, on the other hand, the reader can be exposed to an intuitive discovery. According to Otero et al. (2002), when the reader has high knowledge and when the task involves deep understanding, low coherence brings better interpretative results. There is a likelihood that the highly coherent text brings an "illusion of competence" causing the reader to be prevented from processing the text more freely (Otero et al., 2002). These results explain the need for scientific texts to be based predominantly on explicit coherence and clarity, thus avoiding divergent interpretations based on the reader's subjective knowledge.

2.2 Argumentation

The fact that the universal structure of natural language is recognized, but it is not self-evident and rarely deal with clear and distinct elements, leads us to adopt inference instead of the recommended logical reasoning for scientific texts. The argumentation that directs the content presentation of this book obeys a specific line that we consider more suitable for this purpose: Chaim Perelman's method of argumentation. The reason for this choice lies in the fact that this argumentative method moves away from the ideal and generic certainty that governs scientific knowledge to rely on a regressive reasoning that considers the variability of special situations and values. This aspect of Perelman's theory (Perelman and Olbrechts-Tyteca, 1973) is crucial for our book, because, as we put the scientific branches all together under analysis with their different natures, we could not use a method that would consider them ideally equal, homogenizing them in the name of clarity of logical reasoning. It would, then, be necessary to choose a method that study all branches of science together and consider, at the same time, their specific characteristics.

Our efforts are concentrated on organizing thinking in these strategies: (1) to gather qualitative knowledge about some disciplines related to language; (2) use Perelman's argumentative method to find what is the common element of language that runs through those disciplines. What is common to natural language that can establish a connection between its use by humans in the various scientific disciplines and its use by Artificial Intelligence? To dissolve the shadows of doubt and find an object that has been highly sought after, we bring a look at language that, instead of being based on facts, truths, and assumptions of logical reasoning, will be based on value and context. In this way the argumentation opens the perspective of observing the natural language within its context of apparently contradictory information and theoretical postures.

The path we follow in this book to present ideas is: (1) we verify the scientific truths of each discipline as to what is theoretically established about natural language; (2) then we relate those truths to the context of the discipline in which natural language is being studied, that is, we verify how language behaves within the perspective of each discipline; (3) working in this way, we seek to verify, offering a more comprehensive approach, a pattern that appears repeatedly in all different disciplinary perspectives, something universal that guarantees the coherence of reality and truth. This standard must be taken as a whole; there must be no conflict between facts and truths on which it is based.

In general, the arguments with which Perelman works involve associative techniques to establish reality. There are arguments founded in succession relationships, and arguments that depend on the relationship of coexistence. The former use causes and effects to reach a conclusion; the latter, in turn, associate one element with another indirectly.

The arguments with appeal to the real are classified by Perelman and Olbrechts-Tyteca (1973) in: Arguments of example or model and arguments by analogy. The former takes a unique situation to move toward generalization. Arguments by analogy, on the other hand, establish hierarchies in the observation between two elements; the similarity with another set is observed. The reality perceived through appearances can be misleading. Perelman suggests looking at reality with respect to similarity in relationships.

2.3 Perelman's argumentative techniques

Perelman's (Perelman and Olbrechts-Tyteca, 1973) work has different interpretations: In favor, considering him a traditional logician; and against, considering him an antiphilosopher who would be concerned with the art of persuading without caring about the truth. Regarding the aspects of his work dealt with in this book, we highlight Perelman not as a philosopher writing about logic and ethics. We take advantage of the characteristics of his thought in which a renewing source of apprehension of reality is revealed.

Showing his originality, Perelman and Olbrechts-Tyteca (1973) give a philosophical sense to the argument by creating his method by importing elements of linguistics and logic. According to Schmetz (2000, p. 289), the reality of studies on argumentation in the 21st century is twofold: On the one hand, studies on argumentation mechanisms are found; on the other hand we find general reflections on place and meaning related to human beings. Perelman's creative work describes the argumentative phenomenon: The Perelmanian way of analyzing arguments is not negligible, he distinguishes himself from all other scholars of argumentation (Schmetz, 2000, p. 300). Perelman and Olbrechts-Tyteca (1973) conceive rhetoric as a way of arguing without leaving the field of reason, but at the same time transcending the categories of formal logic. In this way, he establishes the argumentation as a principle of philosophical research.

Starting from certain uncontroversial propositions, already accepted by the recipient before the beginning of the speech, the speaker seeks the audience's adhesion in relation to the thesis he presents. This procedure is carried out using argumentative techniques. We will focus on just a few techniques offered by Perelman in his work on the Argumentation Treaty (Perelman and Olbrechts-Tyteca, 1973).

In search of the auditorium's adherence to a thesis, Perelman and Olbrechts-Tyteca (1973) present two aspects to be observed: (1) the positive aspect in which solidarity is established between the presented thesis and the theses already admitted by the auditorium—connection arguments; (2) the negative aspect that break the solidarity found or presumed between the thesis of the speaker and the theses already admitted by the auditorium—dissociation arguments. We will go deeper into the first, the connection arguments, which can be grouped into three classes: Arguments almost logical, the arguments based on the structure of the real, and those that found the structure of the real (Fig. 1).

Quasi-logical arguments are supported by formal logic, but do not have the same rigor as the latter to eliminate ambiguity or to remove the possibility of multiple interpretations. It is similar to the structure of the logical argument and has a persuasive force dependent on the latter. Quasi-logical arguments, in case they face a contradiction, instead of present absurdity (which would be the result of the univocity of ideas), result in incompatibility.

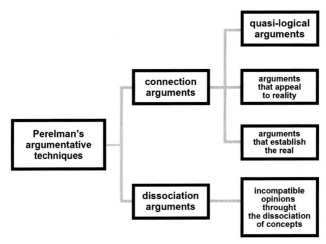

Fig. 1 Perelman's argumentative techniques based on the descriptions of Perelman and Olbrechts-Tyteca (1973).

Arguments that appeals to reality are based on connection between the various elements of reality. Since it is admitted that the elements of the real are associated by a given connection, that connection serves as a basis to argue that there is a passage from one of these elements to each other. This connection can happen by succession or by coexistence. When the argument is based on the structure of the real by succession, there is a cause and effect relationship, there are relationships involving realities of different orders, where one is the essence and the other the manifestation exterior of that essence. The argument based on the structure of the real by coexistence is explained in the next topic along with the argument that establish the real.

Arguments that establish the real are those that generalize something that is already accepted in a specific case (event and relationship) or they transpose to another domain, by means of analogy or metaphor, which is admitted in a given domain.

Finally, dissociation arguments are those that, instead of using the connection and rupture of associations, seek to solve an incompatibility of the discourse, reestablishing a coherent view of reality. Faced with contradiction, the speaker seeks to build a concept of reality as a criterion for judging appearances: Those that conform, are considered valid; those that do not conform, are disregarded. In the dissociation argument, there is a depreciation of what was until then an accepted value, to replace it with another concept that is in accordance with the original value.

2.4 Perelman's liasons of coexistence

Among the multiplicity of argumentative techniques suggested by Perelman and Olbrechts-Tyteca (1973), there is a variety of relationships between the categories that are considered close. Perelman's theory describes mobility between arguments. More than ideal types of arguments, his theory reveals the multiple versions of an argument and the means of passing from one to the other. The instability of the categorization indicates the possibility that the arguments integrate a dynamic dimension in the argumentative analysis of a discourse (Schmetz, 2000, p. 260; 262). It is in this sense that we use two close types—arguments that appeals to reality and arguments that establish the real—to be developed in a systematized set of knowledge from various disciplines.

In the following chapters, we take as a starting point phenomena—widely used or universally accepted in the perspective of various scientific disciplines—not as a description of the content of those disciplines, but taken as a connecting tool that will qualify our argument. The systematic connection of scientific knowledge from various areas that we make in this book is not an accidental or superficial connection. Our argumentative link runs through different realities to reveal an essential element in that link, a common existence within the scientific branches. We look for heterogeneity within a structured guiding thread in the functioning of language, that is, we observe the descriptions of how it behaves in each branch of science and compare these descriptions to highlight a behavior that is repeated, whether in natural intelligence or in artificial intelligence. It is in this common connection that we find the universal structure of language, which is shown to be consistent through the interaction of arguments. Perelman's (Perelman and Olbrechts-Tyteca, 1973) argumentative phenomenon allows for easy reconstruction of the object in question. The axiomatic-logical structure of natural language emerges from the operational effectiveness of the argument that links different theories.

Perelman makes the sciences usually invoked for the study of rhetoric blind to it. In addition, in doing so, he announces another approach, more material than formal, which is also based on a theorization of rhetoric more monstrative than demonstrative. Finally, it provides the theoretical conditions for recognition of what we have called the rhetorical doing since it highlights the inseparability of the rhetorical aspect of discourse and the ideas defended therein, but not their indistinguishability.

(Schmetz, 2000, p. 348).

Perelman rend les sciences habituellement invoquées pour l'étude de la rhétorique aveugles à celle-ci. De plus, ce faisant, il annonce une autre approche, plus materielle que formelle de la question, fondée également sur une théorisation de la rhétorique plus monstrative que démonstrative. Enfin, il fournit les conditions théoriques d'une reconnaissance de ce que nous avons appelé le faire réthorique puisqu'il met en evidence l'indissociabilité de l'aspect rhétorique du discours et des idées qui y sont défendues mais non point leur indiscernabilité.

(Schmetz, 2000, p. 348).

Let us remember that one of the argumentative methods, proposed by Perelman and Olbrechts–Tyteca (1973), is based on the argumentative use of the analogy to verify a similarity of "relationships." It is not based on similarities of situations. The authors' (Perelman and Olbrechts–Tyteca, 1973) proposal is to make links of coexistence between the observed elements, in such a way that the transitivity law remains. They argue that, if the "relationship" between A and B resembles the "relationship" between C and D, we can also establish a link between A and C, although they belong to different areas of knowledge (Fig. 2). This type of argument is built on the structure of reality to connect different levels of the same reality, that is, when we have a recognized connection, we can use it to move from what is accepted to what we want to accept (Perelman and Olbrechts–Tyteca, 1973).

In short: We find a structure of reality that is accepted and apply it to a specific situation with a similar structural functioning. The result of this operation helps us to fill a gap: The similarity of "relationship" between A and B and between C and D allows us to infer that this same relationship

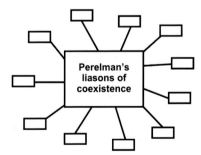

Fig. 2 Perelman's Liasons of coexistence based on the descriptions of Perelman and Olbrechts-Tyteca (1973). There are arguments founded in succession relationships and arguments that depend on the relationship (liasons) of coexistence. The former use causes and effects to reach a conclusion; the latter, in turn, associate one element with another indirectly.

exists between A and D. Thus we move from what is known to what is unknown (Perelman and Olbrechts-Tyteca, 1973). It is in this respect that we work on the universal essence of language: The axiomatic-logical structure gives access to the creation of a condition of similarities between disciplines that apparently have no connection. This is possible because the axiomatic-logical structure of language that we define in this book is invariable.

The methodology (Perelman and Olbrechts-Tyteca, 1973; Pessoa, 2004) focuses on the universal structure of language "functioning" is due to the absence of variation when using language in each of the branches of science. The universal standard that the language holds is exactly the connecting element between the different realities of unequal disciplines. This relationship takes place through the broad concept of natural language in its dynamic functioning. Language as a human phenomenon is the starting point. It is vitally important to apprehend language dynamically to cross the various disciplines and discover that, behind their different perspectives, a structure that unites them remains: The axiomatic-logical structure of language.

Based on the understanding of this immutable structure, we provide suggestions in more detail on how this pattern can help artificial intelligence to draw resources from the specific languages of each discipline (medicine, finance, sport, slang, dialects, trade, etc.) diminishing ambiguity in the construction of algorithms.

We can summarize our model as follows:

(1) we propose a new definition of language structure (axiomatic-logical) which is universal generalizing the known linguistic models;

(2) to legitimize our new definition, we compare the structure of our language model with the technical languages used in some disciplines, showing that these specific languages have, in their essence, the axiomatic-logical universal structure.

We highlight that the human cognitive process has a compelling uniqueness and universality based on the axiomatic-logical model of language, regardless of the area of knowledge in use. In fact the technical language of each discipline is a subset of natural language, and therefore, obviously, technical language inherits the properties of natural language. Similarly, cognitive computing and artificial intelligence are based on the universal structure demonstrated in this book.

In the following chapters, we will deepen our reflections on what the axiomatic-logical structure of language is, and then apply it to some branches of science, without worrying about exhausting them, as this structure is invariable and is at the root of language, regardless of the discipline using that technical language. The axiomatic-logical structure of natural language is supposed to find its existence within a mathematical algorithm, which provides an ethereal feature to it giving a great advantage of going beyond the limitations of any formalized mathematical system that limits and restricts information, homogenizing its differences. Since our base is focused on something that is common to different scientific branches, there is no homogenization. We just point out "what" should be considered by artificial intelligence. This will help to solve computational problems so that they can structure neural networks to design them properly.

References

Otero, J., León, J., Graesser, A.C., 2002. The Psychology of Science Text Comprehension. Routledge.

Perelman, C., Olbrechts-Tyteca, L., 1973. The New Rhetoric: Treatise on Argumentation. Wilkninson, J. (transl), University of Notre Dame Press.

Pessoa, M., 2004. A análise retórica de acordo com Perelmam. In: Linguagem em (Dis) curso—LemD, Tubarão, pp. 135–151. vol. 4, n. 2, jan./jun Tubarão.

Schmetz, R., 2000. L'argumentation selon Perelman: Pour une raison au coeur de la rhétorique. Presses Universitaires de Namur, Belgique.

CHAPTER THREE

The natural intelligence

3.1 Introduction

Human intelligence is described through a variety of perspectives such as theories of intelligence, psychometric theories, cognitive or cognitive-contextual theories, biological theories, brain wave studies, blood flow, and so on. From the context point of Bechtel (2006) view, human intelligence is conceived as the mental quality that consists of the skills to understand abstract concepts, to learn from experience and to adapt to new situations to manipulate the environment. Until today, we observe many attempts by researchers to determine exactly what intelligence is. It is curious that there are a great number of definitions about intelligence mixed with the concept of language such as the intelligence as the ability to think abstractly (for an abstract concept to form, it is necessary to use signs, which refer to the existence of a language). There are also psychometric theories designed to understand the structure of intelligence, seeking to unravel what its parts are and what their forms are using tests of mental skills, of classifying words or recognizing numbers in series. We can see that, although nebulous, the concept of intelligence is somehow linked to learning and understanding, in other words, is connected to language and to the ability of interpreting.

This chapter aims to dispel the mists that cover the conceptualization of natural intelligence and language. To do this, we explain some principles underlying intelligence and then provide some details about brain functioning that will be crucial for understanding what human intelligence is. We make it clear that we follow the line of reasoning put forward in this book: We seek to rely on linguistic theories that consider the importance of context for the constitution of intelligence and language. Then, we make an analogy of these linguistic principles with human physiology, seeking to identify the biological origin of the functioning of natural language that corresponds to each of these linguistic principles until reaching a biological structure that corresponds to the universal structure of language. We believe

The Natural Language for Artificial Intelligence
https://doi.org/10.1016/B978-0-12-824118-9.00003-5

that the identification of the principles in supporting the language function-ing is the first step to make available elements to help the development of machine learning models.

Being aware that there is a new theory about Enactivist embodied cog-nition (Gallagher, 2017, p. 6), based on the same assumptions of this book, such as:

1. *Cognition is not simply a brain event. It emerges from processes distributed across brain-body-environment. The mind is embodied [...]*
2. *The world, (meaning, intentionality) is not pre-given or predefinied, but is struc-tured by cognitions and action [...]*
3. *Cognitive processes acquire meaning in part by their role in the context of action, rather than through a representational mapping or replicated internal model of the world [in our book we explain how and why both are part of the same process]*
4. *[approach] have strong links to dynamical systems theory, emphasizing the rel-evance of dynamical coupling and coordination across brain-body-environment [...]*
5. *[approach] emphasize the extended, intersubjective, and socially situated nature of cognitive systems [...]*
6. *[...] aims to ground higher and more complex cognitive functions not only in sensorimotor coordination, but also in affective and autonomic aspects of the full body [we describe these aspects more generally in the topics where we address otherness]*
7. *Higher-order cognitive functions, such as reflective thinking or deliberation, are exercises of skillful know-how and are usually coupled with situated and embodied actions [we relate this topic to ours on decision-making] (Gallagher, 2017, p. 6).*

We can say that each of these assumptions mentioned by Gallagher (2017)—derived from human biological reality and longtime settled and recognized as guiding the study of language in several publications in the area—are adopted by us in this book over many chapters. The difference between Gal-laher and us is in the viewpoint from which we operate: Gallagher (2017) has as its starting point philosophical conjectures that escape the objective of our research.

The language perspective that we propose in this book is focused on the linguistic theories of cognition that correspond between language and the respective human biological process. Among them are the cognitive-contextual linguistic theories, which will be mentioned quickly and without depth, just to present counterpoints to our theory about the concept of nat-ural intelligence. Those theories study cognitive processes related to context, but do not reach consensus on what intelligence is. We can cite "Intelligence reframed: Multiple intelligences for the twenty first century," by Howard Gardner (1999) and Sternberg (1997) "Successful intelligence" as examples of different ways of describing intelligence. Other theorists claim that intelligence encompasses multiple skills. Gardner claims that intelligences are multiple, including linguistic, logical–mathematical, spatial, musical, kinesthetic-bodily, interpersonal, and intrapersonal intelligence.

Another definition found for "intelligence" is that it consists of the ability to recognize data and assimilate it into an entire image. This definition corresponds to a structural cognition of the human being with interpretive characteristics. There are also theories that describe intelligence as a system that classifies multiple intelligences into notions of polarity, as right or wrong; and others classifying it in terms of opposition to intellectual skills and behavioral attitudes.

In view of this variety of concepts, we need to leave two important aspects established: When speaking about "interpretation" and about "understanding," we refer to language. Without language there is no way to interpret the world. In addition, "skills" must be understood as the result of a "process." If a person has skills in mathematics, music, emotions, languages, those skills have already been processed by intelligence so that they could be understood by the individual. Skills are actions, the final step of processing natural intelligence according to the content of this book. Herrnstein and Murray, in "The bell curve" (1994), talk about heredity, high and low intelligence in a determined population, measuring the intelligence responsible for behaviors and capabilities. They are measuring the result of a process and not the process itself. When we discuss about intelligence, we need to focus on a comprehensive process. If we are concerned with measuring the results, we will not be able to get a conclusion due to the human capacity to produce infinite behaviors and actions.

Following Herrnstein and Murray (1994), and Gardner's (1999) line of reasoning and the theories mentioned earlier, the intelligence test is conceived as a series of tasks designed to measure the ability to make abstractions, learn, and deal with new situations. Among the most used are the Stanford-Binet Intelligence Scale and the Wechsler Scale (1981). The first was inspired by Binet-Simon (Roid, 2003), being used by Stanford University to test children from 2 years of age. It consists of a series of problems whose solution involves arithmetic, memory, and vocabulary skills. Intelligence measurement seeks the intelligence quotient, IQ, a term created by William Stern to measure a person's mental age based on a statistical percentage of people who expect to have a certain IQ, with the categories normal, gifted, and mentally disabled. Tests have also been developed trying to not reflect people's culture, such as the Johns Hopkins Perceptual Test, to measure children of preschool age intelligence using geometric figures.

So far, we can see tests measuring skills. We reinforce that they evaluate the results of processing intelligence. The analysis of geometric figures, for instance, implies interpretation and then, language. We understand that intelligence is a uniform structure prior to those skills, and it should be the focus of our attention so that the results are not as disparate as those that have been collected from the tests developed hitherto.

According to Gardner (1999), the conceptualization of intelligence has not advanced for decades; testing intelligence has focused on technologies useful in selecting people to fill academic or vocational niches. In line with the author (op. cit.), intelligence is the test result, with reasonable predictions about people's school performance. We disagree with his opinion and with the opinion of other theorists we have presented until now. Starting from the next topic, we expose our point of view on the phenomenon of natural intelligence and explain what natural language is and "how" it works. As Gallagher (2017, p. 8) states, "a theory of the mental has to account for processes."

3.2 What natural intelligence is and how it might be assessed?

We can cite among the ideas about intelligence, the concept of general intelligence as the "fluid ability" to integrate "multiple cognitive skills" to solve a new problem. Under this concept, intelligence is perceived as an accumulator of crystallized knowledge that will facilitate higher-level thinking. Spearman (2005), in the early 1900s advocated the existence of general intelligence related to information processing. This hypothesis comes close to the notion of cognition given by neuroscience, which is directly connected to our concept of natural intelligence. The mention of a "fluid capacity" is an indication that there is a previous underlying process. If there is a "multiplicity of skills," they have an origin that cannot be evaluated and that, however, can be accessed indirectly through understanding how the whole process works until it results in those "skills." This line of reasoning guides the next topics.

3.3 Principles underlying human intelligence

Before we carefully analyze the cognitive process, we need to turn our attention to language. As we saw in the previous paragraphs, intelligence assessment is commonly based on the measurement of understanding and skills. These matters refer to the language itself. Language mediates between what is in the outside world and the interior of the individual. Thus it should not be confused with cognition, which we call natural intelligence. So that the reader is not confused, we leave it only didactically established—because these elements are not independent—that: Cognition (natural intelligence) is a dynamic process that becomes viable through language (logical-axiomatic structure).

It is noteworthy that natural language cannot be understood as speech and writing (see Chapters 5 and 8). The first encompasses the complex natural intelligence system playing an important role in the construction of subjectivity, while the latter is restricted to the language rules. Written texts, speech, social context, and subjectivity must be considered linked to both.

Before exposing the functioning of natural intelligence and to make understandable its complexity, we explain, as an introduction, some principles about the role of language in the formation of human beings through the different points of view of Voloshinov (1973), Wallon (1934), and Lacan (1949) to better investigate the influences of external stimuli on it. The theory of these authors has in common one aspect that interests us: The fact that they consider the importance of context in the development of language.

The Sections 3.3.1–3.3.3 are dedicated to three currents of thought about language which represent a deepening in the concept of what language really is and about its role in the construction of the individual and his cognitive system.

We begin with Voloshinov (1973) teaching that the enunciation is influenced by the historical moment to which one belongs, showing that the understanding is not passive. Then, we show some aspects of Wallon's (1995) work, which addresses an important function of natural intelligence through a symbolic system that allows the individual to acquire the notion of "own body" as a global body. For Wallon (op. cit.), this phenomenon integrates psychic life with a symbolic order of operations. Finally, we discuss the morphogenic power of language reported by Lacan (1946/1998). This author explains that the symbolic activity of language interferes with the human being, determining a connection between imaginary ties to

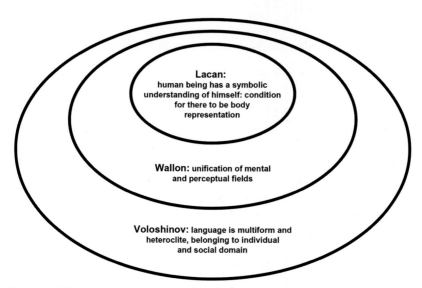

Fig. 3 In addition to being a system of signs, language must be related to the social context (because the historical moment influences the enunciation); to the body (as a symbolic system linked to the biological substrate, distinguishing the body from the externality); and to the other (condition for the individual to represent himself as a "self" in the form of a mental integration).

mental representations. The other, that is the otherness located on the imaginary plane, contributes to the formation of subjectivity (Fig. 3). This theoretical path shows, in an increasing order, the importance of language for cognition through which the human being understands himself as a "self" and understands the world around him.

3.3.1 Language concept given by Voloshinov

The works by the name of Valentin Voloshinov are believed to be authored by Mikhail Bakhtin. One of these works deals with language and ideology: "Marxism and the Philosophy of Language." In this book, Voloshinov (1973) argues that it is a mistake to study language in an abstract and synchronous way, not relating to its context. He justifies his position by stating that words are dynamic social signs and take on different meanings for different historical contexts. Because it is a system of signs endowed with material reality, language is the way for consciousness to emerge. Voloshinov (1973) states that language and human consciousness are associated. He adds that the meaning of words has to do with the active participation of the speaker and the receiver and that the manipulation of the word in each act of individual expression is regulated by social relations.

In his book, Voloshinov (op. cit.) devotes a section to the reported speech, showing that the social and temporal relations between expressions are properties of language. This issue was further explored by Roman Jakobson and influenced linguistic anthropology. The dialogism developed by Voloshinov, integrates meaning, cognition and consciousness in language, interfering in theories that talk about language and cognition. According to Voloshinov (1973), an individual's speech is organized not by individual conscience, but for what is external to him, for the social or extraverbal context. The author states that "all comprehension is dialogical" (op. cit., p. 232). Language mediates this dialogical relation; without it there is no interpretation or meaning. The language, then, is affected by the socio-historical context. This social interpretation of the nature of language is necessary to account for its dynamic and unpredictable nature.

In criticizing the abstract objectivism of language, Voloshinov (1973, pp. 83–84) states that:

> It is necessary to look for the roots of this orientation in the 17th and 18th century rationalism. Such roots plunge into the fertile soil of Cartesianism. It was Leibniz who first expressed these ideas clearly in his theory of universal grammar.
>
> The idea of a conventional, arbitrary language is characteristic of all rationalist currents, as well as the parallel established between the linguistic code and the mathematical code. To the rationalist spirit of mathematics, what matters is not the relationship of the sign with the reality reflected by it, or with the individual who engenders it, but the relationship of sign to sign within a closed system, and not nevertheless accepted and integrated. In other words, they are only interested in the internal logic of the sign system itself; it is considered, just as in logic, completely independent of the ideological meanings attached to it. Rationalists are also inclined to take into account the point of view of the receiver, but never that of the speaker as a subject who expresses his inner life, since the mathematical sign is less susceptible than any other to be interpreted as the expression of the individual psyche; the mathematical sign was, for the rationalists, the sign par excellence, the semiotic model, including for the language. It is precisely these ideas that are clearly expressed in the Leibnizian concept of universal grammar.

Extending his criticism to contemporary tendency for the abstraction, Voloshinov (1973) comments on Saussure's work, demonstrating that the latter, despite understanding what natural language is, abandons this perception to establish his "proton–pseudo" (false premise). Voloshinov (1973, p. 86) begins his debate by exposing the difference that Saussure (1916, p. 25) establishes between what we call conventional language and natural language:

Taken as a whole, the [natural] language is multiform and heteroclite; participating in several domains, physical, physiological and psychic, it still belongs to the individual domain and the social domain; it does not allow itself to be classified in any category of human facts, because it is not known how to isolate its unit. The [conventional] language, on the contrary, is a whole in itself and a principle of classification. From the moment we give it the greatest prominence among the facts of language, we introduce a natural order in a set that does not lend itself to any other classification.

Voloshinov (1973, p. 86).

To this distinction between natural language and conventional language, Voloshinov (1973, pp. 86–87) adds the contrast that Saussure (1916, p. 30) makes between language and speech:

Separating the [conventional] language from speech, it separates at the same time: first, what is social than what is individual; secondly, what is essential than what is accessory and relatively accidental.
The [conventional] language is not a function of the speaking subject, it is a product that the individual passively records; it never supposes premeditation and the reflection there only intervenes for the classification activity that we will deal with. On the contrary, speech is an individual act of will and intelligence within which it is appropriate to distinguish: first, the combinations by which the speaking subject uses the language code to express his personal thought; second, the psychophysical mechanism that allows it to externalize these combinations.

Voloshinov (1973, pp. 86–87).

Based on Saussure's proposals, Voloshinov (1973, p. 87) states that speech, with its individual and accidental character, is sovereign and is governed by laws completely different from those that govern the conventional language system. The way Saussure established the linguistic methodological path, banning speech, left his rationalist spirit, characterizing philosophical-linguistic thinking toward an "irrational domain that corrupts the logical purity of linguistic system" (Voloshinov, 1973, p. 88).

Speech, from the perspective of Voloshinov (1973, p. 90), does not contain any evidence of a system of immutable norms (which would be characteristic of conventional language). On the contrary, it encompasses an uninterrupted evolution of the norms of language.

To say that language, as a system of immutable and indisputable norms, has an objective existence is to make a serious mistake. But a perfectly objective relationship is expressed when it is said that the language constitutes, in relation to individual conscience, a system of immutable norms, that this is the language's mode of existence for every member of a given linguistic community.

(Voloshinov, 1973, p. 91).

Contrary to a purely mechanistic notion of language, Voloshinov (1973, pp. 106–109) argues that the meaning of the word is determined by its context. Isolating the word by stabilizing its meaning outside the context leads the linguist to create the "fiction of a unique part of reality, which is reflected in the language" (op. cit., p. 106). When individuals are born, they do not receive the language ready to be used: "They enter the current of verbal communication; […] only when they immerse themselves in this current does their conscience awake and begin to operate" (op. cit., p. 108). For the author (op. cit., p. 108), language as a system of norms is nothing more than an abstraction; he declares that "this system cannot serve as a basis for understanding and explaining linguistic facts as living and evolving facts." Voloshinov proposes that the true nature of language is a dialectical synthesis between objectivism and subjectivism in language, since even subjective speech (enunciation) has a social nature.

As a conclusion of this approach to language made by the philosopher and linguist Voloshinov (1973, p. 128), we emphasize that, during an enunciation (speech), not only linguistic forms (such as words, morphological and syntactic forms, sounds, intonations) enter the composition. Nonverbal elements are also part of this composition. If we lose sight of these elements, we will not be able to evaluate the concrete enunciation, the one that comes with the historical moment to which it belongs. This attitude leads to failures in understanding the meaning, which is one of the most difficult themes in linguistics and for which we still seek solution. Understanding cannot be passive as Voloshinov teaches:

> Nothing can remain stable in this process. That is why signification, an abstract element equal to itself, is absorbed by [context], and torn apart by its living contradictions, to finally return in the form of a new meaning with an equally provisional stability and identity.
>
> **(Voloshinov, 1973, p. 136).**

3.3.2 The phenomenon of bodily globality described by Wallon

When explaining this topic, it is important to keep in mind that language has a biological substrate, even concerning the symbolic system. To that end, we transcribe in detail some of Wallon's observations regarding the phenomenon in which the individual distinguishes his own body from an externality.

Going beyond communication and understanding shown in Section 3.3.1, and making an incursion into Psychology, an important function of natural intelligence is of encompassing a symbolic system and making it possible for the individual to acquire the notion of "own body" as bodily globality. This phenomenon was observed by the psychologist Dr. Henri Wallon in 1934. He states that bodily globality only exists with the integration of the "psychic life plan, to a different order of operations," in which "symbolic activity" intervenes (Wallon, 1995, p. 192). According to the author, the individual's psychic life (thoughts, emotions, mental representations) only connects to the outside world—in such a way that the former is able to distinguish his bodily unit as something distinct from the reality that surrounds him—through a symbolic system.

The studies by Wallon (1934) on the reaction of the child in front of a mirror, in the work "The origins of the character in the child" brings important reflections on language that, later, were taken up by Psychoanalyst Jacques Lacan in two works: "Family Complexes" (1936) and "The mirror stage as a form of the function of the Self" (Lacan, 1949). Some observations made by Wallon became important questions for Lacan, such as, for example, what does the relationship between the image and the child do? What is the relationship between the image in the mirror and the considerations that Lacan makes about the "self"? What is more about the child that is not present in the chimpanzee studied by Wallon?

Wallon's (1995) study of the symbolic system is important for unraveling aspects of something we take for granted. Wallon and, later, Lacan make clear the role of language in the delimitation of the self, whose conquest is slow, confused and integrated with the organic territory. In this topic, we describe some subjects commented by Wallon that were taken up by Lacan in the study of the role of the "other" (alterity/context) in the construction of the "self."

Cenesthesia or body awareness is not a complete skill at birth. Wallon (1995, p. 167) observed that the phenomenon of the sensitivity of one's own body has the function of opposing that body to the outside world and develops in stages. He reports that the child is born with a dissociation between three functional domains: The interoceptive (of visceral sensitivity), the proprioceptive (of sensations linked to balance, attitudes, and movements), and the steroceptive (of sensitivity toward excitations of external origin), the interoceptive being the earliest and the steroceptive the latest.

Within the domain of interoceptive sensitivity Wallon cites the food function as prevalent over the respiratory and circulatory in the child's psychic development. It states that dietary reflexes mediate between the needs of the organism and the external environment (op. cit., p. 175).

When talking about proprioceptive sensitivity, Wallon relates the system of functions that accompany motor activity to the constitution of the notion of the body itself. He says that proprioceptive sensitivity consists of cohesive "synergistic systems of movements and attitudes" related to muscle and psychic activity (Wallon, 1995, p. 178). This system of reflexes, according to his studies, is archaic when the child is born, and over time the reflexes "overlap one another, orient themselves towards the outside world, in order to respond with a growing appropriation to their varied excitations" (op. cit., p. 179). The author states that proprioceptive functions appear in the first moments of life and, "around the fifth month [the child can already] follow with the eyes for the first time an object that moves" (op. cit., p. 184).

With regard to the concept of natural intelligence and natural language, it is important to note that the human body is endowed with a system of reactions that regulate cohesion in space and time, shaping the "organism according to the opposite forces of the outside world and with objects of motor activity" (op. cit., p. 183). This is an axiomatic feature of language, which we will talk about later in this chapter and, in more detail, in Chapter 6. If its balance is not installed, there will be "instability of unity in action and in the formulas that correspond to it, in the physical and in the moral, [better saying,] in the immediate feeling of one's own body and personality" (Wallon, 1995, p. 184).

According to Wallon's observations, there are systems that capture external stimuli, providing the body with a set of impressions, but, at first, a relationship between own body and exterior is not yet established. Around the third month of the child's life

> *intersensory associations [...] between the interoceptive and proprioceptive domains start to appear, on the one hand and the steroceptive [...] on the other, the sources of excitation are individualized and at the same time the field of perception is unified [so that] the child starts looking with their eyes for the glass that clinked. Even though the excitement ceased, they worriedly sought its source.*
>
> ***(Wallon, 1995, pp. 188–189).***

In this case, the child can establish a relationship between a sound he heard and its external cause: "The orientation of their attention becomes more abstract" (op. cit., p. 189).

The ability to reduce impressions of the same origin into a common source is something that develops in the child over time. According to Wallon, the child becomes more able to detach from the present and *instead of fragmented impressions, which absorb [the child] totally and whose succession will necessarily have to be a kind of psychic fragmentation, the unification of mental continuity operates with their perceptual field.*

(op. cit., p. 189).

Around the age of 4 months, the author realizes, that "the child begins to attract the eye when it comes in contact with an object; their eyes guide when they try to reach it" (Wallon, 1995, p. 190). At the end of the sixth month of age

there is progress of mental activity and anticipatory aptitude regarding the direct perception of things [...]. [The child] looks at some things that have nothing in special as if trying to discover something attractive in them. They anticipate the excitement to arouse it.

(Wallon, 1995, p. 190).

Wallon's (1995, p. 191) insight can be seen in his following observation: "As soon as two objects are able to entertain [the child] simultaneously, [he] cannot prevent himself from combining them [...] and to constitute a single whole with them." The author explains that the simple placement of objects together does not necessarily lead to a combination by the child. There is something more that makes an integration. The simple approximation of things, as evident as their mutual conveniences may seem, does not automatically explain their discovery by man, child, or animal.

A turning point on Wallon's (1995) studies about the children is that their intuition power is what drives them to realize, effectively or mentally, a convenient combination. As a result, Wallon admits that

the system of sensory or motor data corresponding to the object cannot make [the child] perceive as an object unless it is integrated into another plane of psychic life, a different order of operations, in which symbolic activity intervenes [...] the notion of the body itself could not be the result of an automatic combination between different sensibilities.

(Wallon, 1995, p. 192).

Children of different ages, in front of their image reflected in the mirror, demonstrate, by Wallon's (1995, p. 202) observation, the steps that they go through until they "come to integrate, in a whole intuition, everything that is related with their physical personality." The author states that the children recognize their aesthetic aspect, transmitted by the mirror, in two stages: They perceive an image and relate that image to themselves. However, Wallon does not deal with the element that establishes this relationship. Wallon speaks of a "symbolic activity" mentioning successive integrations that link psychological evolution to biological evolution (Gaufey, 1998, p. 31).

In comparison with the monkey, Wallon (1995, p. 205) claims to be a stage that the child does not suddenly reach and for him it seems that.

The reaction of superior monkeys in front of a mirror is of a much higher level. They immediately pass their hand from behind, expressing anger at not finding anything they can grab and from that moment on they refuse to look at it.

The children's manifestation in front of the mirror is intermittent until they reach the sixth month of age, when they start to associate their own image with other reactions, under the impact of an "external circumstance." Wallon's wit comes from observing the case Darwin reported about his own son.

Darwin's son smiles at his image and that of his father, seen in the mirror. However, he finds himself very surprised when he hears him speak behind his back. Therefore, he still did not know how to coincide in time and space the aspect reflected by the mirror and the real presence of his father.
(Wallon, 1995, p. 206).

Wallon states that the auditory excitement coming from the father's voice behind the child led to the discovery of the relationship between the mirror image and the object:

The gesture of attribution that associated the image with the object, and translated its juxtaposition into identity, did not have as a starting point the previous intuition of that identity. This intuition is, on the contrary, consecutive. The gesture prepared it, paved the way for it.
(Wallon, 1995, pp. 206–207).

This discovery of the interference of the other (alterity/context) by Wallon is crucial for our considerations on the meaning construction. Wallon draws attention to the fact that

the verification of a relationship is an act of knowledge [...] the child's behavior really indicates that he does not surrender to a tendency that has become familiar, to a habit that is somewhat unconscious; on the contrary, it is an indication that he is doing something new, resolving a difficulty, integrating in a kind of higher order what until then had no specific connection with him.
(Wallon, 1995, pp. 207–208).

During this period of childhood (6 months of age) the child's intersensory associations allow him to distinguish elements, individualize them and unite them in a higher plane of psychic activity, and this is a language assignment as Lacan explains (see Section 3.3.3).

The presence of a simple juxtaposition instead of an integration is appreciated by Wallon (1995, p. 208) as the mental incapacity of the 6–month–old child in not knowing how to capture the true subordinate relationships. He states that what the child lacks is the ability to raise the representation of things to a higher plane, in which his existence would no longer be substantially linked to that of the images found in the sensorimotor space, but would result from the order to be established between these images, around their ideal center (Wallon, 1995, p. 209).

The representation process that comes from language, according to Wallon (1995, pp. 210–211), takes place in the child when he has an "illusion of reality," that is, "between the immediate experience and the representation of things' there is 'the intervention of a dissociation that highlights the qualities and existence peculiar to the object itself, […] attributing to him, among other essential characters, those of exteriority. There is no representation without it." The author concludes that the representation of the body itself "can only be formed by externalizing it" (op. cit.).

In conclusion, Wallon (1995, p. 214) makes an important contribution to thinking about the design of artificial intelligence. He reflects on the child's ability to unify his self and be able to establish distinctions and relationships in space as a "condition" and not a "consequence" of true learning.

The author establishes this unification as a prelude to symbolic activity and outlines two needs for this to occur:

> *[the child] admitting images that only have the appearance of reality and affirming the reality of images that evade perception.*
> *[and being able] to multiply, through representations, the increasingly differentiated game of distinctions and equivalences.*
> **(Wallon, 1995, p. 213)**

3.3.3 Lacan and the cognitive structuring in stages

As for the principles that govern language seen so far, Voloshinov (1973) taught that enunciation is influenced by the historical moment to which it belongs, and that understanding is not passive. Wallon (1995) shows us that true learning is conditioned by the ability to establish distinctions and relationships that are integrated with a symbolic activity. Lacan (1936), in turn, goes beyond the two authors mentioned, explaining the morphogenic power that this symbolic activity (language) has on the human being.

Lacan (1936) contrasts with Wallon's neuropsychological theory and places the family as an integral part of the psychic phenomena that structure subjectivity. He uses the concept of imago to refer to the unconscious representation that is constituted between the cultural dimension that determines this representation and the imaginary ties that organize it.

The concept of language for Lacan is not detached from the reality in which the individual lives. On the contrary, family complexes are part of the construction of subjectivity and act in the mental identification of the person. Children aged 6 months to 2 years, for Lacan (1949) are located in a "stadium" in which the recognition of a rival, that is, of an "other" as an object, is outlined, and this situation manifests itself only within an age limit. Lacan observes the reactions, of exhibition, seduction and despotism, in this phase of the child's development, and concludes that in a situation of conflict between two opposite attitudes, each partner confuses the other's part with his own and identifies with him. This identification that is based on a feeling of the other, Lacan (1936) calls imago. According to what Lacan (1949) teaches, the "self," in its constitution, is affected by the identification process, which, in turn, can bring the mark of the relationship with the other. In this case, identification can lead to the formation of this "self" according to the model of the other.

The theory of affective identification is called the "mirror stage" (Lacan, 1949), which deals with the moment of the "weaning decline," at the end of the child's 6 months of age. The influence of Wallon's theory here is quite intense. Some elements used for Lacan (mirror stage, declining weaning, delayed physical growth) were already present in Wallon's theory.

Lacan (1949) went further in his text "The mirror stage as the creator of the function of the Self." He describes the individual's psychic/cognitive structuring "in stages, according to images taken from the other" called "projective identifications" (Roudinesco and Plon, 2006, p. 194). The author takes the expression "proof of the mirror" from Wallon (which was conceived as a natural dialectic), and transforms it into the "mirror stage," conceived as a stage in which the human being has a symbolic understanding of himself.

We can observe that the enactivist theory (Gallagher, 2017) defines intercorporeality as a mutual influence of body schemes. Intercorporeality has already been developed by Wallon, Lacan and, also, by phenomenology (Merleau-Ponty, 1968, 2012) as explained by Gallagher (2017), under evidence that baby and caregiver interactions have a shared language.

Lacan goes further than enactivism in our opinion; he mentions the symbolic system. It is through the symbolic system that the individual discovers that he is a "self." We point out that in this process if there is understanding of something, there is mediation of language.

The theory of affective identification is called the "mirror stage" (Lacan, 1949), which deals with the moment of the "weaning decline," at the end of the child's 6 months of age. The influence of Wallon's theory here is quite intense. Some elements used for Lacan (mirror stage, declining weaning, and delayed physical growth) were already present in Wallon's theory. But he realizes that the "jubilatory waste of energy that marks the triumph," indicates that there is a relationship between the image and the child. For Lacan, a subject/self "appears" in the movement between looking at the image in the mirror and looking at the other. By relating the mirror stage to the energetic investment of libido and mental structure, Lacan (1949) goes beyond Wallon's developmentalism. For Lacan (op. cit.), the image in the mirror establishes a relationship (provokes identity) with an intrusion of the other. The mirror image introduces a unity that contributes to the formation of the self.

The "self" is presented by Lacan (1949) as an additional element, responsible for the identity of the subject who sees the image in the mirror. For the author, this element (self) comes from outside and guarantees the formation of an ambiguous structure that comes with the destructive essence of the other: The "self" corresponds to a place of relation between the individual and the space. In this case, there is no juxtaposition between the child and the other, but there is an ability to raise the representation of the image reflected in the mirror to a higher plane: The "self" that apprehends itself as a body among bodies, representing itself distinctly from the other.

The existence of a "primordial symbolism" (Lacan, 1949) of the object, making the latter be related to an "extension outside the limits of vital instincts" or to a "perception as an instrument" is the essence of the symbolization process. Lacan (1949) observes that without this process—in which there is dissociation between the "self" and the other, attributing characters to the exteriority—there is no representation. For there to be a "proper body" (body representation), this condition must be met. The representation of the body itself can only be formed by exteriorizing, that is, being represented by a symbolic process.

These conclusions by Lacan are corroborated by Wallon's observations, when Wallon (1995, p. 211) states that, for the child to be able to unify his self in space, there is a double need: To admit images that only have the appearance of reality and to affirm the reality of images that evade perception, sensitive but not real images, real images but subtracted from sensory knowledge. Wallon (1995) already stated that the notion of existence implies substitutions of images and points of view. It implies the ability to evolve above the present sensorimotor; to evoke, in contrast to current impressions, purely virtual systems of representation; or rather, the ability to subordinate the data of immediate experience to pure representation; and to multiply, through representations, the increasingly differentiated game of distinctions and equivalences. This process is called the prelude to symbolic activity, which can be explained by the following words: By this phenomenon, the individual is able to transmute the data of sensitivity into representations.

The interference of the cultural and social context in the language evidenced by Voloshinov (1973) is corroborated by Lacan (1949) findings, when the latter affirms that the "self," in the identification process, takes the trace of a relationship with the other; it is to the other that the subject identifies himself (Lacan, 1949).

Lacan conceptualized the "symbolic" by relating it to a specific concept of language. For him, language is not immaterial. It is linked to a body with its own dimension: A dimension that at the same time is linked to an instinctive conduct and to the mental field (psyche). Lacan (1953/1998a) defines the symbolic as the signifier that precedes signification, and in 1974 and 1975, he gave his 22nd seminar (unpublished), in which he states that the real, the symbolic, and the imaginary are intertwined. We see, in this way, that the interference of the cultural and social context in the language evidenced by Voloshinov is corroborated by Lacan's findings, when he affirms that the body is affected by language, and the "self," in the identification process, traces a relationship with the other. Is it for the other that the subject identifies himself? As Radej (2020) teaches, Hegel, Peirce, Freud, and Lacan made use of triadic structures to illustrate the placement of an intermediate element in two others, attributing characteristics of irrationality, inconsistency, and transience to the intermediate elements. In this case, triadic thinking is not opposed to dyadic thinking, but incorporates it into a broader and more explanatory scheme.

The description of Wallon (1995) as a child's gesture of attribution in front of the mirror corresponds, in Lacan's view, to the "imago," to the unconscious representation that comes from something external to the individual. According to Lacan (1949), the mirror image seems to be the threshold of the visible world.

In his text "The mirror stage as the creator of the function of the Self," Lacan (1949) writes about the structuring of the self, in stages, in projective identifications with the other (Roudinesco and Plon, 2006). He takes the expression "proof of the mirror," by Wallon, and transforms it into "mirror stage." What was described in Wallon as a natural dialectic, becomes for

Lacan the "mirror stage," a psychic operation, or even ontological, in which the individual identifies with the other who is holding him, describing this phenomenon through the prism of the unconscious (Roudinesco and Plon, 2006). He observes that there is a tension between the anticipation of the child's jubilatory joy for recognizing himself in front of the mirror as a "self" and his own insufficiency in placing himself in front of the mirror, depending, for that, on the support of another person. Thus, the other is part of the construction of the child's "psychic space" (self). This circumstance is exemplified in the Fig. 4.

The importance of discussing Lacan's finding for this book lies in the fact that he understands that the mirror stage is a form of higher psychic activity. This activity is the natural intelligence allowing the child to "understand" himself as a separate entity from the other to assume his own image as "self." This understanding can only happen through a symbolic system (natural language) that allows a mental "representation" of that "self" to exist. We must emphasize that the child's experience of seeing himself in the mirror joins his image projected in the mirror through a form of mental integration. Natural

Fig. 4 For Lacan, the recognition event can take place from the age of 6 months. A baby who, before the mirror, still without having control of the gait or even the upright posture, overcomes in a jubilatory bustle, the obstacles of this support, to sustain their posture and rescue, to fix it, an instantaneous aspect of the image.

language (which promotes mental integration) mediates the reality of what is happening by uniting it with the mental representation of the "self." We observe in this complex picture the functioning of the universal structure of language: The axiomatic element of the experience lived by the child combined with the logical element, in which he makes the relation and integration of the image into a "self."

> The connection between the psychic, the biological and the morphogenic power of the image is demonstrated by Lacan (1946/1998) in an experiment in which he observes that the dove only ovulates in the presence of his fellow men. When the dove is placed in front of a mirror, can ovulate in two and a half months. According to Lacan (1946/1998) the imago gives form to the Self, it has the effect of alienating the subject, because it is in the other that he identifies himself. The imago can be conceived as an 'early maturation of visual perception' and acquires a 'functional anticipation value' in front of the mirror (Lacan, 1946, p. 187) performing a 'resolutive identification' in the imaginary space-time complex (op. cit., p. 189).
> **(Monte-Serrat, 2014, p. 132).**

Lacan's description of the language's morphogenic power is further evidence of its role in putting body and environment in relation. The body interprets the situation because there is a system that puts it "in relation" to the world. It is what we can observe in Merleau-Ponty:

> Erotic perception is not a cogitation that intends a cogitatum; through one body it aims at another body, and it is accomplished in the world, not within consciousness. For me a scene does not have a sexual signification when I imagine, even confusedly, its possible relation to my sexual organs or to my states or pleasure, but rather when it exists for my body, for this always ready power of trying together the given stimuli into an erotic situation and for adapting a sexual behavior to it.
> **(Merleau-Ponty, 2012, p. 159).**

This relationship installed by the structure of language and its resulting morphogenic power can be observed in love emotions, as described by Pierre de Chardin:

> Love dies from the contact of the impersonal and the anonymous. And it unfailingly degrades with the remoteness in space - and even more so with the difference in time. To love ourselves, it is essential to coexist. Never, for as wonderful as his predicted figure is, never could Omega just balance the game of human attractions and repulsions if he did not act with equal power, that is to say with the same padding of Proximity - In love, as in any Another kind of energy is in the existing data that the lines of force have to close at all times. Ideal center, virtual center, none of this is enough (…) To be supremely attractive, Omega must be present.
> **(Chardin, 1956, pp. 296–297).**

Although Merleau–Ponty and Chardin describe eroticism and love based on different theoretical foundations, it is possible to observe that there is a need for an exchange, a relationship that is carried by the symbolic system of natural language (with its biological and rational elements: The axiomatic logical structure). This need of exchange or relationship is implicit in Gallagher (2017, p. 69) concept of behavior when he agrees that

> *Erotic intentionality is not a matter of a propositional attitude or an instrumental rationality; nor is it reducible to a set of observable behaviors, or, even if it does have something to do with desire, to some attributional/inferential link behavior and belief. It's a form of intentionality that seemingly goes beyond the terms of folk psychology.*
>
> **(Gallagher, 2017, p. 69).**

We conclude that the author (Gallagher, 2017) indirectly and in other words, accepts the existence of a morphogenic power of language when describing the following phenomenon:

> *Face perception not just objective patterns that we might recognize conceptually as emotions. It involves complex interactive behavioral and response patterns arising out of an active engagement with the other's face – not simple recognition of objective features, but interactive perception that constitutes an experience of significance or valence that shapes response. Social perception is affective in ways different from object perception. The experience of the gaze of another person directed back at you 'affects' you, even if this affect is not consciously recognized [...] The perception of emotion is itself affective.*
>
> **(Gallagher, 2017, p. 117, highlighted by the author).**

While we classify morphogenic power as an element of language, Gallagher (2017, pp. 118–199) conceives it as a nonrepresentational factor that has a perceptual response: "Such things as affects and effects of respiration and heart rate are not represented as part of my perception; they are nonrepresentational factors that have an effect on perceptual response."

We understand that the nonrepresentational classification given by Gallagher (2017) is contradictory. When the author (Gallagher, 2017, p. 117) states that constituting an "experience of significance or valence that shapes the response" is not a simple recognition, he does not consider that contemplating a "meaning" or "valence" already indicates that there is representation through a symbolic system.

The morphogenic power of language (Lacan, 1946) shifts our gaze to something that is beyond the sensory observation of the environment that would be looking for visual discontinuities or colors. The study of language is complex because it is necessary to consider a subject behind this look that observes the environment. While scientifically describing the individual who looks at or appreciates something, we consider a generic perception in interoceptive and proprioceptive terms as part of the construction of a mental representation. When we put the concept of the individual aside and think of a subject of perception, the look is analyzed from another perspective because the subject's appreciation is charged with subjectivity. In this case, one can think of the mental representation associated with the concept of imaginary registration given by Lacan (1953) combined with the morphogenic power of language (Lacan, 1946).

3.3.4 Conclusion

The most important contribution of the theoretical considerations made in this topic is that the body is an important element in the symbolization process. Foucault (1963) establishes a difference between the Cartesian conception of the body (res extensa) and the notion of body and thought (res cogitans). The human cognitive system unites the biological system with the symbolic system (language). The work in the field of artificial intelligence and cognitive computing must take this union into account. Language is articulated to the body, despite the scientific demarcations in the functions of both.

The psychosomatic manifestations studied by Psychology show that language is incorporated and that the body is not limited to what is natural and observable evidence. Language has its own dimension that interferes with the functioning of the body, regulating it by an instinctive knowledge.

> […] cognition [natural language in our point of view] doesn't exist if there is just a brain without bodily and worldly factors. The mind is relational. It's a way of being in relation to the world' […].
>
> **(Gallagher, 2017, p. 12).**

Wallon (1995), Lacan (1949), and Voloshinov (1973), each within their specialty, leave as a lesson the perception that the individual's body is linked to a symbolic process, and that this process mediates between the individual's mind and his exteriority. This is the reason why we cannot separate language from natural intelligence. The body has contact with the external reality, "picks up" its impressions and "prints" the correspondent of those impressions in the individual's mind. We can conclude that natural language and natural intelligence are conceived within the body. Language here is taken as a whole system that goes beyond a set of rules within a logical chain. Natural language is a complex system attached to natural intelligence to mediate between what is "inside" and what is "outside" of the person's body.

As reinforcement, the influence of the outside world on what goes on inside the individual was not only observed in the humanities but also in the formal sciences, as is the case of the study on the interference of the natural world in the emotion of the couple Romeo and Juliet. Some authors (Sprot, 2004; Strogatz, 1994; Gottman et al. 2002; Radzicki, 1993) wrote about the love relationship of couples and love triangles analyzing the chaotic behavior influenced by the positive and negative external environment. Even starting from simple linear models of love, the authors described complex dynamics faithful to the common human experience. Anyway, this is just an example that it is possible to describe mathematically the love situation (internal emotion) of men and women affected by the surrounding environment. We use these references to consider "love" as a propositional attitude that can be interpreted in a special way involving the symbolic system (language). Cognitive psychology explains that cognition (natural intelligence or mental processes) is determined by extrinsic properties such as history and environmental relations. In this way, cognitive states and processes are constituted by the occurrence, transformation, and storage (in the mind/brain) of structures that carry information (representations) (Pitt, 2020). This construction of semantically evaluable mental objects— as thoughts, concepts, perceptions, ideas, impressions, notions, rules, schemes, images—is intermediated by the symbolic system (language).

Once, we are aware of the role of language in the functioning of natural intelligence, we now provide a detailed analysis of the last one to understand how properties extrinsic to the individual interfere with his cognitive system and, consequently, with his behavior. We can say, in advance, is that our bet, in this book, focuses on the axiomatic-logical structure of language, which is responsible for "translating" information from outside into mental representations.

Having exteriority, body and language linked, how would it be possible to transfer this connection between exterior and interior to the machine design? Can natural intelligence, with its variability and uncertainty, with perception and cognition influenced by the external world, be transformed into machine learning?

From the point of view that language does not reside only in subjectivity but suffers interference from the contextual reality of the individual, this chapter is dedicated to explaining how natural intelligence is processed, causing decision-making. Based on what is established here, it is possible to outline the first impressions about the structural paradigm of cognitive computing, which will be developed in the following chapters, as we show the strategic procedure to be applied to artificial intelligence.

We make, in the next sections, a presentation of what is meant by natural intelligence, innovating in the sense of establishing its foundations to be translated into a universal structure. In this way, it is possible to understand how natural language works so that this knowledge can be replicated in machine learning, making the latter more intuitive and less ambiguous. The other chapters discuss aspects of natural language in more depth until reaching Chapter 10, where some applications of the universal structure of natural language confirm it experimentally.

3.4 Natural intelligence

This book has as its essence the study of the universal structure of language, which is taken also for natural intelligence, since both encompass complex processes for the construction of understanding. Considering a theoretical need, we can differentiate both concepts establishing that the universal structure of natural intelligence is an abstraction. It is an ethereal algorithm that describes "how" natural language operates. Natural language, in its turn, encompasses the complex biological systems that range from the entrance of the stimulus into the body until the moment they are "translated" or understood as such by the individual. Universal structure of natural intelligence would then be the abstract description of the functioning of natural language.

While the natural language is conceived as a living complex system, the universal structure of language (natural intelligence) is the way in which parts of that living complex interact with the ability to generate a new quality of behavior such as emotions, actions, and understanding. The latter can only be replicated in artificial intelligence and cognition computing after having its dynamics mapped and understood. Thus we are going the opposite way to that adopted by Goodfellow et al. (2016):

From a scientific and philosophical point of view, machine learning is interesting because developing our understanding of machine learning entails developing our understanding of the principles that underlie intelligence.
(Goodfellow et al., 2016, p. 99).

Our underlying view is the means to achieve self-learning technologies similar to human cognition. We emphasize that the scope and methodology of both, AI and cognitive computing, overlap precisely because they lay their foundations (consciously or unconsciously) in the universal structure of natural language. The constitutional characteristics of the last one must be present in the machine's algorithm, so that it has an intuitive performance.

Some aspects of fundamental laws that govern the cognitive process are exposed in the following sections so that they can be carried out in mathematical formulations. We present some principles that reside in the universal natural language algorithm (which corresponds to the natural intelligence), so that they not only explain a series of known language facts but also make it possible to include unexpected predictions arising from the language complexity.

There is a concern to describe in detail the interaction of some physiological mechanisms related to natural intelligence so that they can be better mathematically modeled in the machine learning process. This topic focuses on cognition (natural intelligence) at its biological and functional level. We highlight the importance of this approach for artificial intelligence, since the latter has been related, with some success, to neural mechanisms, and experimentally confirmed. We hope that from the understanding of systems hierarchy related to the cognitive process, predictions will open to vast areas in future research.

Being a complex system that works according to a "functional" hierarchy, natural intelligence aims to "build the process of understanding." Where there is understanding, there is language. According to Perlovsky (2016, p. 2), for the success of natural intelligence, there are higher- and lower-level functional interactions. These interactions are bidirectional, and at times, a higher-level model unifies the lower-level ones to create a more abstract and general concept (Perlovsky, 2016). To exemplify this approach, inspired by Perlovsky's physics of the mind (2016), we can classify as natural intelligence: (1) The mechanism of understanding abstract objects, events, and ideas; (2) the instincts, as mechanism of measuring important vital parameters; (3) the emotions, which communicate instinctive needs to the mechanisms of understanding conceptual recognition. The natural intelligence hierarchically structures these elements to govern behavior (decision-making). Then, most human behavior occurs as consequence of the cognitive system functioning, which improves concepts, understanding, and knowledge (Perlovsky, 2016).

The universal structure of language in our opinion encompasses the entire natural intelligence system that aims to build understanding. This universal structure is taken by Perlovsky (2016, p. 3) as "vagueness of mental models." This author states that those models' inaccuracy is fundamental to perception. We establish that this inaccuracy corresponds to an ethereal structure on which perceptions will be combined to correspond to a complex result. Due to its universality, the structure of cognition encompasses large number of combinations. Perlovsky (1998) calls this a combinatorial complexity. What the author states about his vague model describes, in our opinion, the characteristics of the natural intelligence functioning:

> Vague models avoid a need to consider combinations. The vague-to-crisp process is fundamental for self-organization, perception and cognition; vague representations and processes are not conscious, possibly for this reason vagueness of representations has not been appreciated by psychologists and mathematicians modeling the mind, and this is the reason why mind processes have not been mathematically modeled and understood in artificial intelligence (Perlovsky, 2001; Russell and Norvig, 2010).
>
> **(Perlovsky, 2016, p. 3).**

The axiomatic-logical structure of natural language encompasses an infinite series of combinations made by natural intelligence, which will be given as needed, reproducing an image, an emotion, the interpretation of a work of art, the understanding of something that has been said and so on. As an example of this we can cite Perlovsky (2016, p. 3):

> The process 'from vague to crisp' until models match retinal projections take approximately 150 ms. These includes many neuronal operations: about 10 ms per firing of a neuron, while tens of thousands of neurons are participating in parallel. The initial part of this process cannot be accessed by consciousness, vague models and processes are not accessible to consciousness. Conscious perceptions occur only at the moment of model-projections matching object-projections from the retina.

We emphasize the last sentence—that "conscious perceptions occur only at the moment of model-projections matching object-projections from the retina"—to draw the reader's attention toward the characteristic of the structure of language in the construction of sense: Meaning is not born ready but it is built in its relationship with the context. In the case of Perlovsky's quote, consciousness, cognitive understanding occurs when there is a "relationship" between the projections of the model and the projections of the object on the retina. The property of natural language, of constructing the meaning "in relation to" is repeated in different situations, such as those reported in the works of Voloshinov, Wallon, Lacan (already highlighted) and in the works of Saussure, Jakobson, and others, who are mentioned in the next chapters.

Explaining and arguing a little more with support in Perlovsky's work (2016, p. 3), the author states that: "The founder of logic, Aristotle explained to his students that logic is needed to argue what has been already understood, but not for understanding of new phenomena." About natural language, comparatively, we can say that the axiomatic (living) element of the intelligence universal structure "translates" the impressions and stimuli to which the body is exposed, and, in the sequence, the logical element of language takes action based on what has already been "understood" by the body, bringing to consciousness those potentialities which were not yet logical at the first moment.

3.5 Natural intelligence determined by the biological constitution of the individual

Lenneberg (1967) observed that there is a latent structure of cognition determined by the biological properties of the human being. This structure allows forms of categorization based on operational characteristics of the brain's data processing mechanism. The author also noted that cognitive ability performs alternatives to types of input stimuli, exemplifying this statement with language acquisition by deaf people regardless of the processing of acoustic patterns. That is, there is an underlying symbolic mechanism whose existence is structural in human beings (what we call natural intelligence). This symbolic system serves as a basis for the development of conventional language, but, in the absence of conditions to develop the latter, other capacities take its place, as in the case of deaf and blind people who develop language capacities in configurations of physically perceived stimuli.

Cognition is a process that involves the perception of the world and how the individual symbolizes and reacts to it. According to Chardin (1956, p. 39) the two outer and inner faces of the world correspond to each other in such a way that one can move from one to the other, with the sole condition of replacing "mechanical interaction" with "consciousness." There is a dynamic movement of natural intelligence that evolves from vague, fuzzy, and unconscious states to more concrete and conscious states, and thus realizing the essence of perception that can give rise to decision-making (Perlovsky and Kozma, 2007, p. 1).

3.6 Natural intelligence setting alternatives for complementary aspects to emerge in consciousness: The axiomatic-logical structure functioning

To deepen some aspects of natural intelligence and clarify the way in which the symbolic system intermediates the external reality and the individual's mind, we describe the functioning of the natural language logical-axiomatic structure. The symbolization mechanism transports different operators helping the brain to translate aspects of the physical world into information that is intelligible to the biological body. For this task, we adapted the information theory of Abrahan Moles (1978).

The axiomatic-logical structure of natural language provides two faces for the natural intelligence: The process of meaning construction by the cognitive system (biological) and, on the other hand, the information previously provided by the structure of language as a convention (set of rules). It concerns the possibility of giving a specialized organization to the sparse connections of the brain, generating an increasing order of instances within a dynamic system, to integrate them into a persuasion, an information, an understanding, and so on. The universal principles (axioms) of natural language operate as the basis for its following logical deductions.

3.6.1 The cognitive system

Cognitive abilities of natural intelligence process are supported by specific neuronal networks. Human being has a motor hierarchy that functions in an interdependent way: The spinal cord and brainstem are involved in processing the activity of individual muscles such as walking and reflex actions that initiate consciously. There are also the third and fourth levels of that hierarchy:

> *Voluntary movements require the participation of the third and fourth levels of the hierarchy: the motor cortex and the association cortex. These areas of the cerebral cortex plan voluntary actions, coordinate sequences of movements, make decisions about proper behavioral strategies and choices, evaluate the appropriateness of a particular action given the current behavioral or environmental context, and relay commands to the appropriate sets of lower motor neurons to execute the desired actions.*
>
> **(Knierim, 2020, n.p.).**

The motor cortex comprises: The primary motor cortex, premotor cortex, and supplementary motor area:

> The motor cortex comprises three different areas of the frontal lobe, immediately anterior to the central sulcus. These areas are the primary motor cortex (Brodmann's area 4), the premotor cortex, and the supplementary motor area [...]. Electrical stimulation of these areas elicits movements of particular body parts. The primary motor cortex, or M1, is located on the precentral gyrus and on the anterior paracentral lobule on the medial surface of the brain. Of the three motor cortex areas, stimulation of the primary motor cortex requires the least amount of electrical current to elicit a movement. Low levels of brief stimulation typically elicit simple movements of individual body parts. Stimulation of premotor cortex or the supplementary motor area requires higher levels of current to elicit movements, and often results in more complex movements than stimulation of primary motor cortex. [...] the premotor cortex and supplementary motor areas appear to be higher level areas that encode complex patterns of motor output and that select appropriate motor plans to achieve desired end results.
>
> **(Knierim, 2020, n.p.).**

The classical neuroscience defines the brain motor scheme covering the following areas and functions: Broca area; sensory area; somato-sensorial area; auditive area; visual area; Wernicke area; association area; prefrontal cortex (superior mental functions: representation, planning, and execution of the actions; cognition; behavior and emotional control; environment adaptation; working memory). The Figs. 5 and 6 illustrate this classification.

The complexity of cognition system led, in a fMRI study, Benjamin et al. (2017) to identify multiple language-critical areas that includes Broca's and Wernicke Area (inferior and superior), Exner's Area, Supplementary Speech Area, Angular Gyrus, and Basal Temporal Language Area.

Although classical doctrine relates some areas of the brain to language, we propose in this book to think of language linked to natural intelligence. In this way, natural language is conceived as a complex system that goes beyond the network of neurons and supporting cells to provide an understanding (natural intelligence) of the world involving functional mechanisms such as thought, memory, emotion, and sleep.

It is proposed to understand natural language as the system that involves since the capture (input) of the external stimulus made by the body, the passage through the central cognitive system (natural intelligence) that transforms the stimulus into mental representation and exit (output) by human action, all of them working together as an integrated whole.

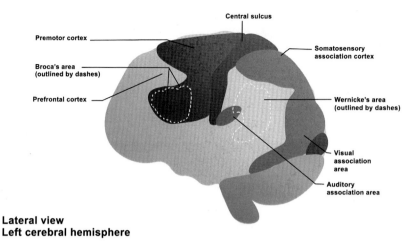

Lateral view
Left cerebral hemisphere

Fig. 5 Central nervous system. *(Based on Copstead, L.E., Banasik, J., 2013. Pathophysiology, fifth ed. Elsevier Inc., p. 866; Patton, K., Thibodeau, G., 2013. Mosby's Handbook of Anatomy & Physiology. Elsevier Health, p. 441; Thompson, E., 2007. Mind in Life: Biology, Phenomenology and the Sciences of Mind. Harvard University Press, Cambridge, MW, with permission from Elsevier.)*

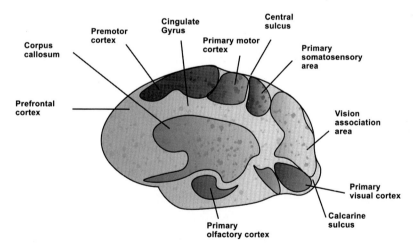

Left cerebral hemisphere

Fig. 6 Lateral view left hemisphere: Central nervous system. *(Based on Copstead, L.E., Banasik, J., 2013. Pathophysiology, fifth ed. Elsevier Inc., p. 866 and Patton, K., Thibodeau, G., 2013. Mosby's Handbook of Anatomy & Physiology. Elsevier Health, p. 441, with permission from Elsevier.)*

The nervous system is traditionally divided into three principal anatomic units: the central nervous system (CNS), the peripheral nervous system (PNS), and the autonomic nervous system (ANS).These systems are not automatically or functionally distinct, and they work together as an integrated whole. Therefore, when function [...] the nervous system is more conveniently divided into sensory, motor, and higher brain functions.

[...] The CNS includes the brain and the spinal cord. Its primary functions are receiving and processing sensory information and creating appropriate responses to be relayed to muscles and glands. It is the site of emotion, memory, cognition, and learning. The CNS is bathed in cerebrospinal fluid (CSF) [and] interacts with the neurons of PNS through synapses in the spinal cord and cranial nerve glia. The cranial and spinal nerves constitute the PNS.

(Copstead and Banasik, 2013, p. 858).

The peripheral nervous systems comprise 31 pairs of spinal nerves and 12 pairs of cranial nerves. Certain areas of the cerebral cortex are associated with specific functions: Frontal lobe is in charge of complex thought, motivation, and morality; the temporal lobe encompasses the auditory center and parts of the language center; the occipital lobe is linked to visual functions; the parietal lobe contains the somatosensory cortex; the limbic area is responsible for memory and emotion (Copstead and Banasik, 2013, p. 877) (Figs. 7 and 8).

The body is somatotopically represented by the spinal cord and the cerebral cortex as taught by Copstead and Banasik (2013, p. 891):

Projections to the somatosensory cortex begin in sensory receptors throughout the body. Receptors send axons to the spinal cord through the dorsal root. Stimulations of the receptors by mechanical deformation, temperature, or chemical alters membrane permeability, resulting in receptor potentials. The intensity of the stimulus is reflected in the rate of action potentials generated.

(Copstead and Banasik, 2013, p. 891).

Stimulation of the primary motor results in movements that travel, crossing the spinal cord through neuronal connections, which produce reflexive alterations in muscle contraction. This is a response to sensory information (Copstead and Banasik, 2013, p. 895) (Fig. 9).

According to Copstead and Banasik (2013, p. 895), although science recognizes that the cerebral cortex is "integral to the elaboration of complex thought, learning, memory, and so-called higher brain functions," little is known about the way the brain fulfills these higher functions. Gallagher (2017, p. 15), on this subject, defends the theory of Enactivism (holistic conception of cognition involving body-brain-environment) in which the body, using the motor control or forward control mechanism "enacts (or re-enacts) a process [...] coupled to a new cognitive action." He

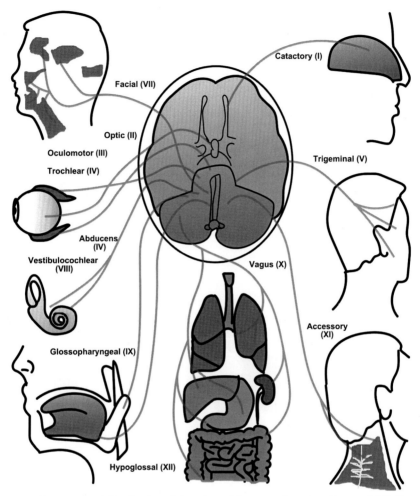

Fig. 7 The origin and distribution of the 12 cranial nerves. *(Based on Copstead, L.E., Banasik, J., 2013. Pathophysiology, fifth ed. Elsevier Inc., p. 872, with permission from Elsevier.)*

(Gallagher, 2017, p. 15) argues that cognitive states like imagining or remembering do not begin in a representational process:

> *In remembering, for example, there may be reactivation of perceptual neural processes that had been activated during the original experience. It has also been shown, using electromyography (EMG) that other non-neural bodily processes, e.g., subliminal tensing of muscles and facial expressions, may be (re)activated in cases of remembering, imagining, reflecting, etc.*
>
> ***(Gallagher, 2017, p. 15).***

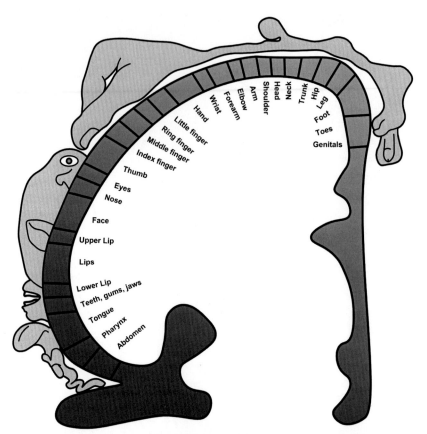

Fig. 8 Illustration of topographic organization of the body on the somatosensory cortex, forming a homunculus map. *(Based on Copstead, L.E., Banasik, J., 2013. Pathophysiology, fifth ed. Elsevier Inc., p. 891, with permission from Elsevier.)*

On the other hand, natural intelligence in our view constitutes a process that encompasses a symbolic system, which gives rise to a representation "translating" bodily processes into values or meanings. In this way, bodily processes are represented mentally by mental signs with respective semantic properties, as we explain in more detail in Section 3.6.2.

3.6.2 Mental representation

Although we use the expression "mental representation," we do not assume that it is itself an object with semantic properties, but rather a process that results in the idealized association of semantic properties with a given object.

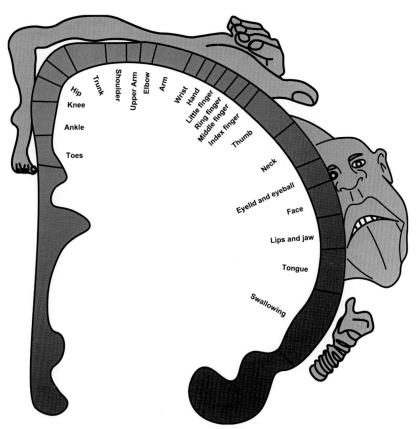

Fig. 9 The cortical representation of the muscles of the body. *(Based on Copstead, L.E., Banasik, J., 2013. Pathophysiology, fifth ed. Elsevier Inc., p. 894, with permission from Elsevier.)*

We give mental representation a more generic format: That of a symbolic process in which there is a union between the represented thing and a mental record of the basic characteristics of that thing. To exemplify, we can understand what a chair is, whatever its model or style because we have "stored" in our mind the structural aspects of a chair, which differentiate it from other objects such as a table, bookcase, and sofa. Something of the essence of language causes this classification to direct our interpretation. We take it for granted but this stems from the axiomatic structure related to the biological aspect of language, associated with its logical aspect, which causes a logical chain resulting in the attribution of a meaning.

[...] the imaginative practice is to manipulate concepts, thoughts, images – take them up and play with them, move them around, in order to solve a problem, or map them onto novel affordance spaces. This is a process that is most frequently scaffolded by language.

(Gallagher, 2017, p. 196).

The classic concept of representation as something that mediates between the self-enclosed mind and the outside world is rejected by Gallagher (2017). The author (op. cit.) states that in his enactivist view of representation that

memory or imagination involves a (re-) activated presentational activity that evokes or brings to presence something that is absent [...] If the product or result of this process is in some sense a representation, representation is not something involved in the production process itself.

(Gallagher, 2017, p. 188).

Citing Thompson (2007), Gallagher (2017, p. 188) adopts a different way than ours to explain that memory and imagination can involve a reconstitution of the activity of an internal process:

'offline', simulated or emulated sensory experience. An emulation represents an activity by reenacting it in a circumscribed and modified way – for example, as an internal process that models but does not loop through the peripheral sensory and motor systems [...]. Remembering could involve emulating earlier sensory experiences and thus reenacting them in a modified way.

(Thompson, 2007, pp. 290–291, apud Gallagher, 2017, p. 188).

According to our point of view, the symbolic system is part of the structure of natural language. This consideration may explain some concerns raised by Husserl (1982, p. 179), about how to explain the origin of the mathematical conceptions that we acquire with everyday practices or why the principles and rules of geometry are applied "with unconditioned generality for all men." Language is structured as a symbolic system and this structure encompasses diverse symbols such as letters, numbers, gestures, and sounds. When we place these symbols within a structure (natural intelligence), they gain a value that will give them meaning. This meaning goes through a continuous updating process (due to the axiomatic face of language) or tends to stabilize (due to the logical face of language).

The symbolic system makes it possible for the input stimulus to become something corresponding stored in the central cognitive system. We agree that mental representation and its result are different things. Mental representation inhabits the human mind and, at some point, this representation in the mind will act as the starting point of an action (output); mental representation must not be confused with action. Thus we can say that the action (output) is a resumption of mental representation in a modified way. If I have an idea represented in my mind, I can reproduce it in writing. Writing is the expression (output) of that idea (mental representation) giving it a different configuration. This understanding can be reinforced by the words of Goldstein and Scheerer (1964).

> Although the normal person's behavior is prevailingly concrete, this concreteness can be considered normal only as long as it is embedded in and codetermined by the abstract attitude. For instance, in the normal person both attitudes are always present in a definite figure-ground relation.
>
> **(Goldstein and Scheerer, 1964, p. 8).**

For us, mental representation goes a step beyond the relationship between thing and meaning, being the origin of the valorization of our attitudes—which Gallagher (2017, p. 200) would call the "right posture." The universal structure of natural intelligence establishes this relationship. When the representation of the thing acquires a generic meaning in terms of differentiating it from other things, it becomes mental representation in the proper sense. Acquiring a value can be appreciated as a "special" thing represented, that is, something from the outside world that is mentally presented again. The attribution of meaning in the mental representation of a thing is closely related to the attribution of value to this thing. That value can vary from individual to individual (if the origin of attribution of that value is axiomatic, biological—perhaps this aspect corresponds to what Gallaher calls affordance-based imagining) (Gallagher, 2017, p. 191); or it can consist of a generic, equal value for all (if the origin of the attribution of this value comes from the logical element of language) (Monte-Serrat, 2013, 2014).

As natural language has axiomatic and logical characteristics in its structure, it is conceivable that we assume that it carries sensory and conceptual representations. This is in accordance with Dretske (1995), who

> Distinguishes experiences and thoughts on the basis of the origin and nature of [conceptual and sensory representations'] functions: An experience of a property P is a state of a system whose 'evolved' function is to indicate the presence of P in the environment; a thought representing the property P on the other hand, is a state of a system whose 'assigned' (learned) function is to calibrate the output of the experiential system.
>
> **(Dretske, 1995 apud Pitt, 2020, n.p.).**

The difference between conceptual representation (which stems from the logical aspect of language) and sensory representation (which stems from the axiomatic aspect of language) can be exemplified through the distinction between analog and digital representation (Goodman, 1976), respectively. Analog representation is continuous (e.g., in the case of imagistic representation, we speak of properties such as being more or less bright or colorful). The digital representation, in turn, is discrete (e.g., a thought cannot be more or less about the sun; either it is or it is not). Perhaps, this differentiation explains the distinction between phenomenal and nonphenomenal properties of representations; nonphenomenal vary continuously (Pitt, 2020, n.p.).

Gallagher (2017, p. 84) discusses the idea of "decouplability" of mental representation, as if the mental representation were "offline" in the memory or imagination of an action or context. If we take into account that language has axiomatic and logical aspects, we can attribute to the logical characteristic of natural language the ability to separate the mental image from the context, as this is a characteristic of logical reasoning (Monte-Serrat, 2013; Pêcheux, 1988).

In contrast, the axiomatic resource of natural language is less dependent on a mental representation, due to the acquired knowledge is experienced in a discriminatory process in which the brain refines the combination of situation and appropriate response. We say "less dependent" because the fact of configuring a discriminative process shows that there is an underlying "previous memory" as a basis for comparison for the refinement of the action.

While Gallagher (2017) questions mental representation and action in the same process,

> An action is not a momentary or frozen snapshot supplemented by representations of past and future movements; it has a unity over time that is accounted for by (and integrated into) the intentional structure of the action itself.
> **(Gallagher, 2017, p. 99).**

We establish a difference in stages, placing the mental representation in an earlier stage, from which the action would be the output.

The axiomatic-logical conception of language ends the questioning as to whether there is decouplability of representation (Gallagher, 2017, p. 100), as both hypotheses are possible. Dynamical system is hooked directly into the real world (axiomatic and biological aspect of natural language). On the other hand, the logical aspect presents a representation that stands in for something that is not present, being "stantiated independently of what is going on in the outside world" (Rowlands, 2012, p. 141).

Enactivism, in accepting that "the activities [...] are themselves thought of as essentially embedded and embodied interactions between organisms and their environments, interactions that occur and are themselves shaped in new ways over time" (Gallagher, 2017, p. 126), does not takes into account that subjectivity also interferes with mental representation and, therefore, with these human activities.

It is possible to assess the difference in the enactivist theory's conception of language and that of this book when considering autism. The autism spectrum is related to a series of developmental disorders that interfere with the social and cognitive abilities of the autistic individual; he reacts in communication situations but does not create an emotional bond, does not evaluate the environment in a subjective way. In our opinion, the concept of language must consider the concepts of mental representation (which establishes valuation, appreciation) and subjectivity (which allows the establishment of a social bond) (Lacan, 1949, 1953). In this way, we understand that language cannot be thought of just in terms of a mentality emerging from "the autopoietic, self-organizing and self-creating, activities of organisms" (Gallagher, 2017, p. 126).

The stimuli that reach the cognitive system are somehow processed by the brain. This processing is intermediated by the symbolic system (Wallon, 1995; Lacan, 1949; Quinet, 2003), transforming these stimuli into cognitive processes (Copstead and Banasik, 2013) with semantic properties such as content, reference, and truth value. The symbolic system is related to the concept of natural language because without language we are unable to interpret the world through ideas, thoughts, concepts, impressions, and so on. Natural intelligence can be understood as any process that starts from the input of a stimulus taken as the starting point of a thought, a belief, a perception output resulting from it.

According to Dewey (1916, pp. 336–337), the brain makes adjustments to the stimuli received (input) and responses (output) so that there is not only a response to sensory stimulation but also that the value of that output determines what the next stimulus will be. It can be thought, then, that the brain is an organ that not only responds to the present stimulus but also that it somehow "stores" information that will interfere with the processing of the next stimulus. This storage is due to a memory where these records that we call mental representation are "stored."

For Dewey (1938), an organism is in a relationship of dependence with the environment.

In actual experience, there is never any such isolated singular object or event; an
object or event is always a special part, phase, or aspect, of an environing expe-
rienced world – a situation.

(Dewey, 1938, p. 67).

What is the "instrument" in charge of establishing this "relationship"? It is
exactly the structure of language, which allows the subject to interpret the
environment that surrounds him. If the individual has a brain injury that
affects regions linked to the functioning of this structure, he will not be able
to interpret the environment properly. An example of this is the person with
hydrocephalus, who is unable to assess time, unable to distinguish between
what will happen tomorrow and what happened yesterday (Monte-Serrat,
2017, 2018).

Between stimuli input and its output, there is the "process" of mental
representation, provided by the natural intelligence, responsible for a transformation: Something in the real world starts to correspond to a mental
image, which acquires a value. Mental representation is not the meaning
itself and it is not neutral: It is a result of a "process" that put things in relation
to house a semantically evaluated image; it relates a content of thought to a
perceptual experience. Just to exemplify, we cite the findings (Kosslyn,
1980; Kosslyn and Pomerantz 1977) in which it is claimed that mental representation has spatial properties—that is, pictorial representations or imagery in other modalities such as auditory or olfactory. Mental representation
works together the axiomatic-logical configuration of natural language. The
last one, being structural and universal, is the appropriate means to integrate
representational units of mental representation, covering the latter's complex combinatorics. Better saying, the means the stimulus is transported until
becoming information in the central nervous system is the (universal) structure that does not contain any value in its own composition. Valuation or
semanticity, taken as construction of a meaning for information, only comes
when the stimulus goes through the mental representation process (provided
by the natural intelligence). This functioning of mental representation con-
firms the suitability of the axiomatic-logical structure of natural language. If
the mental representation presents variability in the representation properties, as in the imagistic representations, we can say that the axiomatic element
is applied in a greater proportion than the logical element. If, on the other
hand, mental representation is related to concepts in terms of having or not a
certain property, there is no variation and, in this case, mental representation
would be more supported by the logical element of the natural language
structure.

In summary: Mental representation results from cognitive functioning (natural intelligence depending on the axiomatic-logical aspect of natural language). The universal structure of language is the only way for natural intelligence to carry out this process: To transport the stimulus to the central cognitive system and, at the same time, to correlate that stimulus to the exterior, imprinting a value on it. Although this process is treated as a theory in cognitive science, Lacan (1949), in his text "Mirror stage," established a difference between imaginary and symbolic when describing the register of consciousness and meaning (Quinet, 2003, p. 126). In his works, he uses logic, topology, literature, psychiatric clinic, the history of philosophy, to establish an "unsuspected unity" between phenomena that we usually observe separately (Gaufey, 1998, p. 17).

The phenomenon of mental representation can be well understood by Husserl's (1931, p. 158) words when explaining that there is a difference in the scope of the word "presentation" related to the perception of things:

> 'Whose front, which is properly seen, always and necessarily represents the rear face of the thing, prescribing a more or less determined content'. If I look at the moon, I see the face that it presents to me and I deduce that behind there is another face that is not present but only represented by that which is given to me directly by experience.
>
> **(Husserl, 1931, apud Gaufey, 1998, p. 56).**

In Section 3.6.3, we explain how subsystems capture stimuli and integrate them into sensations.

3.6.3 Language axes and cognitive operation

According to Perlovsky and Kozma (2007, p. 92), the "language-cognition interaction" accommodates language model-concepts that are not equivalent to cognitive model-concepts. The author differentiates language and cognition stating that

> language models serve to understand language, not the world around. Cognitive models that serve to understand the world are developed in individual minds with the help of language. This development of cognitive models from language models, connection of language and cognition is an important aspect of synthesis.
>
> **(Perlovsky and Kozma, 2007, p. 92).**

The final construction of meaning depends on the restrictions imposed by the inputs of the logical mechanism provided by the language as a convention. Pinker (1994, pp. 323–324) teaches that "naming an object involves recognizing it, looking for its entry in the mental dictionary, accessing its pronunciation, articulating it and perhaps also monitoring the output for errors when listening to it." There are several operations involved in combining words. Pinker (1994, p. 312) says that words are "strung together in order, but do not need to be directed in several directions." Therefore there is a logical sequence in the construction of meaning coordinated by Broca's area "configured innately to be involved in the anticipations and predictions that define the syntactic structures of linguistic expression" (Turner and Ioannides, 2009).

Perlovsky, Pinker, and Turner and Ioannides are clear in establishing that the logical sequence of language is imposed on the cognitive system through the rules of language such as: Grammatical rules; or a convention and its input signals that establish values which are previously given to the individual auditory and visual systems. These signs and values will join with other subsystems to integrate sensations.

The location of these mental processes can be done by magnetic resonance imaging, "which can measure [...] how hard the different parts of the brain are working during different kinds of mental activity" or by the "Magneto-Encephalography, which is like EEG but can pinpoint the part of the brain that an electromagnetic signal is coming from" (Pinker, 1994, p. 324). An example of this occurs in the "Wernicke's area [which] is adjacent to the part of the cortex that processes sound," and "seems to have a role in looking up words and funneling them to other areas, notably Broca's, that assemble or parse them syntactically" (Pinker, 1994, pp. 317–318).

We can state from these assumptions that the universal structure of natural intelligence, with all the operations to construct meaning, works in cooperation with the structure of the prefrontal cortex linked to conventional language with its grammatical rules and logical reasoning: The motor part of the brain is associated with sound, simultaneously producing a cognitive operation in which grammar is an instrument for meaning construction. Language as a convention is the tool underlying cognitive operation to give rise to a reconstruction (representation) of the external world in the individual's mind.

In this way, regarding to natural intelligence, the "input" (stimulus) of the language as a convention from another person is an external force that gives rise to the cognitive process. This "input" can occur through visual, tactile hearing systems, for example. The "force" (given by language as a convention) leads to the natural language movement. We bet that the conventional language "input" in the cognitive system comes together with a

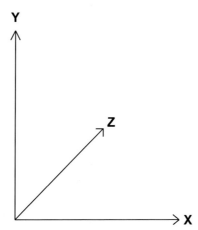

Fig. 10 Simulation of 3D point rotation to represent language as a convention: its *x* and *y* axes determine the limits of space (*z* axis) to be occupied by probability events. This figure represents a three-dimensional space in which natural language operates.

value previously established by the set of rules of first one. The result is making the cognitive process less chaotic. Thinking of language as a convention, its *x* and *y* axes determine the limits of space (*z* axis) to be occupied by probability events (Monte-Serrat, 2017) (Fig. 10).

Jakobson (1990, 2010) transformed geometric spaces into Cartesian coordinates when describing the conventional language in two sets: The set of the paraphrastic axis (*y*) and the set of the metonymic axis (*x*), translating the language into mathematical arguments. The author (Jakobson, 1990, 2010) states that these two axes (paradigmatic, *y*; syntagmatic, *x*) cover two realities of conventional language: Operational and structural. These realities are selected in two sets: One of elements associated by similarity, and the other of elements associated by contiguity.

The works of Whorf (1942), Jakobson (1990, 2010), and Pêcheux (1988) allow us to distance ourselves from this traditional method of seeing language, to articulate it with neurolinguistics and time. The relationship between conventional language with the paradigmatic (*y* axis) and metonymic (*x* axis) axes is successful while studying writing, which operates in two-dimensional space. This description is insufficient to explain the natural language that is temporarily influenced by speech. Thus it becomes necessary to study language considering yet another axis, the *z* axis, which represents the element of time (considered as a three-dimensional space in which natural language works) (Monte-Serrat, 2017). The vector space occupied by the *y* axis is considered a space of probabilities and, therefore, instead of providing bivalent values, it offers a probability for falsehood or for truth (Monte-Serrat, 2017).

The temporal organization of language is revealed in rhythm, assuming a spatial extension in the syntax (x axis), which determines new elements in contiguity (Monte-Serrat, 2017). The way "how" words are brought together is important in the formation of meaning. Words brought together by reason of the rhyme have a critical component of the y axis inserted in their meaning, which cannot be ignored in the machine design, for example.

For Whorf (1942), language encompasses all symbolism, all symbolic processes, all processes of reference and logic. Each language has specific characteristics in the propagation and flow of speech. The author (op. cit.) points out that words and speech are not the same, and that the patterns of sentence structure are more important than words. Thus the words gathered by reason of the rhyme have a critical component of the y axis inserted in its meaning, which cannot be ignored in the design of the machine, for example.

3.6.4 Stimuli integrating sensations in natural intelligence

As for the axiomatic characteristic of natural intelligence, it can be mathematically represented by Perlovsky and Kozma's (2007) idea, with low values of similarity for less conscious states; and for more conscious states, such as perceptions, cognitions, and concrete decisions, the description can be made by concrete models of high values of similarity (which are better adapted to the input signals). This conception allows us to conceive that the unconscious is a state of natural language in which there is little or no interference from language as a convention input. In this way, neurodynamics moves from a chaotic and vague dynamic to a logical dynamic that evolves through a cycle of action and perception motivated by the model of increasing clarity (similarity value presented) as the cognitive cycle progresses (op. cit). According to Perlovsky and Kozma (2007, p. 83), "dynamic logic is a convergent process. It converges to the maximum of similarity, and therefore satisfies the knowledge instinct."

The value of similarity given by the universal structure of the natural language comes from outside of the individual because it is provided previously by the rules of the language as convention (Monte-Serrat and Belgacem, 2017). It is imposed from the outside in, through the learning of those grammar rules, through the symbolic dimension of the language (Lacan, 1949; Monte-Serrat, 2020).

If likelihood is used as similarity, parameter values are estimated efficiently (that is, in most cases, parameters cannot be better learned using any other procedure) [...] it is proven that the similarity measure increases at each iteration. The psychological interpretation is that the knowledge instinct is satisfied at each step: a NMF [Neural Modeling Fields] system with dynamic logic 'enjoys' learning. [...] the fundamental property of dynamic logic is evolution from vague, uncertain, fuzzy, unconscious states to more crisp, certain, conscious states.

(Perlovsky and Kozma, 2007, p. 84, highlighted by the author).

According to the content we exposed in this chapter, we describe a closed circuit for the natural intelligence functioning as a process of perception/learning. For this purpose, some concepts of information theory based on Moles (1978, p. 14) were adopted by us. The author (op. cit.) establishes the following assumptions about the axioms that represent the man integration in the physical–chemical universe:

1. *The individual is an open system whose behavior, in the smallest details, is determined entirely by the sum:*
   (a) of a hereditary bag giving the general structure of its organism;
   (b) the events of his particular history, inscribed by his conditioned reflexes and his memory in that organism and which define his 'personality';
   (c) of his present environment [we learn language as a convention. It is part of the environment because it comes from the people who live with us], against which his organism reacts.
2. *All modalities of current or future behavior of this individual can be enunciated with a degree of precision equal to that of the description of a physicochemical system, insofar as the three determining factors are known.*
3. *This perfect knowledge of the heredity, the history and the environment of the individual at a given instant, being practically an asymptotic ideal, the individual, like any other system, is determinable only in a statistical behavior that is proper object of experimental psychology. (Moles, 1978, p. 14).*

A perception-reaction (learning) cycle describes, in our opinion, in a simplified way, the modes of behavior of humans are governed by vast systems of equations. We adapted a closed circuit of the perception/learning process using some concepts from information theory (Moles, 1978). The cognitive process can be described as follows: The individual receives messages (input) from the environment through various channels (visual, audible, tactile, for example); these messages can have a spatial or temporal nature (speech and music are pure temporal messages, which are modulations of duration); and the spatial message is transformed into a temporal message. The symbolization process carried out by the cognitive system allows the transformation of something from the real world into a representation through the symbolic process that can end in an action (output). In this sense, we agree with the enactivist theory:

> Enactivist versions of EC [embodied cognition] emphasize the idea that perception is 'for' action, and that action-orientation shapes most cognitive processes.
> **(Gallagher, 2017, p. 5, author's highlight).**

The temporal signs allow the transposition of the messages dimension into each other (Moles, 1978, p. 33) and the "value or quality of a message must be based on the capacity of the ultimate recipient who [...] is always the human individual" (op.cit., p. 35). In this case, as the individual learns the conventional language, the value of the message starts to integrate him in the following terms:

> If a message is what serves to modify the behavior of the receiver, the value of a message is the greater the more capable it is to make modifications to this behavior [...] since what is already known is integrated by the receiver and belongs to his interior system.
> **(Moles, 1978, p. 36).**

A message will cause reaction of the individual if there is an "a priori" statement indicating that it "should be interesting" and if the individual knows how to organize it (Moles, 1978, p. 97). The rules of the language as convention act as an "a priori," putting the hypothesis, the anticipated value for the individual to interpret reality (Monte-Serrat, 2017). Or, in other words, the language as a convention place limits to the probability distribution to organize the meaning formation by the cognitive process (natural intelligence).

What marks the intelligibility of a message are symbols and rules that perform the same function: "One and the other contribute to define a repertoire." A symbol is a mode of constant grouping of elements, known "a priori." A rule defines a set of meeting modes that respect that rule (Moles, 1978, p. 98). So the intelligibility has to do with predictability that gives the receiver the ability to know

> in the order of message development, whether temporal or spatial, which will follow from what has been transmitted, extrapolating the temporal or spatial series of the element its message, to imagine the future of a prediction that is nothing more than a degree of coherence of the phenomenon, a rate of regularity [...] The existence of a degree of predictability is a statistical link between the past and the future, expressing a coherence, a correlation between what has happened to the time that will occur in time $t+r$.
> **(Moles, 1978, pp. 100–101).**

In this sense, we can conclude that the logical structure of language as convention organizes and makes intelligible the broad complex of natural language functioning, and consequently structures the individual (Monte-Serrat 2018). This is the way language as a convention is matched to input signals (Perlovsky and Kozma, 2007, p. 2).

The complexity of the learning system needed to train a simple input-output according to Werbos (2007, p. 119) is greater than the complexity of the input–output system itself. Kozma (2007, p. 136) states that "the relatively slow macroscopic order parameters 'enslave' the faster microscopic elements and produce large-scale spatiotemporal cooperative patterns in a system at the edge of stability." This process results in Kelso and Tognoli's (2007) concept of metastable brains that produces complementary effects of general coordination and the disintegration of individual components. While language as a convention inputs some patterns in the brain, the complexity of the cognitive system (natural intelligence) as a whole is counting on several inputs systems to produce several parallel sensations intermingling elements like energy, cells, waves, organs, chemical elements, and systems.

Kozma (2007, p. 136) describes the basal state of the brain as a high/chaotic attractor over which the influence of external stimuli will produce an activity pattern, a synchronization of neural electrical activity while completing cognitive tasks. For the author, this is possible in the mathematical theory of chaotic itinerancy that describes the trajectory of a dynamical system visiting intermittently "Ruins of Attractors," a phenomenon that helps to interpret the key features of EEG measurements.

Neural signal propagation through axonal effects [...] supports synchronization over large areas of cortex [...]. This creates small-world effects [...] in analogy to the rapid dissemination of information through social contacts. 'Small-world' networks can be generated by certain preferential attachment rules between vertices. [...] Preferential attachment rule simply states that, during the network evolution, new nodes will be connected to the old nodes in proportion to the degree of the old nodes. As the result, a highly connected node (= a node with high degree) is likely to get even mode connections. This rule can lead to a special hub structure [...].

(Kozma, 2007, p. 138).

According to Kelso and Tognoli (2007, p. 42), brain dynamics is coordinated in space and time: "Neurons in different parts of the brain oscillate at different frequencies [...] These oscillations are coupled or 'bound' together into a coherent network when people attend to a stimulus, perceive, think and act." They (Kelso and Tognoli, 2007, p. 42) state that "this is a dynamic, self-assembling process, parts of the brain engaging and disengaging in time," to reach conscious states, better saying, natural intelligence.

> the 'informational code' lies in the transient coupling of functional units, with physiological significance given to specific phase-lags realized between coordinating elements [...], [they] propose that phase relationships carry information, with multiple attractors (attracting tendencies) setting alternatives for complementary aspects to emerge in consciousness [...].
>
> **(Kelso and Tognoli, 2007, p. 42).**

Gallagher (2017) elucidates the difference between action and behavior in the following words:

> [...] an action involves certain mental processes that lead up to bodily movement. On the Cartesian view, what makes a certain behavior an action is the contribution of these mental processes. Without such processes we have mere behavior, the sort of thing possible for automata and animals. Unless the action takes place in the mind first – in some cases acted out explicitly in imagination - then the external behavior is not really an action. Action on this definition is always intentional action. If my bodily movement is not intentional, then there is mere behavior, something like reflex behavior. If my bodily movement is determined by something other than my own reflective thought, then it is involuntary movement, but not action.
>
> **(Gallagher, 2017, p. 134).**

3.6.5 Cognitive computing and decision-making: How the logical characteristics of language structure interfere with the meaning construction?

Cognitive computing is a new branch of artificial intelligence charged with the task of making the machine imitates the human brain in decision-making. This theory is intended to make the machine reason and respond to stimuli in a manner adjusted to a previously chosen situation. Cognitive computing makes it possible: To adapt its characteristics progressing as requirements evolve; to interact with the user or with other processors; to help defining a problem and finding solutions; or to identify context information.

Reality-based tasks are the support of cognitive computing, that is, the appreciation falls on the "result" of natural intelligence. We observe that this situation of cognitive computing takes into account the action resulting from stimuli already processed by human cognition. Our suggestion for the machine to be intuitive like the human being is that it incorporates information about the context/reality on which it is beginning to build its decision-making.

Since the machine is based on reality to form its answer, it is important to elucidate, based on linguistic theory, the difference between virtual reality and "real" reality. This is an important contribution of this book to cognitive computing. Monte-Serrat et al. (2017) show that the conditions of language production to generate meaning can be based on assumed or not assumed conditions. Using discursive theory (Pêcheux, 1988), the authors (Monte-Serrat et al., 2017) identify interpretations that have an anticipated meaning as a starting point, whose effect is to decontaminate other sense possibilities. They compare discursive functioning to a mathematical structure of logical reasoning (classical logic), which puts in advance a "perceived truth" to eliminate alleged ambiguities, without the reference to a special meaning or context. However, as natural intelligence is not crystallized, it can play a dual role: That of disclosing subjection to the previously established sense (value) by classical logic or subverting that sense, and thus breaking the vicious circle of logical reasoning.

Cognitive computing must consider that, in addition to the classic logic establishing true—also, it must be able to make the multipurpose logic computable, foreseeing a new class of problems between the true-false values. This means that the machine must be adapted to complex situations characterized by ambiguity and uncertainty in a fragmented and unpredictable way, to deal with human types of problems. Natural intelligence presents dynamic features and artificial intelligence must follow this behavior to deal with changing information. Multipurpose logic works with possibilities instead of previously establishing false-true values. It rejects the principle of bivalence by bringing a third element, the indeterminate (I). In this case the fluid nature of the information will make the machine redefine its objectives, offering a synthesis of information and also perfecting its own "way of acting" in different contexts and ideas to suggest the "best solution" instead of the "right answer."

Human symbolic processes harbor ideology in linguistic actions. Ideology imposes a sense on the discourse, interfering in the individual's decision without him realizing that there are other possibilities of meaning (Pêcheux, 1988; Monte-Serrat, 2013). To understand this process, it is necessary to assume that the construction of meaning comes from a constitutive division, that is, meaning can result from the knowledge acquired through logical and supposedly neutral discourse, or it can result from the subjective appreciation of the individual.

When it is stated that the conditions of language production (context) interfere with meaning (Voloshinov, 1973; Lacan, 1949; Wallon, 1995; Fig. 3 based on Monte-Serrat creation; Pêcheux, 1975, 1988), the Saussurian theory of value (Saussure, 1916) is considered in the sense that the meaning of words is relational.

If a discourse is supported by systematic reasoning, it depends on a body of techniques directing conjectures and predictions, emphasizing a certain perspective of knowledge (Peirce, 1877, 1908). Logical reasoning presents hypotheses, such as conjectures based on preconceived knowledge and under controlled conditions, to determine and anticipate logical consequences. This discursive functioning anticipates the result in the sense that it interferes with the decision-making eliminating other possibilities of choice/meaning.

> [There] is a mathematical structure in discourse which puts a 'perceived truth' beforehand to eliminate supposed ambiguities. This is how logical reasoning imposes general patterns to thinking, without reference to a particular meaning or context. This kind of discursive functioning works as a shift of the orientation of knowledge and establishes self-evident truths that are considered to be obvious. There is a 'right order' of thinking which starts from a true statement 'known' to be true to reach a true truth. Criteria of rationality are coherence between thought and action and between means and end.
> **(Monte-Serrat et al., 2017, p. 4).**

Classical logic is defined as a set of principles and methods of inference or valid reasoning (Mortari, 2016, p. 435). Logic is concerned with whether the premises are a good reason to support the conclusion.

> Classical logic starts from statements we know to be true and, if each statement is true, we can reach a true conclusion. In this process, we are interested in the form rather than in the content of an 'implication', of an 'assertion that if one particular statement is true, then another particular statement is true' (Eccles, 2007, p. 10). These conditional propositions start from explicit or implicit hypotheses to demonstrate an outcome: If the hypothesis is valid, then, so is the thesis. There is a right order of mathematical language that provides a kind of necessary certainty, anticipating a systematic mathematical interpretation. The principle of bivalence governs classical logic, which is: every proposition is True or False.
> **(Monte-Serrat et al., 2017, p. 6).**

Classical logic is associated with virtual reality (Pêcheux, 1975, 1988; Monte-Serrat, 2013), since it anticipates a truth in its structure. Mathematically speaking, classical logic works with a true or false "proposition," which is the key to avoiding ambiguity in the result. We call attention to what happens before the result is reached. In logical reasoning, before stating whether something is true or false, an investigation is carried out using techniques based on true or false assumptions and conjectures to gather information that provides evidence of veracity or falsehood. In other words, the result is achieved through a standard or model in which veracity or falsity is established in advance, disconnecting the result from the "real" reality. For this reason, the result of logical reasoning is considered a virtual reality based on a previously stated hypothesis "If P then Q." The result or proof of logical reasoning is defined as:

> *a sequence of statements starting from statements we know to be true and finishing with the statement to be proved. Each statement is true because the earlier statements are true. The justification for such steps usually makes use of the idea of 'implication'; an implication is the assertion that if one particular statement is true then another particular statement is true.*
>
> **(Eccles, 2007, p. 10).**

On the other hand, there is intuitive reasoning that has been associated with multipurpose logic. The polyvalent logic is associated with intuition because it assumes the possibility that there are values different from true and false, rejecting the principle of bivalence: If the principle of bivalence implies determinism, it implies the absence of free will (Mortari, 2016, p. 463). The polyvalent logic works with a third value, the Indeterminate (I), which is evaluated under conditions of uncertainty (Mortari, 2016, p. 467). In this way, it can be considered that the interpretation leading to decision-making may be based on more than two options. It shifts from the rigidity of the proposition "If P then Q" making us think of another order of reasoning that takes into account a third option: That of indeterminacy, through which data existing between what is false and what is true are appreciated, and which would be discarded by classical logic.

The content developed in this chapter on natural intelligence added to the lesson by Bechtel (2006, pp. 24–25), allows us to conclude that human beings observe a sequence of sensory events and not the causal relationships (cause and effect) which are unobservable. For this reason, polyvalent logic is more suitable for cognitive computing, making it more intuitive: It works with a degree of indeterminacy and gives an opportunity for intuitionist probability to appreciate different assumptions in observable events.

The interpretation of reality has no direct access but it is mediated by language. The appropriate choice of a procedure that exposes interpretation to cognitive computing is essential in this quest to design intuitive machine learning inspired by natural intelligence, in such a way that the more opaque levels of the collected data are also part of the result sought. When we combine linguistic theory with machine design, we can come up with interpretations that will chart new paths for artificial intelligence decision-making.

If we intend to imitate the functioning human brain, we need to realize that the individual cannot be thought of as a conscious, rational, and logical-operative strategist (Pêcheux, 1988). This concept of the human being is a myth, as there are symbolic and unconscious interactions that affect his activity (op. cit.). Goodfellow et al. (2016, p. 54) explain that machine learning makes use of probability theory, although many branches of computer science deal with deterministic and certain data.

> *Probability theory is a mathematical framework for representing uncertain statements. It provides a means of quantifying uncertainty and axioms for deriving new uncertain statements. In artificial intelligence applications, we use probability theory in two major ways. First, the laws of probability tell us how AI systems should reason, so we design our algorithms to compute or approximate various expressions derived using probability theory. Second, we can use probability and statistics to theoretically analyze the behavior of proposed AI systems.*
> **(Goodfellow et al., 2016, p. 53).**

Although mathematics deals with truths, they are assumed propositions. Intelligence, whether natural or artificial, reasons according to truths by definition and, also, deals with uncertainties. Goodfellow et al. (2016) claim that there are three possible sources of uncertainty:

> **1.** *Inherent stochasticity in the system being modeled. For example, [...] quantum mechanics [describing] the dynamics of subatomic particles as being probabilistic [and scenarios with] random dynamics [...]*
> **2.** *Incomplete observability. Even deterministic systems can appear stochastic when we cannot observe all of the variables that drive the behavior of the system. [...]*
> **3.** *Incomplete modeling [which] discard some of the information we have observed, the discarded information results in uncertainty in the model's predictions. (Goodfellow et al., 2016, p. 54).*

There is a difference in the application of probability with respect to quantitative research and qualitative research. According to Goodfellow et al. (2016, p. 55), in quantitative research, the tool for an artificial intelligence application will fall on the frequency of events. The calculation of the probability of the occurrence will be based on the repetition of the event (frequentist probability). As for the application of probability in qualitative investigations, there are levels of belief related to qualitative levels of certainty (Bayesian probability).

In conclusion, we can say that the universal structure of language, which carries axiomatic and logical elements, is sufficient to incorporate the algebraic structures of logical reasoning (classical logic and polyvalent logic) and also deterministic or nondeterministic quantities as starting points for decision-making. With the condition that this structure is transferred to the machine design, cognitive computing will be able to make decisions based: On classic logical reasoning, founded on a hypothesis (a virtual truth given previously); or on polyvalent logical reasoning, established on a set of axioms observed at the space of indeterminacy (I).

According to Cohn (1981, p. 41) and Goodfellow et al. (2016), algebraic structures, which involve defined operations, can coexist with nonalgebraic structures.

Probability can be seen as the extension of logic to deal with uncertainty. Logic provides a set of formal rules for determining what propositions are implied to be true or false given the assumption that some other set of propositions is true or false. Probability theory provides a set of formal rules for determining the likelihood of a proposition being true given the likelihood of other propositions.

(Goodfellow et al., 2016, p. 56).

References

Bechtel, W., 2006. Discovering Cell Mechanisms. Cambridge University Press, Cambridge.

Benjamin, C., Walshaw, P., Kayleigh, H., Gaillard, W., Baxter, L., Berl, M., Polczynska, M., Noble, S., Alkawadri, R., Hirsh, L., Constable, R., Bookheimer, S., 2017. Presurgical language fMRI: mapping of six critical regions. Hum. Brain Mapp. 38, 4239–4255.

Chardin, P., 1956. Tome I: Le phénomène humain. Les Éditions du Seuil, Paris.

Cohn, M., 1981. Universal Algebra. Springer.

Copstead, L.E., Banasik, J., 2013. Pathophysiology, fifth ed. Elsevier Inc.

Dewey, J., 1916. Essays in Experimental Logic. University of Chicago Press, Chicago.

Dewey, J., 1938. Logic: The Theory of Inquiry. Holt, Rinehart & Winston, New York.

Dretske, F., 1995. Naturalizing the Mind. The MIT Press, Cambridge, MA.

Eccles, P., 2007. An Introduction to Mathematical Reasoning: Lectures on Numbers, Sets, and Function. Cambridge University Press.

Foucault, M., 1963. Naissance de la Clinique. Presses Universitaires de France, Paris.

Gallagher, S., 2017. Enactivist Interventions: Rethinking the Mind. Oxford University Press, Oxford.

Gardner, H., 1999. Intelligence Reframed: Multiple Intelligences for the 21 Century. Basic Books, New York.

Gaufey, G., 1998. El lazo especular. Un estudio traversero de la unidad imaginaria, Leguizamón, G. (trad.). Edelp SA, Argentina.

Goldstein, K., Scheerer, M., 1964. Abstract and Concrete Behavior: An Experimental Study With Special tests. vol. 53 Northwestern University, Evanston, IL, p. 2. Reprint of Psychological Monographs, 1941.

Goodfellow, I., Bengio, Y., Courville, A., 2016. Deep Learning. MIT Press, Cambridge, MA.

Goodman, N., 1976. Languages of Art, second ed. Hackett, Indianapolis, IN.

Gottman, J.M., Murray, J.D., Swanson, C.C., Tyson, R., Swanson, K.R., 2002. The Mathematics of Marriage. MIT Press, Cambridge, MA.

Herrnstein, R., Murray, C., 1994. The Bell Curve. Free Press, New York.

Husserl, E., 1931. Méditations cartésiennes. Introduction à la phénoménologie. A. Colin, Paris.

Husserl, E., 1982. The origin of geometry. D. Arr. (transl.). In: Derrida, J. (Ed.), Introduction to the Origin of Geometry. University of Nebraska Press, Lincoln, NE, pp. 155–180.

Jakobson, R., 1990. Two aspects of language and two types of aphasic disturbances. In: Language. Harvard University Press, Cambridge, pp. 115–133.

Jakobson, R., 2010. Linguística e Comunicação. Bliknstein, I. e Paes, J. (trad.). Ed. Cultrix, São Paulo.

Kelso, J.A., Tognoli, E., 2007. Toward a complementary neuroscience: metastable coordination dynamics of the brain. In: Perlovsky, L., Kozma, R. (Eds.), Neurodynamics of Cognition and Consciousness. Springer-Verlag, Berlin, Heidelberg.

Knierim, J., 2020. Motor system. In: Neuroanatomy Online. McGovern Medical School at UTHealth, Department of Neurobiology and Anatomy, University of Texas, Houston, TX (Chapter 3).

Kosslyn, S., 1980. Image and Mind. Harvard University Press, Cambridge, MA.

Kosslyn, S., Pomerantz, J., 1977. Imagery, propositions and the form of internal representations. In: Cognitive Psychology. vol. 9, pp. 52–76.

Kozma, R., 2007. Neurodynamics of intentional behavior generation. In: Perlovsky, L., Kozma, R. (Eds.), Neurodynamics of Cognition and Consciousness. Springer-Verlag, Berlin, Heidelberg.

Lacan, J., 1936. Les complexes familiaux. In: Wallon, H. (org), Encyclopédie française, vol. VIII, La vie mentale. Paris.

Lacan, J., 1946. Formulações sobre a causalidade psíquica. In: Lacan, J., Escritos, Ribeiro, V. (trad). Jorge Zahar, Rio de Janeiro, pp. 152–194. 1998.

Lacan, J., 1949. Le stade du miroir comme formateur de la fonction du Je, telle qu'elle nous est révélée dans l'expérience psychanalytique. Rev. Fr. Psychanal. 13 (4), 449–455.

Lacan, J., 1953. Função e campo da fala e da linguagem em psicanálise. In: Lacan, J., Escritos. Jorge Zahar, Rio de Janeiro. 1998a.

Lenneberg, E., 1967. Biological Foundations of Language. John Wiley and Sons, New York.

Merleau-Ponty, M., 1968. The Visible and the Invisible. Evanston, A. (Transl.). Northwestern University Press, Evanston, IL.

Merleau-Ponty, M., 2012. Phenomenology of Perception. Landes, D. (Transl.). Routledge, London.

Moles, A., 1978. Théorie de l'information et perceptionesthétique. Paris: Flamarion. Portuguese version Cunha, H. (transl.). Ed Tempo Brasileiro Ltda, Rio de Janeiro.

Monte-Serrat, D., 2013. Literacy and Juridical Discourse, USP-RP 2013. thesis guided by Tfouni, L. Retrieved from http://www.teses.usp.br/teses/disponiveis/59/59137/tde-14032013-104350/. (Accessed 28 July 2020).

Monte-Serrat, D., 2014. A questão do sujeito: Perspectivas da análise do discurso, do letramento e da psicanálise lacaniana. Ed. Pedro e João, São Carlos.

Monte-Serrat, D., 2017. Neurolinguistics, language, and time: investigating the verbal art in its amplitude. Int. J. Percept. Public Health 1 (3).

Monte-Serrat, D., 2018. Inclusion in linguistic education: neurolinguistics, language, and subject. In: Psycholinguistics and Cognition in Language Processing. IGI-Global.com.

Monte-Serrat, D., Belgacem, F., 2017. Subject and time movement in the virtual reality. Int. J. Res. Methodol. Soc. Sci. 3 (3), 19.

Monte-Serrat, D., Belgacem, F., Maldonato, M., 2017. Decision making: the complexity of choice processes. Int. J. Res. Methodol. Soc. Sci. 3 (4), 22. Oct–Dec 2017.

Mortari, C., 2016. Introdução à lógica. Editora UNESP, São Paulo.

Pêcheux, M., 1975. Les vérités de La Palice. Linguistique, sémantique, philosophie (Théorie). Maspero, Paris.

Pêcheux, M., 1988. Discourse: Structure or Event. Illinois University Press, Champaign, IL.

Peirce, C., 1877. The fixation of belief. Pop. Sci. Mon. 12, 1–15. November.

Peirce, C., 1908. A neglected argument for the reality of god. Hibbert J. 7, 90–112.

Perlovsky, L., 1998. Conundrum of combinatorial complexity. IEEE Trans. Pattern Anal. Mach. Intell. 20, 666–670.

Perlovsky, L., 2001. Neural Networks and Intellect: Using Model-Based Concepts. Oxford University Press, New York, NY.

Perlovsky, L., 2016. Physics of the mind. Front. Syst. Neurosci. 10, 84.

Perlovsky, L., Kozma, R. (Eds.), 2007. Neurodynamics of Cognition and Consciousness. Springer-Verlag, Berlin, Heidelberg.

Pinker, S., 1994. The Language Instinct. Harper-Collins Publishers Inc., New York.

Pitt, D., 2020. Mental representation. In: The Stanford Encyclopedia of Philosophy. Stanford University, Spring Edition, Stanford, CA.

Quinet, A., 2003. Le plus de regard: Destins de la pulsion scopique. Étude psychanalytique. Ed. du Champ lacanien, Paris.

Radej, A., 2020. Triadic structures in Hegel, Pierce, Freud and Lacan. In: Slovensko drustvo evalvatorjev. 27 marca. Retrieved from https://www.sdeval.si/2020/03/27/triadic-structures-in-hegel-peirce-freud-and-lacan/. (Accessed 30 July 2020).

Radzicki, M.J., 1993. Dyadic processes, tempestuous relationships, and system dynamics. Syst. Dyn. Rev. 9, 79–94.

Roid, G., 2003. The Stanford-Binet Intelligence Scales, SB5, fifth ed. Riverside Publishing.

Roudinesco, E., Plon, M., 2006. Dictionnaire de la psychanalyse. Fayard, Paris.

Rowlands, M., 2012. Representing without representations. Avant 3 (1), 133–144.

Russell, S., Norvig, P., 2010. Artificial Intelligence: A Modern Approach, third ed. Pearson.

Saussure, F., 1916. In: Bally, C., Sechehaye, A. (Eds.), Cours de linguistique Générale, third ed. Payot, Paris.

Spearman, C., 2005. The Abilities of Man: Their Nature and Measurement. The Blackburn Press.

Sprot, J., 2004. Dynamical models of love. In: Nonlinear Dynamics, Psychology and Life Sciences. vol. 8. University of Wisconsin, Madison. n. 3. July 2004.

Sternberg, R., 1997. Successful intelligence: a broader view of who's smart in school and in life. Int. Sch. J. 17 (1), 19.

Strogatz, S.H., 1994. Nonlinear Dynamics and Chaos: With Applications to Physics, Biology, Chemistry, and Engineering. AddisonWesley, Reading, MA.

Thompson, E., 2007. Mind in Life: Biology, Phenomenology and the Sciences of Mind. Harvard University Press, Cambridge, MW.

Turner, R., Ioannides, A.A., 2009. Brain, music and musicality: inferences from neuroimaging. In: Malloch, S., Trevarthen, C. (Eds.), Communicative musicality: Exploring the basis of human companionship. Oxford University Press, New York, pp. 147–181.

Voloshinov, V.N., 1973. Marxism and the Philosophy of Language. Matejka, L.; Tutunik, I. (Transl.). Harvard University Press, Cambridge, MA. 1929.

Wallon, H., 1934. Les origines du caratère chez l'enfant. Boivin, Paris.

Wallon, H., 1995. As origens do caráter na Criança. pinto, H. (trad.). Nova Alexandria, São Paulo.

Wechsler, D., 1981. Wechsler Adult Intelligence Scale (Revised Edition), WAIS-R. Psychological Corporation.

Werbos, P., 2007. Using ADP to understand and replicate brain intelligence: the next level design? In: Perlovsky, L., Kozma, R. (Eds.), Neurodynamics of Cognition and Consciousness. Springer-Verlag, Berlin Heidelberg.

Whorf, B., 1942. Language, mind and reality. In: Theosophist. Madras, India. January and April. Theosophical Society.

CHAPTER FOUR

Artificial intelligence

4.1 Introduction

This book joins efforts to understand how the cognitive system works at a structural and algorithmic level. The content described here sometimes crosses the field of computational neuroscience and the field of deep learning (DL). DL is concerned with creating intelligent computer systems, while the field of computational neuroscience is concerned with building more accurate models of how the brain really works. In this chapter, we provide a general overview on artificial intelligence (AI), without the ambition to be exhaustive on the subject, to make comparisons and insights on how to replicate the structure of natural intelligence in the AI.

According to Goodfellow et al. (2016), the emergence of AI was due to the search for a quick solution to problems that are intellectually difficult for human beings. The machine solutions can be described by a list of formal and mathematical rules, but the real challenge to AI is the intuitive resolution that seems automatic to humans, such as recognizing spoken words or faces in images. The intuitive approach for the computer to understand the world according to a hierarchy of concepts, under the point of view of Goodfellow et al. (2016), "avoids" the need for human intervention to specify knowledge to the computer, because it becomes able to build complex concepts from of the simplest. We highlight the word "avoids" because, in fact, AI depends on, at least, human intervention at the starting point of its functioning.

Machine learning (ML) is a learning algorithm whose data are adjusted by human (external) intervention in search of patterns to be repeated in new data. In this book, we suggest ways for the machine to become more intuitive so that it learns to interpret the world by relating simpler concepts from image, sound, or writing. In this way, the knowledge of the machine is based on generic concepts about "how" the data should be generated. This fact reduces the possibility of an early human intervention in the composition of the data by the machine. It is believed that this knowledge on the part

The Natural Language for Artificial Intelligence
https://doi.org/10.1016/B978-0-12-824118-9.00009-6

of AI or cognitive computing would prevent the human operator from specifying in advance all the knowledge necessary for the computer, interfering with the results.

As we explained in the Section 3.6.5 on decision-making, the starting point of the simplest concept will direct the work of computer cognition. Therefore as an example of human interference in AI, we can observe that the DL will explore the hierarchy of concepts from a simpler concept that was previously given by an individual while providing the algorithms with the resources they "need" to succeed. This fact implies that the computer does not completely prevent human intervention, as there is someone behind the system who has previously established the values for there to be this hierarchy.

Starting from the premise that there is an initial human intervention, one can think about the classification given by Goodfellow et al. (2016, p. 98) that ML algorithms can be divided into: Supervised learning and unsupervised learning categories.

> Most machine learning algorithms have settings called hyperparameters that must be determined external to the learning algorithm itself; we discuss how to set these using additional data. Machine learning is essentially a form of applied statistics with increased emphasis on the use of computers to statistically estimate complicated functions and a decreased emphasis on proving confidence intervals around these functions; we therefore present the two central approaches to statistics: frequentist estimators and Bayesian inference.
>
> **(Goodfellow et al. 2016, p. 98).**

AI is most successful when a list of formal rules, provided by the operator in advance, is required. World knowledge, in its turn, requires intuitive knowledge that has a different process from the formal way. What is most sought after in terms of AI is to provide computers with intuitive thinking. To achieve this, there must be an intense effort on encoding knowledge about the world in formal language. We note that the error is at the beginning point: We try to teach the computer to reason in terms of logical inference without providing it with the necessary information that is already implicit in natural language (axiomatic element along with logic one). The fact that projects on formal language are not successful is due to the inference comes from a database that, although created by humans under complex formal rules, does not describe the world sufficiently. The lack of machine-coded knowledge suggests that AI systems need to acquire the ability of building their own knowledge to extract patterns from raw data. This is called ML, which allows the computer to interpret the world and make decisions.

The progress that is great desired by AI resides, in our view, in the content that we develop in this book. We are presenting topics that take ML to the next frontier, because we have identified the universal structure of language, which, being a common structure that appears in AI and cognitive computing, gives rise to the universal language algorithm. In short, we explain the standard structure that, being present in cognitive computing and, also in AI, allows the two elements to be applied interchangeably.

In Chapter 10, we present a solution to this problem: We suggest using the language representation property. So, the system will not only be able to map the representation, but also it will discover the representation itself, with minimal human intervention. The ML will make it possible for one to obtain a set of resources through a simple task, moving away from resources that require complex, time-consuming tasks and human effort.

Goodfellow et al. (2016) suggest that autoencoder (which combines encoding and decoding) is an excellent example of a learning algorithm. The authors (op. cit., p. 4) also state that when designing resources or algorithms for learning resources, there is a problem in separating the "factors of variation" which will explain the observed data. Thus they work with separate sources of influence that will reflect the construction of the human being in the observed data. This is an important difficulty in many applications of AI, because some factors of the real world are excluded influencing all the data that we can consider.

The "representation property" that we suggest in this book (see Chapter 10) is different from the authors' concept of "representation learning" (Goodfellow et al., 2016, p. 5). We work on the structure, in the process of "how" the machine will perform. The authors (Goodfellow et al., 2016, p. 5) explain "representation learning" as factors that have already gone through human discernment to observe quantities, which may interfere with the observation of the physical world. An example of a solution for interpreting abstract data while ignoring factors of variation (such as a speaker's accent being identified by the machine) is given by the authors (Goodfellow et al., 2016). They (Goodfellow et al. 2016, p. 5) emphasize that the functioning of DL solves the central problem in the representation learning introducing representations "expressed in terms of others, simpler representations," building "complex concepts from simpler concepts." The reader is asked to read Chapter 10 to better understand through figures that how a DL system can represent concepts by combining simpler concepts. We suggest that our definition of this process as the "representation property" of natural language should be applied to AI instead of "representation learning" (Goodfellow et al., 2016). In this way, AI can work with more precision, allowing "logistic regression" (Goodfellow et al., 2016, p. 7).

The representation property of natural language (Chapter 10) consists of an AI approach because it is a process designed to improve ML making it more intuitive. ML, according to Goodfellow et al. (2016, p. 8), is the only viable approach to build AI systems designed to operate in complex real-world environments. The flexibility of ML adapting the machine to the observed context is what is most wanted in terms of representation of the world. This is possible when organizing representation comes in a hierarchy of concepts, in which each concept is defined in relation to the others. This principle rules the natural language universal structure (see Chapter 3).

To better understand AI, Goodfellow et al. (2016, p. 9) had drawn concentric circles placing AI in the largest and DL in the smallest and most internal.

4.2 Artificial intelligence being modeled by the natural intelligence

ML that works from data from a wide variety of experiences, according to Goodfellow et al. (2016, p. 99) inspired by Mitchell (1997), should be defined as:

> A computer program is said to learn from experience E with respect to some class of tasks T and performance measure P, if its performance at tasks in T, as measured by P, improves with experience E.

Goodfellow et al. (2016) do not provide a formal definition of what experiences (E), tasks (T), and performance measures (P) would be. Those elements are essential for building the machine algorithm. In this book, we provide, inspired by the functioning of natural language, the common structure that permeates each of these elements, so that we arrive at their mathematical definition (see Chapter 10). This strategy paves the way for the construction of an algorithm with universal structure intended to be the basis for the configuration of specific ML algorithms.

Following the model of the natural intelligence, ML tasks are conceived as the result of a process, configuring "output." These tasks (T), under

Goodfellow et al. (2016, pp. 100–103) point of view, can take varied actions such as: Classification, in which the machine is asked to specify categories such as, object recognition; classification with missing inputs in which the computer needs to map the function of a single input to replicate it; regression, in which the machine predicts a numerical value, for example, to define insurance premiums; transcription, in which ML transcribes data into a textual form, such as an optical character recognition of an image of text, deciphering it into a textual sequence; automatic translation, in which data from one language are converted to symbols in another language; anomaly detection, in which atypical objects are detected, such as, for example, the detection of credit card fraud. The authors (op. cit.) conclude that because there are many tasks performed by AI, their categorization becomes ineffective or impractical.

In addition to the tasks, the resources or data collected by the ML also present a qualitative or quantitative measure (value) previously given:

An example is a collection of example features that have been quantitatively measured from some object or event that we want the machine learning system to process. We typically represent an example as a vector $x \in Rn$ where each entry xi of the vector is another feature. For example, the features of an image are usually the values of the pixels in the image.

(Goodfellow et al., 2016, p. 99).

[…] In order to evaluate the abilities of a machine learning algorithm, we must design a quantitative measure of its performance. Usually this performance measure P is specific to the task being carried out by the system.

(Goodfellow et al., 2016, p. 103).

AI accommodates prior interference designed to establish value, whether given by context or human intervention. To exemplify this fact, we describe some processes such as: For classification tasks, classification with missing inputs and transcription, there is an accuracy measurement of the model based on the proportion of examples that produce the correct output. In tasks related to density estimation, a previous model is provided to score the continuous value to establish an average probability as a measure.

From the moment, we understand ML according to the functioning of natural intelligence, we can better understand what AI is. The performance of the latter will be improved if it is adapted to performance measures that copy the real world. If real world and measure of performance (value) are used independently, the latter will hardly correspond to the desired behavior of the system. A description task taken out of its context results in ambiguity.

It is known that in natural language there are other elements of context that interfere with the formation of the final meaning: The world we live in "prints" mental representations by connecting the brain to reality. Linguistically, it is possible to describe this link through semantics, whereby the analysis of a sentence is made considering elements of the real world (Monte-Serrat et al., 2020).

Goodfellow et al. (2016, p. 104) teach that measuring the accuracy of the system is an impractical task because we only know what quantity we would ideally like to measure, or we deal with probability distributions only implicitly. The authors (op. cit.) suggest that an alternative criterion be established to project an approximation of the desired criterion. We clarify in this book what is the generalized structure in which the specific and desired criteria must be supported: The universal structure of the natural language.

The concept of experience (E) presented by Goodfellow et al. is the following:

> *Machine learning algorithms can be broadly categorized as unsupervised supervised by what kind of experience they are allowed to have during the learning process.*
>
> ***(Goodfellow et al., 2016, p. 105).***

This definition corresponds to the entry of stimuli into the human cognitive system, in our view. The authors (op. cit.) claim, under informal definition, that experience (E) can be supervised or unsupervised. As it is about receiving stimuli by a machine, it is unlikely to be unsupervised, due to prior human intervention determining what values are placed in the machine so that it chooses which are the "best" stimuli it will absorb: "A classic unsupervised learning task is to find the 'best' representation of the data" (Goodfellow et al., 2016, p. 146). Goodfellow et al. state that:

> *The distinction between supervised and unsupervised algorithms is not formally and rigidly defined because there is no objective test for distinguishing whether a value is a feature or a target provided by a supervisor.*
>
> ***(Goodfellow et al. 2016, p. 145).***

In terms of natural intelligence, we would say that unsupervised stimuli are those that the human body receives daily for being exposed to the environment. Supervised stimuli are those to which the individual undergoes to investigate specific results, such as stimuli during an fMRI session in which the subject repeats movements to investigate which areas of the brain have greater blood oxygenation.

The concept of ML is based on an algorithm that improves the performance of a computer program in a specific task. For Goodfellow et al. (2016), the training of an ML model is subject to error, which needs to be reduced or eliminated. The authors suggest the following path:

> *The central challenge in machine learning is that we must perform well on new, previously unseen inputs—not just those on which our model was trained. The ability to perform well on previously unobserved inputs is called 'generalization'.*
> **(Goodfellow et al., 2016, p. 110, highlighted by the authors).**

This solution was found for the linear regression model in which a generalization error is assumed, defining the expected value of the error in a new input, hoping that the system will find it in practice. The authors note that.

> *If the training and the test set are collected arbitrarily, there is indeed little we can do. If we are allowed to make some assumptions about how the training and test set are collected, then we can make some progress.*
> **(Goodfellow et al., 2016, p. 110).**

ML memorizes a set of properties from a space of previously given hypotheses. In the universal algorithm that we propose in this book, we predict the generic structure through which the complexity of the task to be performed will be guided.

The optimization of a machine model depends on its capacity in terms of the number of input resources it has and the parameters corresponding to those resources. The universal model that we describe specifies the generalized (the simplest one) function—in relation to—to which the learning algorithm functions will be adapted to generate a representational capacity of the model. Some difficulties so far are in finding the best function for the learning algorithm, resulting in errors. Working with the "in relation to" structure decreases the discrepancy by not managing loose boundaries to determine the capacity of DL algorithms. Our suggestion of a generalized and simple path "in relation to" is the solution to design the capacity of the ML. We are going in a different direction from the following ones we observed in Goodfellow et al.:

> *[...] averaged over all possible data generating distributions, every classification algorithm has the same error rate when classifying previously unobserved points. In other words, in some sense, no machine learning algorithm is universally any better than any other. The most sophisticated algorithm we can conceive of has the same average performance (over all possible tasks) as merely predicting that every point belongs to the same class.*
> **(Goodfellow et al., 2016, p. 116).**

[...]

This means that the goal of machine learning research is not to seek a universal learning algorithm or the absolute best learning algorithm. Instead, our goal is to understand what kinds of distributions are relevant to the 'real world' that an AI agent experiences, and what kinds of machine learning algorithms perform well on data drawn from the kinds of data generating distributions we care about.
(Goodfellow et al., 2016, p. 118).

[...]

The no free lunch theorem has made it clear that there is no best machine learning algorithm, and, in particular, no best form of regularization. Instead we must choose a form of regularization that is well-suited to the particular task we want to solve. The philosophy of deep learning in general and this book in particular is that a very wide range of tasks (such as all of the intellectual tasks that people can do) may all be solved effectively using very general-purpose forms of regularization.
(Goodfellow et al., 2016, p. 120).

From the viewpoint of the contents of this book, the universal structure of the algorithm (in relation to) facilitates the task of controlling the performance of the representation learning algorithms, as it directs the type of functions allowed to extract solutions. The universal structure helps to circumvent problems such as:

One difficulty pertaining to clustering is that the clustering problem is inherently ill-posed, in the sense that there is no single criterion that measures how well a clustering of the data corresponds to the real world [...]
It is still not entirely clear what the optimal distributed representation is [...] but having many attributes reduces the burden on the algorithm to guess which single attribute we care about, and allows us to measure similarity between objects in a fine-grained way by comparing many attributes instead of just testing whether one attribute matches.
(Goodfellow et al., 2016, p. 150).

There is an advantage in using the universal algorithm in terms of applying it in a small or large data set, because instead of a statistical uncertainty, an estimated result will be obtained according to the specified task. This positive result is also reflected when the data set presents hundreds of thousands of examples, and thus avoiding the typical use of estimators whose variation is based on average error which is cited by Bengio and Grandvalet (2004).

Inspired by the definition by Goodfellow et al. (2016, p. 152), we suggest that the characteristic elements of the universal language algorithm combine: A representation property application (see Chapter 10), a function determining whether the value is fixed or arbitrated, an optimization procedure and a model that will be specified according to the specific case.

An in-depth discussion of each of the elements of the algorithm would be more appropriate in a book aimed specifically at the field of AI. This book focuses on the theory of linguistics and neurolinguistics to understand brain functioning and apply that knowledge to AI and ML. It is important to note that we design a generalized algorithm (see Chapter 10) that will serve as a framework for the algorithm to be applied in a specific circumstance, which will be decisive for the choice of the relationship between the elements, for example, combination of models, functions, and optimization algorithms.

The central problem of AI, according to Goodfellow et al. (2016, p. 154) continues to be speech recognition or object recognition. The authors claim that the development of DL was created from the failure of traditional algorithms to generalize AI tasks.

We emphasize that the generalization of the data to be processed by ML sanitizes some aspects that are not evaluated in the result, leading to an idealized and not real result. This phenomenon is called "curse of dimensionality" (Goodfellow et al., 2016, p. 154) because the number of possible different configurations of a set of variables increases exponentially as the number of variables increases. The relative success of DL in working on relating the data preserves essential characteristics carrying them for the obtained result (see Chapter 10).

We believe that working with high-dimensional data and with mechanisms that achieve generalization in traditional ML will continue to bring unsatisfactory results as they do not preserve the characteristics of the initial data. On the other hand, the structure of DL preserves the value relationship with the initial data, as described by Goodfellow et al. (2016):

Feedforward neural networks are called networks because they are typically represented by composing together many different functions. The model is associated with a directed acyclic graph describing how the functions are composed together. For example, we might have three functions f(1), f(2), and f(3) connected in a chain, to form f(x) = f(3)(f(2)(f(1)(x))). These chain structures are the most commonly used structures of neural networks. In this case, f(1) is called the first layer of the network, f(2) is called the second layer, and so on. The overall length of the chain gives the of the model. It is from this terminology that the depth name 'deep learning' arises. The final layer of a feedforward network is called the output layer.

(Goodfellow et al., 2016, pp. 167–168).

[…] these networks are called neural because they are loosely inspired by neuroscience. Each hidden layer of the network is typically vector-valued. The dimensionality of these hidden layers determines the of the model. Each width element of the vector may be interpreted as playing a role analogous to a neuron. Rather than

thinking of the layer as representing a single vector-to-vector function, we can also think of the layer as consisting of many that act in parallel, units each representing a vector-to-scalar function. Each unit resembles a neuron in the sense that it receives input from many other units and computes its own activation value. The idea of using many layers of vector-valued representation is drawn from neuroscience. The choice of the functions $f^{(i)}(x)$ used to compute these representations is also loosely guided by neuroscientific observations about the functions that biological neurons compute.

(Goodfellow et al., 2016, p. 168).

In this example, we simply demonstrate the DL solution in representing a real situation. There can be billions of model parameters and billions of training examples. What we need to make clear is the need to find parameters that produce a margin of error very small. The solution that we describe in the universal algorithm is sensitive to the values of the initial parameters, which is applied in DL, as can be seen in the next topic.

4.3 Deep learning

We chose to develop some details of the DL story because it is the closest one to our design of the universal artificial language algorithm, although a comprehensive understanding of DL is beyond the scope of this book. The historical context in which DL arose, according to Goodfellow et al. (2016, pp. 12–13), revealed some key trends such as: Having received several names that reflect different philosophical points of view; it became more useful when it was able to increase the amount of training data available; its models increase in size over time; it obtained the ability to solve increasingly complicated applications, with greater precision over time. Some lines about DL emerging as an exciting new technology are written by Goodfellow et al. (2016, pp 12–13). Generally saying there were three currents of DL: In the 1940s to 1960s, from 1980 to 1990, and re-emerged in 2006. The authors Goodfellow et al. explain these trends below:

Two of the three historical waves of artificial neural nets research, as measured by the frequency of the phrases [were] 'cybernetics' and 'connectionism' or 'neural networks' [...] The first wave started with cybernetics in de 1940s–1960s, with the development of theories of biological learning [...] and implementations of the first models, such as perceptron [...] enabling the training of a single neuron. The second wave started with the connectionist approach of the 1980–1995 period, with backpropagation [...] to train a neural network with one or two hidden layers. The current and third wave, deep learning, started around 2006 [...] and is just now appearing in book form as of 2016. The other two waves similarly appeared in book form much later than the corresponding scientific activity occurred.

(Goodfellow et al., 2016, p. 13).

The wave of cybernetics was marked by the predecessors of modern DL, which consisted of simple linear models marked by the neuroscientific perspective.

These models were designed to take a set of n input values values $x_1, ..., x_n$, and associate them with an output y. These models would learn a set of weights $w_1, ...,$ w_n and compute their output $f(x,w) = x_1 w_1 + x_2 w_2 + ... + x_n w_n$.

(Goodfellow et al. 2016, p. 14).

Those linear models had flaws, according to Goodfellow et al. (2016, pp. 13–14), which negatively influence biological inspiration for ML, making neural networks less popular. The authors (op. cit., p. 14) state that Neuroscience is still considered an important source of inspiration for DL researchers, but it has a reduced role because until then there was not enough data on cognitive functioning. To arrive at the universal algorithm of machine language, it is necessary to obtain a deep understanding of the universal structure of language that encompasses neuronal activity and other biological systems, as explained in Chapter 6 (on the universal structure of language). Goodfellow and colleagues are in line with the content we propose in this book by stating that:

Neuroscience has given us a reason to hope that a single deep learning algorithm can solve many different tasks. Neuroscientists have found that ferrets can learn to 'see' with the auditory processing region of their brain if their brains are rewired to send visual signals to that area [...]. This suggests that much of the mammalian brain might use a single algorithm to solve most of the different tasks that the brain solves.

(Goodfellow et al., 2016, p. 15).

In the 1980s connectionism emerged as the second wave of research in neural networks, based on the interdisciplinary approach to cognitive science, combining several different levels of analysis. Symbolic reasoning models were studied. The central idea in this model, according to Goodfellow et al. (2016, p. 16) is to work with large number of simple computational units to obtain intelligent behavior when connected in a network. Several key concepts of this movement remain in the DL. Among them, we find the one of the distributed representation (each input of a system must be represented by many resources, and each resource must be involved in the representation of many possible inputs).

In the 1990s sequence modeling based on neural networks was perfected with the introduction of the short-term long-memory network (LSTM), which is used today in natural language-processing tasks at Google (Goodfellow et al., 2016, p. 17).

In 2006 the first learning algorithms based on the way learning happens in the brain appeared. A type of neural network emerged that used layered planning as a strategy which would later serve to train many other types of deep networks, making the use of "deep learning" popular, and surpassing AI systems based on other ML technologies. The researchers' focus is now on new unsupervised learning techniques and on the ability to generalize deep models from small data sets (Goodfellow et al., 2016, p. 18).

One of the names that DL has come to be is artificial neural networks (ANNs). ANNs are computational models of learning inspired by the biological brain. It is worth mentioning that the knowledge of how natural language works is important for understanding the brain and the principles underlying human intelligence. Only with this comprehension can we hope to make it possible to design successful models of ML.

DL, according to Goodfellow et al. (2016, p. 13) builds AI by the reverse engineering of the computational principles behind the brain, proving that the intelligent behavior of the machine is possible. This is already an achievement. Our book goes a step further, explaining that biological functioning alone is not enough as a basis. As AI reproduces an artificial language, it must work according to the universal structure of natural language, within the terms defined it in Chapter 6 and not in conformity with Natural Language Processing.

What matters most for AI today is to provide algorithms with the resources necessary for the machine to work from what is recorded. All records are centralized in a data set for the ML application. ML works best when estimation starts from an algorithm suited to the context of a small amount of data, and then applied to larger numbers of data in a way that exceeds human performance.

The choice of the universal ML algorithm implicitly establishes a set of previous principles or beliefs about what kind of function the algorithm should learn. The generalized algorithm has previously established that we will work with the composition of several simpler functions, since learning—which aims at representation—consists of discovering a set of underlying variation factors that must be described in the form of other simpler underlying variation factors.

It is emphasized that the task of the machine will be successful if the work with smaller data sets is very well directed. Hence the importance of the content of this book: The special focus on how natural language works help to better understand and apply the structural functioning of human language to AI, making it work with large amounts of data without supervision.

4.4 Language information given to computational models

The subject of AI is very extensive. It should be stressed that there is an important point in the discussion on AI: What information about the language structure should be transmitted to the machine so that the machine's performance is more intuitive? A computational model that still needs to be improved is the one based on the natural logic of the brain searching for the principles by which it is guided. It must be established that logic and semantics are mutually exclusive. According to Sánchez (1991, p. 15), "what is known is that semantics [related to the context] ends where the system of evidence begins." The logical conclusion dispenses with context in an interpretation. Linguist Charles Peirce reinforces this statement by saying that:

So far, we have a language, but still no algebra. For an algebra is a language with a code of formal rules for the transformation of expressions, by which we are enabled to draw conclusions without the trouble of attending to the meaning of the language we use.

(Peirce, 1976, p. 107).

Peirce (1976, p. 108) states that the inference must be seen as elimination and introduction of formulas: "We require that the rules should enable us to dispense with all reasonings in our proofs except the mere substitution of particular expressions in general formulae." Often the interpretation of the computational system is defective because it does not consider the context: The problem with logical systems is that Modus Ponens is closed and when some axioms are presented, it is done under "universal closures formulas," limiting the machine's range or leading to ambiguous interpretation. "One can say that Peirce's system lacks a real rule of introduction for the universal quantifier and a real elimination rule for the existential quantifier" (Sánchez, 1991, p. 188). No matter how much one tries to introduce formal logic in natural language, there will be no success, as the interpretation goes beyond the syllogistic borders and, to obtain good results, it is necessary to consider the context. Peirce's (1976) formal logic is successful for application to formal language but fails in natural language because the latter is a dynamic system, which needs to be thought very carefully about the computational model.

Another issue to be addressed regarding the construction of computational models concerns the hypothesis that the statistical laws of language are subject to a biological law. Spoken language escapes the formality of writing. Even the transcription of texts remains subject to the phonological rules that establish correspondence between speech and writing. In this case, oral communication transcribed at the word and phoneme level forms a standard corpus and, if it enters the standard, there has already been human intervention in the machine's intelligence to find the corresponding symbolic unit. If human choice is not adequate, the system will fail. A solution to this is proposed in this book: We indicate the universal structure of language, which is the simplest, and how to work with it.

4.5 The key principle for artificial intelligence

An important lesson that can be learned about the functioning of human cognition is that neural networks and neurons work in connection with each other. Isolated they are not useful for the cognitive process. This is the way human language works: It is the result of the cognitive process that goes through several subsystems until reaching a central system (see Chapter 3 on natural intelligence). If we see natural language as a result of the functioning of brain isolated regions, we will never fully understand it. Language is the product of several densely connected biological subsystems of the natural intelligence.

Researchers claim that current ANNs are smaller than that of vertebrate animals such as frogs (Goodfellow et al., 2016, p. 21). Our wager to increasing model sizes is "in relation to" operation, which provides DL with the ability to represent more complicated functions. This concept is central to this book and is described in more detail in Chapter 10. Sequence-by-sequence learning for machine translation is proof that this model is on the right track (Bahdanau et al., 2015).

Thinking about this topic within a formalized system, it would be possible to check whether presenting proof is correct since it is established in an instinctive and complicated notion of the truth. In this way, according to Penrose (1988, p. 507), "whatever formal system is used, there are statements that we can see are true but which do not get assigned the truth-value 'true' by the formalist's proposed procedure." And he (Penrose, 1988, pp. 507–508) continues his reasoning saying mathematical truth goes beyond mere formalism: "When mathematicians carry out their forms of reasoning, they do not want to have to be continually checking to see whether or not their arguments can be formulated in terms of the axioms and rules of procedure of some formal system," guiding themselves by "intuitive understanding of what is 'self-evidently true'." There is in this attitude a certain distance from the context.

Some connectivity principles of natural language have been successfully applied in AI. Examples of them are found in the Convolutional Neural Networks, whose layers of neural networks multiply matrices through a matrix that serves as a parameter, so that the output unit interacts with the input unit.

> Convolution leverages three important ideas that can help improve a machine learning system: Sparse interactions parameter sharing equivariant representations.
>
> **(Goodfellow et al., 2016, p. 335).**

We can cite, also, the valid convolution, in which

> all pixels in the output are a function of the same number of pixels in the input, so the behavior of an output pixel is somewhat more regular. However, the size of the output shrinks at each layer. If the input image has width m and the kernel has width k, the output will be of width m + k − 1.
>
> **(Goodfellow et al., 2016, p. 350).**

We can say that parameter sharing and regularity in the behavior of convolutional networks are successful because they follow principles of natural intelligence. It is known that the main design principles of neural networks were inspired by neuroscience. Hubel and Wiesel's (1959, 1962, 1968) discoveries about cat neurons that respond more intensely to a given light pattern led scientists to detect a simplified structure of brain function responsible for preprocessing the image without substantially altering its representation (Goodfellow et al., 2016, p. 365). From these findings, the convolutional network layer was designed to capture: (1) two-dimensional structures captured on a spatial map; (2) the activity of a simple cell that has a linear function as a characteristic; and (3) invariant aspects of complex cells (through pooling strategies) (op. cit., p. 365).

Regarding these strategies repeatedly applied to the various layers of the brain, Goodfellow et al. (2016, pp. 365–366) claim that they found a "specific concept" invariant to many input transformations:

> As we pass through multiple anatomical layers of the brain, we eventually find cells that respond to some specific concept and are invariant to many transformations of the input. These cells have been nicknamed 'grandmother cells' - the idea is that a person could have a neuron that activates when seeing an image of their grandmother, regardless of whether she appears in the left or right side of the image, whether the image is a close-up of her face or zoomed out shot of her entire body, whether she is brightly lit, or in shadow, etc.
>
> **(Goodfellow et al., 2016, p. 365–366).**

The authors (op. cit.) claim that these "grandmother cells" exist in the human brain, located in the temporal lobe. We claim that what they call "grandmother cells" are not cells but a universal structure present in the cells that gives rise to these findings. This universal structure acts on object recognition tasks because it carries invariant aspects of information.

As an example, we can observe the recurrent neural networks (RNNs), in the sequence modeling used for processing sequential data. RNNs process a sequence of values $x^{(1)}$, ..., $x^{(\tau)}$. Although convolutional networks are scaled to image, recurring networks can be scaled to long sequences. In order that the information does not lose its characteristics, it is necessary to share parameters in a generalized way, so that specific information can occur in various positions within the sequence through the sharing of the same weights in various stages of time.

Comparing the convolutional network and the RNNs, although each one presents special aspects, we can observe an invariant functioning: The generic sharing of parameters in which each element of the output is a function of the previous members of the output. There is the use of the same update rule, preserving the characteristics of the information in the sequence even if it is long. There is an "in relation to" operation in the observed sequence. Otherwise the information may vanish or explode exponentially in a large number of steps.

Once we understand that human language results from a cognitive process that runs through several subsystems until it reaches a central system (see Chapter 3 on natural intelligence), we can transfer that knowledge to AI. If natural language is conceived only as resulting from the functioning of isolated regions of the brain, we will never fully understand it. Natural intelligence stems from several densely connected biological subsystems.

These basic principles of natural cognition will provide conditions for the human visual system, which is integrated with other senses, to be replicated by AI not only as purely visual convolutional networks. In this way it will be possible for AI to interpret entire scenes, including relationships between objects, interacting with the world.

Organizing the idea of Goodfellow et al. (2016) regarding simple cells:

> *So far we have described how simple cells are roughly linear and selective for certain features, complex cells are more nonlinear and become invariant to some transformations of these simple cell features, and stacks of layers that alternate between selectivity and invariance can yield grandmother cells for very specific phenomena. We have not yet described precisely what these individual cells detect. In a deep, nonlinear network, it can be difficult to understand the function of individual cells. Simple cells in the first layer are easier to analyze, because their responses are driven by a linear function.*
>
> **(Goodfellow et al., 2016, p. 368).**

We can affirm that the authors' finding is revealed, in fact, in a structure that underlies these simple cells, complex cells, "grandmother cells": A structure that does not vary, in short, a universal structure.

The key principles of natural language seen under the concept that we propose in this book are evidenced in the way that language works: Natural language results from a process that goes from the external stimulus, passing through several subsystems until reaching a central system (see Chapter 3 on natural intelligence). Thus natural intelligence cannot be understood as the result of the functioning of isolated and independent brain regions.

As a product of several subsystems network, natural language is linked to a central system that makes intelligence an intensely connected product, becoming excellent at storing implicit knowledge (resulting from the axiomatic element responsible for the perception of stimuli by the organs; these stimuli reach a system central located in the brain) and explicit knowledge (due to logical reasoning, responsible for processing information in a sequence of steps, specifying the way the inputs are inserted in a neural network). This is how natural intelligence is modeled: There is an intuitive system response to information whose input is given by stimuli; there is a response due to reasoning related to information whose input parameters are modified by the ability to reason, imposing a given sequence on that information.

References

Bahdanau, D., Cho, K., Bengio, J., 2015. Neural machine translation by jointly learning to align and translate. In: Computer Science, Computation and Language. Cornell University, Ithaca, NY.

Bengio, Y., Grandvalet, Y., 2004. No unbiased estimator of the variance of k-fold cross-validation. In: Thrun, S., Saul, L., Schölkopf, B. (Eds.), Advances in Neural Information Processing Systems 16 (NIPS'03), Cambridge, MA. MIT Press, Cambridge, p. 122.

Goodfellow, I., Bengio, Y., Courville, A., 2016. Deep Learning. MIT Press, Cambridge, MA.

Hubel, D., Wiesel, T., 1959. Receptive fields of single neurons in the cat's striate cortex. J. Physiol. 148, 574–591. 364.

Hubel, D., Wiesel, T., 1962. Receptive fields, binocular interaction, and functional architecture in the cat's visual cortex. J. Physiol. 160, 106–154. 364.

Hubel, D., Wiesel, T., 1968. Receptive fields and functional architecture of monkey striate cortex. J. Physiol. 195, 215–243. 364.

Mitchell, T.M., 1997. Machine Learning. McGraw-Hill, New York.

Monte-Serrat, D., Cabella, B., Cattani, C., 2020. The Schrödinger's cat paradox in the mind creative process. Inf. Sci. Lett. 9 (3), 1–10. https://doi.org/10.12785/isl/paper_new.

Peirce, C., 1976. The New Elements of Mathematics by Charles S. Pierce i-iv. Mouton, Paris.

Penrose, R., 1988. On the physics and mathematics thought. In: Herken, R. (Ed.), The Universal Turing Machine. Kammerer & Unverzagt, Berlin.

Sánchez, V., 1991. Studies on Natural Logic and Categorial Grammar. Dissertation, University of Amsterdam. January.

CHAPTER FIVE

Computer language and linguistics

5.1 Introduction

Mathematics and linguistics deal with the representation of thought from a theoretical perspective of understanding the guiding structure of language functioning. They are disciplines that work with symbolic language, following rational and logical principles.

In this chapter, we explain that computer language is a formal symbolic language which depends on some linguistic principles of natural language. Computing combines grammar and semantics to regulate the machine's behavior when performing specific tasks. We suggest that the logical-axiomatic principle of natural language is the algorithmic core of computational methods. The application of this axiomatic-logical structure to the machine language involves an underlying learning algorithm capable of generalizing the execution of a set of factors, that is, a unifying algorithm that will give the machine intuitive capacity, leaving it less dependent on human intervention.

According to Wolfram (2002, p. 1103), in 2002, there were more than 140 human languages and 15 computer languages. In 2019 there were approximately 6500 spoken languages and over 700 programming languages in the world. These numbers prove that, until 2020, it has been practically impossible not only to identify specific characteristics of the various existing languages but also to circumvent the growing modifications by means of rules well defined by a grammar that determines how the sentences should be constructed.

The number of existing languages is not the main problem for artificial intelligence; we believe that understanding the complexity of language functioning is its biggest challenge. Cassirer (1972, p. 7) states that, in order for man to come to know the world, two general conditions must be present: The delimitation of the main ways in which man can "understand it,"

The Natural Language for Artificial Intelligence
https://doi.org/10.1016/B978-0-12-824118-9.00005-9
89

together with the identification of a "morphology" of the spirit established in accordance with a general theory of forms of expression. The author (op. cit.) states that the formation of concepts and judgments in the natural sciences makes it possible to define the natural "object" in its constituent characters and understand the "object" of knowledge in its dependence on cognitive function. We assume that these elements are not enough when we take into account the domain of pure subjectivity, which seems to work (in terms of evaluation) whenever a given perspective, applicable to all phenomena, assigns a specific configuration to the object of knowledge.

Cassirer (1972) calls "universal linguistic philosophy" what would open the way for a descriptive theory of meanings. From our point of view, such a theory would only be successful if it described the universal process under which meaning is formed in a painting, sculpture, writing, etc., that is, regardless of the means of expression of the idea. In this book, we provide details on how the universal structure of language works giving rise to the birth of meaning, which can happen on two fronts: Either meaning is formed under the prevalence of logical reasoning or it is formed under a subjective approach. This chapter deals with those aspects of language.

An important step to unveil the characteristics of the natural language that will be programmed for the machine is the differentiation between two perspectives on the concept of language: (1) as a human capacity to use complex communication systems; (2) as a set of signals used to encode and decode information.

We organize these concepts so that one is not taken over by the other. It is accorded that language as a human capacity to establish communication corresponds to "natural language" and, on the other hand, the set of signals intended to encode and decode information corresponds to the expression of "conventional language."

Linguistics as a science aims to describe or explain human verbal language. According to this theory, it is through signs that man

> communicates, represents his thoughts, exercises his power, elaborates his culture and identity etc. The signs are fundamental, because they give man his symbolic dimension: This connects him to other men and to nature, this is his social and natural reality.
> There are, in addition to the signs of verbal language, many other kinds of signs that populate the life of man: Painting, mime, traffic code, fashion, artificial languages etc. Signs, in general, both in non-verbal and verbal languages, are objects of a general science of signs: Semiology.
>
> **(Orlandi, 2002, pp. 10–11).**

The approach we take to language in this book concerns the general theory of signs, since all the time we refer to a universal structure responsible for the construction of meaning, making intermediation between the environment and the human mind. Our approach is broad, involving any type of sign, be it image, number, letter, sculpture. In this chapter, we make a foray into some theories that, while dealing with specific aspects of language, present arguments that apply to the universal structure of natural language.

Saussure (1916) inaugurates linguistics as a science by reflecting on aspects of verbal language (oral or written) from the perspective of conventional language, that is, addressing the signs produced by the human being when speaking or writing. Saussure (1916) introduced the structuralist view of language, in which it is understood that the formulation of underlying abstract rules generates observable linguistic structures. Chomsky (1957), on the other hand, studies language from the perspective of prescribing norms or correction rules and is one of the main defenders that a set of phrases can be generated from a certain set of rules. Their works are valid until the moment when we face challenges caused by the dynamic system of language, the main problem whose solution is sought by artificial intelligence. According to Cassirer (1972, p. 16), the conceptual system of physics will account for all the relationships that exist between real objects and understand how they depend on each other, through a theoretical perspective that unifies them. This stance is in line with our understanding of the structure that governs the functioning of language.

Linguists, in general, work with language as a "representation of thought" showing that languages obey rational and logical principles (Orlandi, 2002, p. 12). Taking as a principle that all languages follow rational and general principles, linguists argue that ideas should be expressed in a precise and transparent way, in an attempt to achieve what would be an "ideal language—universal, logical, unambiguous language, able to ensure the communication of the human being" (Orlandi, 2002, p. 12).

We show in this book that linguists were unable to arrive at this universal structure because they considered language as a convention with its rules. The perspective of linguistics as a science is questioned by us for considering only the logical aspect of language (present in conventional language), disregarding its axiomatic character (it is a dynamic system, a biological phenomenon). The universal structure of language is axiomatic–logical and should involve an interdisciplinary discussion. Scientific fragmentation is detrimental to the understanding of this complex phenomenon, as it gives language a unidirectional perspective that makes it impossible to recognize all the elements that constitute it. The recognition of an integrality or universality of language has to do with language as a dynamic system, with a perspective that results from a process of "relations" of elements and not from a "sum" of the elements that compose it.

If the language is always updating, what would be the number of computational steps needed to reproduce something from its shortest description? The set of rules becomes insufficient. The most sensible thing to do is to search for the most essential language and teach that essence so that the machine can make the modifications and adaptations required by the context.

Linguists (Saussure, 1916; Harley, 2013), therefore, "agreed" what language is, leaving aside other aspects of natural language that could not be circumvented by the rules. This agreement does not mean that language comes down to what experts conceive as language. The work of some linguists (Saussure, 1916; Jakobson, 1963, 1965, 1975, 1990, 2010; Pinker, 1994) is exposed in this chapter in due measure as an example of the hard work of circumventing the language dynamic process. Then the views of philosophers and linguists (Foucault, 1963, 1966, 1969, 1971; Pêcheux, 1975, 1988; Lacan 1949) who realized that the study of human language must consider the historical context, is presented, showing that the latter interferes with the meaning formation.

The study of computer language and artificial intelligence is very extensive, with several different approaches to language. The aim of this book is to show the key point of "how" natural language works. Foucault (1969), Pêcheux (1975), and Lacan (1949) succeeded in theoretically describing the interface between language and context. We developed a broad concept of language in Chapter 6 establishing it as the essence of a universal algorithm for the machine: Understanding "how" the language works, this must be implemented in the computer's language. Among the essential elements of machine learning (experience, "E"; task, "T"; and performance measure, "P"), Goodfellow et al. (2016, p. 99, our highlight) agree that "task" is different from learning: "Learning is our 'means of attaining the ability to perform' the task."

For the reasons just outlined, the difference between the concept of language given by linguists and the concept of natural language that we present in this book will directly interfere with the development of artificial intelligence. If someone draws a machine algorithm model and work according to conventional language, they will get a constrained outcome due to the limited concept of language taken as a starting point. If one aims at implementing an intuitive artificial intelligence, they need to work with the concept of natural language, describing its essence to be replicated in the machine. In this way, the computer—through cognitive computing paradigms and guided by the structural functioning of the human cognitive system (which is dynamic and encompasses conventional language)—will be successful in reproducing the natural language process.

5.2 Computer language

A computer language is a formal language, that is, it does not arise from an evolution as the natural language. Human intervention, through mathematics, logic, and computer science makes use of characters to produce formal language from a combination of grammar and semantics. This type of language controls the behavior of the machine so that it performs specific tasks or produces specific meanings to facilitate communication or a task. The logical sequence, as a finite set of rules, aims not only to organize speech and writing (in which rules are applied serially) but also to organize the space (where the rules are applied in series and in parallel), such as, to add edges and points to obtain shapes (Stiny and Gips, 1972; Stiny, 1980). In the world what we perceive is never its reality, but only the repercussion of physical forces on our sensory organs (Hall, 1966, pp. 56–57) which organize the input stimuli. Computational language, therefore, creates systems that organize information attempting to imitate the way natural intelligence organizes information achieved by the human body.

According to Wolfram (2002, p. 1103), computer languages are based on grammars without context, which causes occasional deviations from the model making interpretation particularly difficult.

> *The idea of describing languages by grammars dates back to antiquity [...]. And starting in the 1800s extensive studies were made of the comparative grammars of different languages. But the notion that grammars could be thought of like programs for generating languages did not emerge with clarity until the work of Noam Chomsky beginning in 1956. And following this, there were for a while many efforts to formulate precise models for human languages, and to relate these to properties of the brain. But by the 1980s it became clear - notably through the failure of attempts to automate natural language understanding and translation - that language cannot in most cases (with the possible exception of grammar-checking software) meaningfully be isolated from other aspects of human thinking.*

The fact that grammar is not solely responsible for language was one of Turing's concerns (Gandy, 1988). Turing wondered about the relationship between the logical machine and the physical world. At one point, he realized that he could treat symbolic logic as a way of introducing semantics, making quantifiers be appreciated "in relation to" objects. He theoretically conceived of the machine as a mechanical behavior reduced to simpler operations, which correspond more closely to the idea of intuition. This will be seen in the next topic.

5.3 Computer logic

According to Beeson (1988, p. 191), the word "computational" is related to calculus and it is accompanied by logic. Calculus is linked to mathematics, and proof is understood as the heart of this formal science. In this way, one can understand mathematics as logic plus computation. It is worth noting that computation and natural language are both accompanied by logic: "From the beginning of mathematics there have been intimate connections between logic and computation. The exact nature of these connections is still being investigated" (Beeson, 1988, p. 192). Mathematics is a form of symbolic language that presupposes linguistic models as its foundation. Based on this reasoning, mathematical signs are determined by the axiomatic-logical principle of language to express ideas. Therefore automated deduction deals with the computerization of the logical aspects of mathematics, present in language (Beeson, 1988, p. 192).

Arguing that logic is computation, Beeson (1988, p. 193) states that there is a "universal language into which any argument could be translated." He (Beeson, 1988, p. 197) also provides more details about this by mentioning Turing solution for the machine operation as:

> [the] step-by-step computations of a computer could be described by formulas of logic [...] The computer is a completely deterministic machine, and it proceeds in discrete steps, governed by an internal clock; if we start the computer in a certain configuration, the configuration one step later is completely determined. Turing's insight is that the relationship between the configuration now and the configuration one step later can be described 'logically'.
>
> **(Highlighted by the author).**

Beeson (1988, p. 199) teaches that the built-in algorithms to implement the resolution method provide easy-to-use matching and searching capabilities. Matching and searching are fundamental processes in artificial intelligence.

While the author (op. cit.) quotes Turing to state that computer programs "could" be modeled in logic, we, on the other hand, state that logic dwells inside the fundamental structure (underlying unit) of language and this condition allows for an efficient version of the resolution algorithm. According to Beeson (1988, pp. 200, 209), the exact sciences professionals confirm that mathematics consists of algorithms involved in logic: "Like waves and particles, logic and computation are metaphors for different aspects of some underlying unity [...] algorithms, or computational methods, are central in mathematics and the logical aspect of mathematics is 'wrapped around' this algorithmic core."

The axiomatic-logical algorithmic nucleus as a guiding principle of natural intelligence must be replicated for the machine design, so that the latter keeps track of the various objects being manipulated. According to Beeson (1988, p. 209), the algorithmic core is not visible and has the function of providing "pyramidal definitions of complicated concepts." We argue that this function corresponds to the axiomatic-logical structure of natural language that results from an invisible and comprehensive cognitive process (natural intelligence) which works in the construction of the meaning by conventional language (visible part).

In this way, it can be concluded that there is no program designed to solve any mathematical problem. The focus is to emphasize that the programs need to be designed on a necessary structure, which we defend to be the theoretical foundation of language computation: The axiomatic-logical structure.

Rewriting the symbolic nature of natural language for artificial intelligence, it is necessary to consider that the language physical signs are determined by principles that are independent of the representation of the language in terms of phonetic symbols (Chomsky, 2006, p. 107). Language has nonsymbolic aspects that also interfere with meaning, such as, for example, different intonations, which have semantic consequences. "These variations cannot be explained—by construction—using symbolic language representations, and therefore one would not expect physical measures to follow the linguistic laws without an additional explanation" (Torre et al. 2019, p. 2).

It is also important to emphasize that written communication is not a mere consequence of speech: Speech is idealized by writing, both are not corresponding (Monte-Serrat, 2019). The key to drawing the machine intelligence is to look for a structure common to speech and writing that allows generating, for instance, an explaining model for the distribution of speech duration at a given linguistic level. The organization of the cognitive process into levels is shown as a by-product of physiological processes (derived from the axiomatic principles of language, see Chapter 8). Knowing better the universal structure that governs the laws of language, the scope of oral communication processes will be clarified. "Written corpus is a discrete symbolization that only captures the shadow of a richer structure present in oral communication in which linguistic laws truly emerge, with a physical origin that written texts would only capture partially" (Torre et al., 2019, p. 19).

5.4 Generative model in machine learning

The encoding and decoding of information in natural language is regulated by a mechanism capable of generalizing the incorporation of complex and high-dimensional data in a latent space of thought representation. It is in this way that the human being can generate new data that is similar to the original one. We seek to replicate this capacity of human cognition for the machine so that the latter intuitively identifies the data of interest, identifies patterns, causal structures, or even correlates independently of human intervention.

Machine learning seeks to understand the underlying structure of real-world data and deep generative models are the appropriate means to unravel that structure (Fraccaro, 2018). Traditional approaches to data analysis only model simple distribution and do not handle complex, high-dimensional data (Fraccaro, 2018).

Supervised learning, that is, with human intervention in requesting the mapping of an input variable to an output variable, is prone to errors in the result presented due to machine error or human scorer assessment error. The generalized function in supervised learning is based on this training data, with no real elementary organization of the data. On the other hand, there are unsupervised learning models, which combine probabilistic modeling and deep learning and are called generative model models. Generative models can find the underlying structure (interesting patterns, cluster, statistical correlation, and causal structures of the data) and generate data like it (Fraccaro, 2018). Examples of generative model are the adverse generative networks and variational autoencoder.

Unsupervised learning is rated as being more difficult than supervised learning because it learns a hidden structure of data distribution (Fraccaro, 2018). We understand that both suffer human intervention and that the difficulty lies in transmitting to the machine the structure on which the label or value will be worked. We suggest a structure that serves static or sequential data with relational criteria capable of replicating the characteristics of the original data.

Latent variables parameters can be used in deep neural networks (Fraccaro, 2018). The machine must, then, learn a complicated probability distribution with only a limited set of high-dimensional data points extracted from that distribution (op. cit.). We understand that the weak point of this theory is working about probabilistic terms, which does not reflect the reality. We suggest that the axiomatic-logical structure of natural language be applied to the machine and, also, that the context of exterior reality must be considered (see Chapter 9). This strategy involves an underlying learning algorithm, which generalizes the execution of a set of factors through a relational criterion, making the machine act intuitively.

5.5 Introduction to linguistics

The concept of language is broad and complex. "Without language, there is no access to reality. Without language, there is no thought" (Araújo, 2004, p. 9). Using linguistic and nonlinguistic signs, men express ideas and signify behavior to provoke reactions. For this reason, language is not restricted to signs (op. cit.). Among language's most critical attributes is its unlimited combinatorial nature from a limited set of elements, resulting in the hierarchy of linguistic units. If there is a hierarchy, it means that there is value going through words, phrases and sentences. The biggest challenge posed to the linguist is to analyze and represent speech because, unlike writing (whose acoustic signals/values are given previously), it has no limits in its hierarchical linguistic structure (Ding et al., 2016). Ding et al. (2016) identified a hierarchy of time scales for neural speech processing underlying the grammar-based internal construction of the hierarchical linguistic structure. This finding points to the axiomatic-logical nature of natural language. But language was not always considered that way.

The construction of linguistics in the 19th century is due to the use of language to speak of language, that is, it uses symbols to speak of language itself (metalanguage).

Every science must have a metalanguage, through which it establishes its definitions, concepts, objects and analysis procedures.

There are formal metalanguages (which use abstract symbols, such as physics [...]) and there are non-formal metalanguages (which use ordinary language, such as history, anthropology, the humanities in general). Linguistics, although it is a human science, has valued formal metalanguage [...] as its own writing, which has given it a prominent position among the humanities.

[...] With the American linguist Noam Chomsky, in the 1950s, Linguistics came to a rigorous formal writing, integrated with the theory of systems, of Mathematics. But this is not a peaceful issue for those who reflect on language. There are those in favor of formalization and those who consider that it leaves out the most defining aspects of language.

(Orlandi, 2002, pp. 16, 18).

At the foundation of the science of Linguistics, Ferdinand de Saussure (1916) abandoned speech and dedicated himself to studying writing. This topic is intended to cover some essential aspects of the study of language to lead the reader to understand what the concept of language we are trying to design for artificial intelligence. We start with the linguistic turn in the nineteenth century, with Saussure, until arriving at the change of perspective given by the theory of discourse, which highlights the effects of context on the language production.

It is important to note that in the history of linguistic thought there are two main trends: One that is concerned with the psychic path of language, relating language, and thought (formalism); another that relates language and society (sociologism) (Orlandi, 2002, p. 18). According to the perspective adopted by this book, the universal structure of language encompasses both a psychic and a social path.

5.5.1 Ferdinand de Saussure and the foundations of linguistic science

According to Araújo (2004, pp. 19–20), language was practically ignored until the 19th century, when it was confused with "ideas in the mind." Philosophical or linguistic studies of language were rare. Among them we can mention the works of Augustine, the Grammar of Port-Royal, Locke and Hobbes. For first century BCE Stoics language involves intellection, a process of signification with three elements: The meaning, the sign and the thing.

The value of the sign depends on whether it relates to a previous fact. For example: 'smoke' must relate to fire. With each occurrence of fire, the occurrence of smoke is inferred, which shows that the signs are formulated in propositions, that is, expressions of language articulated by the fact of expressing significant facts.

(Araújo, 2004, p. 20).

In 1660, with the advent of Port-Royal Grammar, the word became more important, dissociating it from the things it expresses. This reasoning followed Descartes theory, who left language in the background to emphasize the mind and thought. The theory that thought provides the rules of saying has repercussions until today, considering the works of "Chomsky on internalized language, in the manner of a universal grammar" (Araújo, 2004, p. 24).

Next, Locke's empiricism (1632–1704) stands out, in which it is stated that knowledge is born with experience and ideas are the content of the cognitive process: "Locke suggests that knowledge demands, for its development, language, which is learned and exercised" (Araújo, 2004, p. 26). Hobbes, in the 17th century, reinforces the idea that language is a decisive factor in the knowledge process.

Linguistics as an autonomous and independent science has four disciplines that correspond to different levels of language analysis: "Phonology (study of sound units); syntax (study of sentence structure) and morphology (study of the form of words) that together make up the grammar; and semantics (study of meanings)" (Orlandi, 2002, p. 22).

This modern linguistics was built on the "General Linguistics Course," a book published in 1916 from class notes by two Saussure's students, Bally and Sechehaye. Despite all the rigor of the theory taught, Saussure produced a work of deciphering (Anagrams of Saussure) according to the hypothesis that the texts would have a "latent background, a secret, a language under language" (Orlandi, 2002, p. 22). This work was rejected by the critic, being considered decipherer and kabbalist. Saussure was recognized for the linguistic theory he developed in the General Linguistics Course.

The object of study of linguistics is language, which is conceptualized as a "system of signs" in which sign is conceived as an "association between signifier (acoustic image) and meaning (concept)" (Orlandi, 2002, pp. 22–23) (Fig. 11). For this branch of science,

> the acoustic image is not to be confused with sound, as it is, like the concept, psychic and not physical. It is the image we make of the sound in our brain.
> It does not matter that when I say 'river', in the many times I repeat that word, I can modify the way I pronounce it a little [...] The acoustic image is what matters, and it will always be the same. Just as the various forms of the different 'rivers' that exist are not of interest, it is always the same meaning 'river' that comes to mind when I pronounce 'river'.
>
> **(Orlandi, 2002, p. 23).**

acoustic image: **concept:**

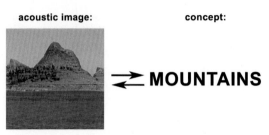

Fig. 11 Acoustic image related to its concept. *(Based on Saussure, F., 1916. In: Bally, C., Sechehaye, A. (Eds.), Cours de linguistique Générale, third ed. Payot, Paris.)*

Linguistics is limited to "langue" and not to "parole" (speech) (Saussure, 1916, p. 92). The reference is not considered part of the language system (conventional language) to preserve the scientific character of the linguistics. Saussure (1916, p. 17) explains that (conventional) language—as "langue"—is "a social product of the language faculty and a set of necessary conventions adopted by the social body to allow the exercise of this faculty in individual." For this reason, all individuals, united by language—langue—will reproduce approximately the same signs united to the same concepts, and the psychic part, called "parole," is left out because it is always act of individual will and intelligence (Saussure, 1916, pp. 21–22).

> *[Conventional language] is a well-defined object in the heterogeneous set of facts of language. It is located at determined portion of the circuit in which an auditory image is associated with a concept. It is the social part of language, external to the individual, who, by himself, can neither create nor modify it; it exists only because of a kind of contract established with the members of the community.*
>
> **(Saussure, 1916, p. 22).**

The linguistic sign unites a concept (meaning) with an acoustic image (signifier) through an arbitrary bond, that is, it is unmotivated and has no link of reality (Saussure, 1916, pp. 81–83). The language system is formed by abstract and conventional units, with no reason why a dog should be called a "dog." Once this name is assigned, it acquires a value in the language, as it is associated, in the human brain, with the idea of a dog so that a dog cannot be confused with a cat (Orlandi, 2002, p. 23).

> *It is through [a] relationship of difference that signs constitute the system of language. One sign is always related to another sign that it is not. That is why it is said that the value of the sign is relative and negative: 'dog' means 'dog' because it does not mean 'cat', it does not mean 'rat' and so on.*
>
> **(Orlandi, 2002, pp. 23–24).**

Although Saussure (1916, p. 85) states that the sign is immutable because it is imposed by the language community, he admits that time produces changes in signs, causing a "displacement between signified and signifier" (op. cit., p. 89).

A language is radically incapable of defending itself from the factors that shift, from minute to minute, the relationship between the meaning and the signifier. It is one of the consequences of the arbitrariness of the sign. [...] time changes everything; There is no reason for the language to escape this universal law.
(Saussure, 1916, pp. 90–91).

By this time Saussure (1916, pp. 94–95) considers that linguistics has duality: There are static linguistics (synchrony) and evolutionary linguistics (diachrony). He claims that this dual characteristic is present in all sciences that operate with values. Regarding to Linguistics, the "time factor" creates special difficulties resulting in the division of this science. For this reason, Saussure excludes diachrony from the domain of linguistics to devote himself to the notion of system, working with the concepts of "language," "value," and "synchrony." The notion of system implies the idea that each element of the language only acquires a value if it is related to the whole (Orlandi, 2002, pp. 24–25).

In this way, the study of the language is linked to the concept of value, that is, a "system of equivalence between things of different orders [...] a signified and a signifier" (Saussure, 1916, p. 95). For this reason, works on language should alert the reader about which axis is operating: (1) the axis of simultaneities (AB) in which time intervention is excluded and the coexistence in the relationship between the elements is studied, being those elements considered one at a time; (2) the succession axis (CD), in which all elements are considered together with the respective transformations (Fig. 12). For him (Saussure, 1916, pp. 95–96), the science of Linguistics

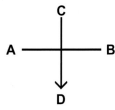

Fig. 12 Inspired by Saussure's (1916) description of AB axis of simultaneity; CD axis of succession.

deals with "a system of pure values that determines nothing outside the momentary state of its terms," and "in Linguistics, natural data has no place."

These axes of simultaneity and succession illustrate a complex system, present in language (Saussure, 1916, p. 96). The multiplicity of signs that explains the continuity of language prevents it from being studied, at the same time, in its temporal relations and system relations. Linguist studies, according to Saussure (1916, pp. 97; 109), must ignore diachrony and work with synchrony characteristic of the language, giving it a sense of order, a principle of regularity: "We cannot describe the language or set norms for its use without putting ourselves in a certain state."

The correspondence between factors and logical categories of language is explained as follows:

> [These notions] do not differ essentially from what we call 'values'. A new comparison with the chess game will make us understand [...] Take a horse; will it be an element of the game by itself? Certainly not, because in its pure materiality, outside its place and other conditions of the game, it does not represent anything to the player and does not become a real and concrete element but coated with its value and embodying it. Suppose that, during the game, that piece will be destroyed or lost: can it be replaced by an equivalent one? Certainly: not only a horse, but a figure devoid of any resemblance to him will be declared identical, as well as the same value is attributed to it. It can be seen, therefore, that in semiologic systems, such as language, in which the elements are mutually balanced according to determined rules, the notion of identity is confused with that of value, and vice versa.
>
> **(Saussure, 1916, p. 128, highlighted by the author).**

> [...] Try to determine the unit, the reality, the concrete entity or the value, and this will always raise the same central question that dominates all static Linguistics [...] It cannot be said that linguists have never placed before this central problem, nor they have understood the importance and the difficulty; in terms of language, they were always content to operate with ill-defined units. However, despite the capital importance of the units, it would be preferable to approach the problem by the aspect of value, which is, as we see, its primary aspect.
>
> **(Saussure, 1916, pp. 128–129).**

This suggestion given by Saussure, that the aspect of value in language should be the object of greater attention, was not followed by the structuralist theory of language, which gave greater importance to the functions performed by linguistic elements, under the phonic, grammatical, or semantic aspects. These distinctions were used to classify grammatical and semantic units and led linguists to encounter problems such as: "what is the trait that would distinguish, for example, at the semantic level, 'love' from 'affection'" [...]? (Orlandi, 2002, p. 26).

Attempts to resolve were toward the use of oppositional and contrasting relationships.

> [...] oppositions and contrasts constitute the two axes, the paradigmatic and the syntagmatic, which are the support of the general organization of the language system. The paradigmatic axis is that which organizes the opposition relations (or/or), in which the units are replaced [cry/fry]; and the syntagmatic axis is the one that represents the contrast relations (e + e) in which the units are combined [f + l + y = fry].
>
> **(Orlandi, 2002, p. 27).**

Although structuralists maintain that language is based on the substitution and combination of forms, this does not solve the semantic analysis of meaning, which, according to Orlandi (2002, p. 27), disturbs this theory.

5.5.2 Recurring effects of structuralism

Saussure's linguistic theory inspired scholars to form groups to discuss certain aspects of language: the Moscow Linguistic Circle (which studied language and the effects of poetic production); the Linguistic Circle in Prague (dealing with phonology and poetics); the Copenhagen Linguistic Circle (which considers Mathematical Logic to develop a universal linguistics). It is in this Prague Circle that an "abstract and logical radicalization of Saussure's thought" takes place (Orlandi, 2002, p. 36), separating the logical plane of communication from the affective and poetic plane. This fact opened the opportunity for the appearance of the Vienna Circle, which worked on debugging language, "to free it from irrationality, to reform it towards a language according to reason" (op. cit., p. 36).

The Vienna Circle removed phenomena such as misunderstanding, ambiguity, and nonsense from the linguistic discussion, separating the meaningful statements from those considered meaningless, building an ideology of communication without defects:

> [...] this ideology of precise communication, of the logical, of the universal, establishes a completely aseptic, formal and transparent conception of language: the metallic language [...] endowing [men] with a rational, refined and without language the 'undesirable' effects of affectivity.
>
> It is in this theoretical environment that the conjuncture is formed in which American linguistics will develop from Noam Chomsky's structuralism to generativism.
>
> **(Orlandi, 2002, pp. 37–38).**

Since linguistics was taken as a science, the foundations laid by Saussure continue to be refined in the incessant search for a flawless and universal language. Two theoretical currents stand out in this attempt. That is what will be covered in the next topic.

5.5.3 Mechanization attempts: The search for a criterion that leads to the universalism of language

Bloomfield founds a new structuralist theory of language called distributionalism. He argues that language analysis should be based on sets of statements—corpus—looking for regularity in them (distribution of units) without relating them to a context, that is, words are analyzed from a set, not to mention their meaning. The units are detected, and equivalence classes are established between them to compare the words of the same classes. This theoretical rigor is intended to make this method automatable, but it has not been successful on the issues of meaning construction (Orlandi, 2002, pp. 33–34).

Also linked to the distribution theory, Noam Chomsky proposes, instead of emphasizing the classification of words, that the theory of logical tradition of language studies be given priority. In this way, he suggests that the language be explained from an autonomous level, that is, "it allows, from a limited number of rules, to generate an infinite number of sequences that are phrases, associating them with a description" (Orlandi, 2002, p. 38).

> The mechanism that this [Chomsky's] generative theory installs is deductive: it starts from what is abstract, that is, from an axiom and a system of rules and reaches the concrete, that is, the phrases existing in the language. This is the conception of grammar: a set of rules that produce the phrases of the language. Basing his study of language on this system of rules, [Chomsky] intends for linguistics to leave its stage of mere observation and classification of data. According to his proposal, the theory of language is no longer just descriptive but explanatory and scientific.
>
> **(Orlandi, 2002, pp. 38–39).**

Chomsky's theory gives Linguistics characteristics of Logic and Mathematics, as it starts from the idealized competence of the human being to produce and understand sentences. This idealization and universalization despise specific performances of the speakers, to define the language as an infinite set of phrases, in which creativity would be governed by rules: "The language is defined not only by the existing phrases, but also by the possible phrases, those that can be created from the rules" (Orlandi, 2002, p. 40). Chomsky's ideal speaker leads to a "supposed" universalism. "Supposed" because it does not cover all human language issues, being restricted to the path of language under the domain of reason.

The formal rigor with which Chomsky defines language has grown over the years, shrinking the object of study of linguistics. He reformulates his theory several times under "methodological fencing" to account for criticisms made by other theorists, who, in turn, try to broaden the field of linguistics (Orlandi, 2002, p. 47).

> *The cuts and exclusions made by Saussure and Chomsky leave aside the real situation of use (speech, in one, and performance, in the other) to stay with what is virtual and abstract (language and competence) [...].*
> *Although this formalist tendency dominates in the twentieth century, there are others that coexist or compete with it.*
> *These other trends develop studies that focus precisely on heterogeneity and diversity, looking for a way to systematize the concrete uses of language by real speakers.*
> *In general, these studies favor the notions of data, context of situation, society, history.*
>
> **(Orlandi, 2002, pp. 48–49).**

Before discussing other trends, in the next two topics on Saussure and Jakobson, we analyze some elements pointed out in structuralism that go beyond the limitations imposed on language and, in our opinion, are characteristics of natural language in its dynamic and logical aspect.

5.5.4 Language is a form, not a substance

Despite the efforts of language scholars, the universality (real one and not ideal as Chomsky proposed) of language was not achieved because they did not consider all its elements in a relationship. The hygiene of language, removing emotion and subjectivity, leads to a theoretical idealization that, when put into practice, proves to be incapable of describing language as a "whole."

The universality of language cannot neglect subjectivity, ambiguity, and lapses. We now resume Saussure's work and his commitment to the construction of meaning. Although his theory referred to an idealized language, he found elements that are structurally repeated in speech as well. According to Saussure the meaning construction occurs in the relationship of one word with others. This relational structure is taken to a broader scope by the theory of discourse (Pêcheux, Foucault, see Section 5.5.6): The enunciation of the subject is related to the context. We understand that this relational structure that Saussure finds in the sentence and that Foucault and Pêcheux find in the discourse account for language in all its aspects. According to this relational structure, language can be understood, at the same time, as a dynamic system (with characteristics of living beings) and as a logical system, revealing itself to be a universal structure, with axiomatic-logical characteristics, which is the most sought after structure of natural language.

"Without the use of signs, we would be unable to distinguish two ideas clearly and steadily" states Saussure (1916, p. 130).

> [The meaning] is the counterpart of the auditory image. Everything happens between the auditory image and the concept, within the limits of the word considered as a closed domain existing by itself.
>
> But here's the paradoxical aspect of the question: On the one hand, the concept appears to us as the counterpart of the auditory image within the sign, and on the other, this same sign, that is, the relationship that unites its two elements, is also, and likewise, the counterpart of the other signs of the language.
>
> Since language is a system in which all terms are solidary and the value of one results only from the simultaneous presence of others, according to the scheme:

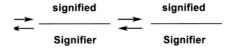

> how does it happen that the value, so defined, gets confused with the meaning [...]? [...] Even outside the language, all values seem to be governed by [a] paradoxical principle [constituted]:
>
> **1.** for a dissimilar thing, susceptible of being exchanged for something whose value remains to be determined;
> **2.** for similar things that can be compared with the one whose value is at stake.
>
> **(Saussure, 1916, pp. 133–134).**

In short, according to these principles, for there to be value: We can exchange one thing for a different one; we can compare it with something else within the same system. Applying this to the language, a word can be exchanged for an idea (dissimilar thing—in this case we get meaning) and can also be exchanged for another word (same nature—in this case we get value, comparing it with the words that can oppose it) (Saussure, 1916, p. 134).

> [...] instead of ideas given beforehand, values emanate from the system. When it is said that the values correspond to concepts, it is understood that they are purely differential, defined not positively by their content, but negatively by their relations with other terms of the system. Its most accurate feature is to be what others are not.
>
> **(Saussure, 1916, p. 136).**

The most important point of this topic is the explanation of "how" the language works when creating meaning. The axiomatic aspect of natural language serves as a support for the logical (incorporeal) aspect to establish itself, constituting meaning and value through a chain of differences and similarities. "The proof of this is that the value of a term can be modified without being touched either in the meaning or in the sound, just because a neighboring term has undergone a change" (Saussure, 1916, p. 139). This axiomatic-logical principle is so essential that it applies to all situations in which there is language and interpretation, since the value of an element (word, sound, image, etc.) only works by reciprocal opposition (how) within a defined system, composed of a certain number of elements. The cognitive system with its neural mechanisms controls cognition, regardless of the system of sign production (Saussure, 1916, p. 139). Meaning is produced automatically, regardless of whether the individual devotes attentional resources. The language has a balance of complex terms that condition each other, which makes it "a form and not a substance" (Saussure, 1916, p. 141).

5.5.5 What is language according to Roman Jakobson

Structural Linguistics dwell on the study from the smallest significant unit—phoneme—to the largest significant unit—the sentence. There is, however, another universe that is that of language as a communication tool, which involves semantic theories. From the works of Benveniste, Katz, Fodor, Roman Jakobson, the language came to be understood in its syntagmatic relationships (horizontal—elements that govern the construction of sentences) and paradigmatic relationships (vertical—elements that occupy the virtual place of each sign vertically). The difficulty of studying semantics is that the meaning can change according to the circumstances, being necessary "to build a theory that could account for the context of this immense universe of the speaker and the innumerable and variable speech situations" (Araújo, 2004, p. 42). We disagree with the author. Our book points to another path: We bet on understanding "how" language builds meaning, rather than building theories that describe the complexity of linguistic functioning; this is the structure (essence) of language that, according to Saussure (1916, p. 141), consists of a "form" and not a "substance."

Chomsky stopped at syntax because he understood that semantics does not belong to the solid branch of science. Katz and Fodor tried to restrict semantics to a dictionary with lexical items, rules that determine how each of these items can be integrated with phrases, information, semantic markers

(Araújo, 2004, p. 43). These limitations leave aside the context, the fundamental relationship that explains the meaning in relation to the reference: The speech situation gives semantic value to the sentence. The codes themselves are insufficient when faced with the power of expressiveness, argumentation, rhetoric, the game of metaphors, connotations, etc.

> [The] structural level, [...] of signs and their combinations, depends on the discourse and not on the grammatical phrase [...] It is necessary to leave the exclusively structural limits of the language [avoiding] the myth of monosemy, that is, that the meaning is ready, crystallized in a kind of dictionary [...] The language is not [...] a code that transmits information. It is in it and through it that a culture lives [...] Language is not a solitary and self-sufficient game.
>
> **(Araújo, 2004, pp. 45–46).**

The germ of Jakobson's linguistic thought is to see in the poem a hierarchy of functions in which sound is linked to meaning (Blikstein, 2010, p. 11). The author (Jakobson, 1990, 2010) realized that the phonic architecture of language has a significant structure, "valid at levels other than the simple phoneme, that is, valid at the level of the word, phrase, paragraph" (Blikstein, 2010, p. 12). Jakobson discovered that the semantic effect stems from the nexus between sound and meaning, stating that there is an overlap of the principle of similarity over the principle of contiguity. When observing people with aphasia, Jakobson noticed that there is aphasia of substitution and aphasia of association, and with that, he was able to describe the formative mechanism of language by deepening the concepts of metaphor and metonymy, expanding the notions of similarity and contiguity. These discoveries led Jakobson to deal with the linguistic phenomenon as something that overlaps the science of different languages, focusing on the structure and function present in the various conventional languages.

The limitation of linguistics in branches serves to focus on limited problems, which are different modes of experimentation but do not mean that they are exclusive points of view. The elements of the language cannot be isolated: "We become increasingly aware of the fact that our supreme goal is the observation of language in all its complexity" (Jakobson, 1990, 2010, p. 19).

Jakobson (1990, 2010, p. 31) disagrees with Saussure's complete separation between synchronic and diachronic linguistics, stating that these concepts are outdated and that "the history of a language can only be the history of a linguistic system that undergoes different mutations." Diachrony and synchrony are therefore coexisting systems.

An important contribution by Jakobson (1990, 2010, p. 35) in the study of language is his statement that "all linguistic significance is differential":

At the semantic level, contextual and situational meanings are found. But only the existence of invariant elements allows to recognize variations. Both at the level of sense and at the level of sound, the problem of invariants is a crucial problem for the analysis of a language given stage.

(Jakobson, 2010, p. 35).

An important aspect of Jakobson's work is his considerations about language in relation to speech disorders. He complains about the omission of language scholars because they neglect these problems, pretending that disorders in the way of communication are not related to language.

Language disorders reveal that language is linked to the individual's body, to the psychological and neurological characteristics of the latter. Jakobson (1990, 2010, p. 51) states that the elements of language are linked to the code by an internal relationship and linked to the message by an external relationship. The author (Jakobson, 1990, 2010, pp. 51–52; 73) noted that speech disorders can affect an individual's ability to combine or select linguistic units. Based on this finding, he theorized that language has a bipolar structure with an axis of selection and a contiguity axis. In the selection axis, "the context is an indispensable and decisive factor" and the aphasic individual changes the word "fork" for "knife," "smoke" for "pipe," "eating" by "toaster" (Jakobson, 1990, 2010, p. 61). On the other hand, the disturbance in the combination axis (contiguity) leads to the deterioration of the individual's ability to "combine simpler linguistic entities into more complex entities," "the syntactic rules, which organize the words in higher units, are lost [...] the links of coordination and grammatical subordination, whether in agreement or in regency, are dissolved" (Jakobson, 1990, 2010, p. 64). Jakobson (1990, 2010, p. 76) adds that the symbolic process of language harbors competition between two procedures: Metonymic and metaphorical.

"A dichotomous principle [...] underlies the entire system of distinctive features of language" (Jakobson, 1990, 2010, pp. 93–94). In the latter there is

a conventional transformation, usually term-to-term and reversible, through which a given set of information units is converted into others: for example, a grammatical unit in a sequence of phonemes and vice versa.

[...] A comprehensive view of the dynamic symmetry of the language, implying the coordinates of space and time, should replace the traditional model of descriptions arbitrarily limited to the 'static' aspect.

(Jakobson, 2010, pp. 97; 100 highlighted by the author).

In short, we can find in Jakobson (1990, 2010, p. 153) that language shares properties not only with the conventional language and its words but also with the world and the extra-linguistic values of the discourse because linguistic phenomena expand in time and space where there is an underlying stream of meaning.

We find in Jakobson a perspective of language that considers, albeit in a precarious way, the body that receives the stimuli of information. While Saussure manages the rigor of the use of signs, Jakobson works with the perception that there is a domain of operations prior to these signs and that it is linked to the moment of enunciation. More abstract structures that regulate phonetics, syntax, and semantics are part of the reality of the language and its functioning and dysfunctions. There are, therefore, internal elements of language functioning and, also, external elements such as the environment closely related to the construction of meaning in a message.

5.5.6 What is language in the discursive theory

5.5.6.1 Introduction

After devoting attention to the formalist tendency in language studies (Section 5.5.3) and delving into some theoretical aspects developed by Saussure and Jakobson (Sections 5.5.4 and 5.5.5), we do a quick tour through the history of the studies of language to justify the emergence of the discursive perspective, which tries to systematize its concrete uses considering the context of situation, society and history. The purpose of this analysis of the historical path is intended to enlighten the reader about the difficulties of circumventing all aspects that involve natural language. Our point of arrival is the certainty that language is plastic, that is, it does not involve imprisonment by rigid rules. Its way of functioning and building meaning is fruitful and has its own movement.

There is no single way of thinking about language. There are several. But a person still will not be free of a dominant discourse that seeks to define 'one' path for Linguistics. This is a stance that hardens perspectives and confuses institutional interests with truth and scientific authority. There are those who allow themselves to be trapped in this posture, as well as those who resist and there are those who propose other speeches. The latter are those who perceive that the object of science is also the object of desire. And around it they weave their reflective adventures, becoming scientists at the same time while instituting different forms of knowledge about language.

(Orlandi, 2002, p. 66, highlighted by the author).

Founded by Saussure as a science of language, linguistics has the specific object of language as a system of classification and explanation (Orlandi, 2002, p. 66). Since then, theories have emerged that repel or accept the existence of a relationship between language and society. Among them, Sociolinguistics, Ethnolinguistics and Sociology of language stand out.

Sociolinguistics observes reflexes of social structures in language and tries to systematize the effects of variation in language caused by speakers in their communities, that is, it explains linguistic variation through social factors. It is based on phonological, syntactic, and morphological analysis recommended by Saussure's structuralism and Chomsky's generativism to correlate them to social factors.

Saussure and Chomsky's structuralism deals with designation (combination of signs and rules in the formation of language sentences), moving away from denotation (phrases that refer to things or state of things). "The question of whether the sign [...] corresponds or not corresponds to reality [...] belongs to the scope of philosophy" for these authors, but for Peirce "signs are not limited to an interrelation regulated by the language system" (Araújo, 2004, p. 57).

Occupying a theoretical position diametrically opposed to Sociolinguistics, there is Ethnolinguistics, which considers language as a cause, and not a reflection, of social structures, giving language the role of organizing the world in which we live. This current follows the Sapir-Whorf hypothesis, that "language interpenetrates experience, in such a way, that the deeper categories of thought are different in different cultures" (Orlandi, 2002, p. 53).

Another theory goes beyond Sociolinguistics and Ethnolinguistics, proposing that there is interpenetration between language and worldview, which gives language a concrete, usable characteristic, giving more importance to the study of meaning: [...] Pragmatic [...] includes, beside the study of the relationship between the signs (syntax) and the study of the relationship between the signs and the world (semantics), the study of the relationships between the sign and its "users" (Orlandi, 2002, p. 55, highlighted by the author). There is another aspect of Pragmatics that studies language more as a means for the individual to engage in an action than as a means of transmitting information: "Even when considering the value of truth, in this theory, this truth will depend on the situation of speak with your rules" (Orlandi, 2002, p.58). Especially related to Pragmatics is the enunciation theory, which focuses on the enunciation process, on the "way in which the subject is marked in what he says" (op. cit. p. 59). This theory marks the beginning of the study of subjectivity in language:

> *Communication appears [...] only as a consequence of a more fundamental prop-*
> *erty of language: That of the constitution of the subject. Property that demon-*
> *strates the speaker's ability, when saying something, to propose himself as a*
> *subject.*
> *From this capacity comes the category of 'person'. In other words: the speaker, in*
> *the exercise of speech, appropriates the forms that the language has and to which*
> *he refers to his person, defining himself (as 'I') and his interlocutor (as 'you'). It is in*
> *this interlocution relationship that the linguistic foundation of subjectivity lies.*
> *In short, language is not only an instrument of thought or an instrument of com-*
> *munication. It plays a decisive role in the constitution of 'identity'.*
> **(Orlandi, 2002, pp. 59–60, highlighted by the author).**

5.5.6.2 *The importance of context for language*

So far, we have seen the formalist-logicist theories of language outlined by scholars such as Saussure, Jakobson, and Chomsky. We also saw some historical theoretical lines about language through Sociolinguistic, Ethno-linguistic, and others.

In this topic, we describe some approaches that show the importance of context in the study of language so that, in the next topic, we can deepen the discussion on the theory of French Discourse Analysis (Pêcheux, 1975), which gives importance to context in the construction of meaning by language, without forgetting that the latter has characteristics of subjectivity.

Plato was the first to worry about the connection of words in a sentence and the corresponding state of things. Formal semantics establishes that "it is precisely the possibility of establishing conditions of truth that gives intelligibility to phrases [...] Once the calculations that establish the truth value are specified, it is possible to formalize natural languages and thus heal all the errors" (Araújo, 2004, p. 59).

Different approaches to the relationship between meaning and reference were made by linguists, with different solutions, which were criticized by many other experts on the subject. What remains essential in these discussions about the problem of reference "is to take into account the effective act of speech," as human beings do not communicate only through propositions governed by formal semantics (Araújo, 2004, p. 62).

Araújo (2004, p. 63) teaches that Frege distinguishes between referring and meaning: "Thoughts differ from representations, since the latter belong to a given person, are attributable to someone in a time and space. Thoughts are not of someone in special, they remain in their identity, even though individuals, times and places vary." We would like to highlight that, just as meaning and representation are for the individual, thoughts, as a process, are for men.

Subjective representations make translations difficult. The thought, the idea, in turn, remains the same and, for this reason, we associate it with a process, a "way of being" in the subject's interpretation of the world: Its content remains the same, even if apprehended by different people at different times (Araújo, 2004, p. 66). "What allows knowledge, progress, science, according to Frege, are phrases with meaning (thought) [...] and with truth value (reference) [...]" (Araújo, 2004, p. 67).

The adoption of the point of view that "facts can only be said if they can be formulated in a logical way, otherwise they would not be thinkable" (Araújo, 2004, p. 81) was overtaken by the adoption of language as "behavior, as a way of life [making no sense] to seek the representation of the combinatorial possibilities of facts" (Araújo, 2004, p. 105). The uselessness of trying to tie up all linguistic uses was realized because, although they have connections in some uses, unforeseen situations arise, new uses due to peculiar uses and to the context.

> *Contextualizing speech, seeing its multiple uses, is discarding the structural hypotheses for which language is a set of rules that make it possible to generate all and only those sentences of the system, of the 'langue', of competence.*
> **(Araújo, 2004, p. 112, highlighted by the author).**

Dewey explains meaning as a quality of language, derived from sounds, movements, and characteristics:

> *Language is a natural function of human association, and its consequences interfere with other events, physical and human, giving them meaning and significance.*
> **(Dewey, 1958, p. 33).**

5.5.6.3 Language under discourse analysis theory

After going through structuralist and logical-semantic approaches, language starts to be discussed from the point of view of the theory of discourse analysis (Pêcheux, 1975, 1988), which takes the communication processes in use, that is, the discourse.

It is worth mentioning the discursive theory (Pêcheux, 1975, 1988) because language is not explained only through brain function. We tend to think that language, context, individual and subjectivity are different things. The discursive theory raises important questions regarding these factors, which are appreciated together with the neuroscience data in this book. For discursive theory, social interaction has a power over the individual to the point of transforming the way the latter interprets the world and makes decisions.

The deepening of discursive theory is not the aim of this book, but we will address some aspects that are of interest in discussing the cognitive process and the structure of natural language.

We start with Miaille (1979, p. 88) and his definition of the word "person," which has its origin in the Greek "mask." The author explains that when people assume their roles in the "social game," they integrate a system of relations determined by "norms that will establish the measure of these social relations."

Courtine and Haroche (1988, pp. 38–39) affirm that the "unity of the person" that corresponds to the mask of a public character overlaps the "interiority of the private person," interfering with the individual's forms of enunciation:

> Man as social subject [...] is, effectively, a double man, at the same time being and appearance, because that is the condition of every being exposed to the human eye [...] He gives himself, or receives from the other, something that is a mask, double, wrapper, detached skin.
>
> **(Courtine and Haroche, 1988, pp. 38–39).**

The authors (op. cit., p. 41) add that the individual's body is immersed in the social context under an "immediate apprehension." Something in the order of politics covers the subjectivity of that individual, regulating his ways of thinking, speaking, and acting (Monte-Serrat, 2014).

In the discourse situation, social and cultural practices make language work as a "vehicle and target for complex relations of knowledge and power in the so-called 'disciplinary society'" (Araújo, 2004, p. 204). Thus the function of value and truth goes beyond the domain of logic, as it concerns complex social relations that imply a notion of power, whether what is said is lawful or appropriate, for example. In "discursive practice [...] institutional, social, epistemic, historical factors must be considered" (Araújo, 2004, p. 205); not only is the transmission of information at stake but also "how" linguistic activities give meaning to the world. The way of referring and transmitting information is not stable in the language. The fact that cognition obeys adaptable, unstable, and context-dependent patterns is of interest to discursive theory. An example of this is the significance of the piano in a concert and as being a heavy piece of furniture to transport (Araújo, 2004, p. 210).

The discourse analysis theory suspects any description of the world that claims to be unique, universal, and timeless, as science does, which aims at an aspect of reality and legitimizes it through a concept, transforming a specific reality into a "thing" described by the history of science. The discourse analysis perspective calls this fact into question, arguing that "there is no stable way of referring"; that "language is plastic and allows adaptation to the context" and that "the lexicon changes according to the communication needs and not according to a brain programming" (Araújo, 2004, p. 210). With these premises, we make it clear that in the theory of French discourse analysis, language is conceived as a "relationship" operation with the environment.

The complexity of the natural language leads it to be treated not only as a code system but also as an activity situated in a context. That is why the theory of discourse analysis is imbued with a force that combats the idea that language is neutral, not ideological, and apolitical.

Michel Foucault is considered one of the main inspirations of the theory of discourse analysis, showing that "language does not serve to 'say' the 'reality' [because] there is simply no meaning on one side (words), which would represent things […] that would be on the other side" (Foucault, 1966 *apud* Araújo, 2004, p. 216). For Foucault (1966), speaking is a practice that creates the dimension of discourse. "Discourses are not set of signs (significant elements that refer to contents or representations), as they do more than designating: They are practices that form the objects they speak about" (Araújo, 2004, p. 223).

Thus the referential in the discursive theory,

is not constituted by 'things', 'facts', 'realities' or 'beings', but by laws of possibility, rules of existence for the objects that are named, designated or described in it, by the relationships that are stated in it or denied. The referential of the statement forms the place, the condition, the emergency field, the instance of differentiation of individuals or objects, of the state of affairs and of the relationships that are put into play by the statement itself; it defines the possibilities of appearance and delimitation of what gives the sentence its meaning, the proposition its value of truth […] The statement makes of a phrase or a series of symbols, a phrase that can or cannot to mark a meaning, a proposition that may or may not receive a truth value.

(Foucault, 1969, pp. 120–121).

The context, as taught by Foucault (1969, p. 129) "is the set of elements of the situation or language that motivate a formulation or determine its meaning." It can be said then that, according to the discursive theory, the sentence alone is not enough to complete the formation of meaning. It is necessary to take into account adjacent elements that update this statement, for example, to which field of experience it belongs: "The statement is not identified with a fragment of matter; but its identity varies with the complex regime of material institutions" (Foucault, 1969, p. 135). Things are "duplicable not only by the copy or translation itself, but also by exegesis, by comment, by the internal proliferation of meaning" (Foucault, 1969, p. 157), they are disconnected from its founding subjectivity because there is a domain of science that establishes, organizes, and distributes procedures regarding what can be said (Foucault, 1971).

Another French philosopher and linguist, Michel Pêcheux (1975) says that discourse analysis cannot ignore subjectivity. He describes this theory as being traversed and articulated by a theory of subjectivity of a psychoanalytic nature (Pêcheux and Fuchs, 1975, pp. 163–164). According to Pêcheux (1975), the individual can identify himself with a discursive formation given by the sociohistorical context in which he is inserted. But there can also be a "disidentification" with this context, leading to a "transformation-displacement of the subject-form" through the "breakdown-rearrangement" of ideological formations and discursive formations (Pêcheux, 1975, p. 217).

Subjectivity in language stems from its own symbolic order (Lacan, 1949). No matter how much the social structure determines a meaning to the subject's speech, at any time that meaning can be turned and modified (Lacan, 1961–1962). The signifier plays and wins, in the game of Witz, in the joke, surprising the subject (Lacan, 1964).

The individual's sociohistorical context conditions him through discursive processes and other significant systems such as rituals, gestures, and behaviors constituting specific practices. The discursive complexes of a social formation are metabolized psychically by the subject, to the point of producing the effects expected by the social structure, which imposes its objective conditions of existence (Sercovich, 1977, p. 53).

Jacques Lacan develops the theory of psychoanalysis based on incursions in the field of language using structures such as speech-language, enunciation, signifier-signified, signification, being influenced by linguists such as Saussure, Jacobson, and Benveniste. Before him, Freud established relationships between psychoanalysis and language through studies on speech pathologies (aphasias), the model of the psychic apparatus as a language apparatus, the theory of the discourse of the unconscious, the universal conception of symbolism (Dunker, 2011).

Psychoanalysis is admitted by Lacan as a science supported by the sciences of language. Lacan (1970) thinks of the unconscious as a way of symbolic figuration, as a condition for linguistics. The author (Lacan, 1952) explains that the discursive structure harbors a kind of ambiguity, a diplopia on the surface of the discourse in which the symbolic function that does not peacefully cover the reality of the world. Lacan finds opacity in discourse through properties of language such as diplopia, ambiguation, inversion of meaning (Dunker, 2011).

5.5.6.4 Conclusion
In this chapter, we could observe a growing expansion of the concept of language. We saw that Saussure defines what the science of linguistics is, putting aside speech, due to the difficulty of circumventing it, and he stopped at the study of conventional language with its rules. Then we have the contribution of Jakobson who, through studies on aphasia, shows the importance of taking biological aspects into account in the study of language, making linguistic science more comprehensive.

We aligned some theories to illustrate the cleanliness they did in the concept of language, discarding speech, lapses, context, and subjectivity. We finally come to the French discursive theory that brings two important contributions: it highlights the importance of subjectivity in the analysis of language and emphasizes the relational aspect of language with the context.

The discursive theory starting with Foucault argues that there is interference from the context on the individual's speech. For Foucault, the context gives a "place" from which the subject is given an identity to speak as a priest, as a doctor, as a lawyer, as a teacher, and others. Lacan and Pêcheux who, each in their linguistic specialty emphasizing the importance of context in the construction of meaning, go further, explaining that, although there is an identification of the subject with the position from which he speaks, there is an unexpected adversity in thought (Pêcheux, 1975, p. 294).

Michel Pêcheux explains that the identity that the sociohistorical context gives the subject to act as a writer, as a doctor, as a priest, as an engineer, and others, is the "subject-form of discourse" constituted by these individuals. In this subject-form, "interpellation, identification and production of meaning coexist," causing "the material conditions of existence of men to determine the forms of their conscience," through "the eternal repetition of descriptive evidence" (Pêcheux, 1975, p. 295). Concomitantly with this identification of a subject constructed by the sociohistorical context, Pêcheux (1975, pp. 298–299) is devoted to the notion of "disidentification," which stands as a paradox to the unifying power of identification. The author (op. cit., p. 300) shows that the formation of meaning imposed by the socio-historical context coexists with the formation of meaning arising from subjectivity, and that both "are inscribed in the simultaneity of a beat, of a 'pulse' by which the unconscious 'non-sense' keeps returning to the subject and to the meaning that is intended to settle in him" (Pêcheux, 1975, p. 300). Thus the construction of meaning cannot be conceived as a static thing, but as something that admits lapse, the flawed act, failures in which one word is taken by another. In this case, the construction of the meaning slides into a different direction from that determined by sociohistorical ideological interpellation, making a new meaning appear, from another order (Pêcheux, 1975, p. 301).

What Pêcheux and Lacan propose is that there is a subjectivity that underlies identity. This subjectivity emerges and gives another direction to the discourse meaning construction. For both authors, the formation of meaning is not unique, as another unexpected meaning may appear, giving rise to the existence of ambiguity, to diplopia of speech.

References

Araújo, I., 2004. Do signo ao discurso. Introdução à filosofia da linguagem. Parábola Editorial, São Paulo.

Beeson, M., 1988. Computerizing mathematics: logic and computation. In: Herken, R. (Ed.), The Universal Turing Machine. Kammerer & Unverzagt, Berlin.

Blikstein, I., 2010. Prefácio. In: Jakobson, R. (Ed.), Linguística e Comunicação. Bliknstein, I. & Paes, J. (Trad.). Ed. Cultrix, São Paulo.

Cassirer, E., 1972. La philosophie des formes symboliques. La pensée mythique. Editions Minuit, Paris.

Chomsky, N., 1957. Syntactic Structures. MIT Press, Cambridge, MA.

Chomsky, N., 2006. Language and Mind. Cambridge University Press, Cambridge.

Courtine, J., Haroche, C., 1988. O homem perscrutado—semiologia e antropologia política da expressão e da fisionomia do século XX. In: Lane, S.(org.), Sujeito e texto. EDU, São Paulo, pp. 37–60.

Dewey, J., 1958. Experience and Nature. Courier Corporation, USA.

Ding, N., Melloni, L., Zhang, H., Tian, X., Poeppel, D., 2016. Cortical tracking of hierarchical linguistic structures in connected speech. In: Nature Neuroscience. vol. 19, pp. 158–164.

Dunker, C., 2011. Estrutura e Constituição da Clínica Psicanalítica: Uma arqueologia das práticas de cura, tratamento e psicoterapia. AnnaBlume, São Paulo.

Foucault, M., 1963. Naissance de la Clinique. Presses Universitaires de France, Paris.

Foucault, M., 1966. Les mots et les choses. Gallimard, Paris.

Foucault, M., 1969. L'archéologie du savoir. Gallimard, Paris.

Foucault, M., 1971. L'ordre du discours. Gallimard, Paris.

Fraccaro, M., 2018. Deep Latent Variable Models for Sequential Data. Technical University of Denmark, Kongens Lyngby.

Gandy, R., 1988. The confluence of ideas in 1936. In: Herken, R. (Ed.), The Universal Turing Machine. Kammerer & Unverzagt, Berlin.

Goodfellow, I., Bengio, Y., Courville, A., 2016. Deep Learning. MIT Press, Cambridge, MA.

Hall, E., 1966. The Hidden Dimension. Ed. Anchor Books.

Harley, T., 2013. The Psychology of Language: From Data to Theory. Psychology Press, New York.

Jakobson, R., 1963. Essais de linguistique générale. Les Éditions de Minuit, Paris.

Jakobson, R., 1965. À la recherche de l'essence du langage. In: Diogène, 51. Gallimard, Paris.

Jakobson, R., 1975. Les règles des dégâts grammaticaux. In Kristeva, J., Milner, J.C. et Ruwet, N., (org.) Langue, discours, société. Paris: Seuil,11–25.

Jakobson, R., 1990. Two aspects of language and two types of aphasic disturbances. In: Language. Harvard University Press, Cambridge, pp. 115–133.

Jakobson, R., 2010. Linguística e Comunicação. Bliknstein, I. e Paes, J. (trad.). São Paulo: Ed. Cultrix.

Lacan, J., 1949. Le stade du mirroir comme formateur de la function du Je telle qu'elle nous est révélée dans l'experiénce psychanalytique. In: Revue Française de Psychanalyse, France, Octobre 1949, pp. 449–455.

Lacan, J., 1952. O Mito Individual do Neurótico. Jorge Zahar, Rio de Janeiro. 2007.

Lacan, J., 1961-1962. The seminar of Jacques Lacan. In: Book IX Identification. Karnac. Übersetzt Von C. Gallaghan. Translated from unedited French typescripts for private use only.

Lacan, J., 1964. O inconsciente freudiano e o nosso. In: Lacan, J. (Ed.), O seminário. Livro 11. Os quatro conceitos fundamentais da psicanálise. Jorge Zahar, Rio de Janeiro. 1998.

Lacan, J., 1970. Radiophonie. Seuil, Paris.

Miaille, M., 1979. Uma Introdução Crítica ao Direito. Prata, A. (trad.). Moraes Editores, Lisboa.

Monte-Serrat, D., 2014. A questão do sujeito: Perspectivas da análise do discurso, do letramento e da psicanálise lacaniana. Ed. Pedro e João, São Carlos.

Monte-Serrat, D., 2019. A fala idealizada pela escrita. In: Lorenzatti, M., Bowman, M. (Eds.), Educación de Jóvenes y Adultos. Ed. UniRio, Córdoba, pp. 35–52.

Orlandi, E., 2002. O que é linguística. Editora Brasiliense, Campinas.

Pêcheux, M., 1975. Les vérités de La Palice. Linguistique, sémantique, philosophie (Théorie). Maspero, Paris.

Pêcheux, M., 1988. Discourse: Structure or Event. Illinois University Press, Champaign, IL.

Pêcheux, M., Fuchs, C., 1975. Mises au point et perspectives à propos de l'analyse automatique du discours. In: Languages. vol. 37. Armand Colin, pp. 7–80.

Pinker, S., 1994. The Language Instinct. Harper-Collins Publishers Inc., New York.

Saussure, F., Bally, C., 1916. In: Sechehaye, A. (Ed.), Cours de linguistique Générale, third ed. Payot, Paris.

Sercovich, A., 1977. El discurso, el psiquismo y el registro imaginário. Nueva Visión, Buenos Aires.

Stiny, G., 1980. Introduction to shape and shape grammars. Environ. Plann. B. Plann. Des. 7 (3), 343–351.

Stiny, G., Gips, J., 1972. Shape grammars and the generative specification of painting and sculpture. In: Information Processing. vol. 71. North Holland Publishing Company, pp. 1460–1465.

Torre, I., Luque, B., Lacasa, L., Kello, C., Hérnandez-Férnandez, A., 2019. On the physical origin of linguistic laws and lognormality in speech. R. Soc. Open Sci. 6, 191023.

Wolfram, S., 2002. Processes of perception and analysis section: human thinking. In: A New Kind of Science. Wolfram Media, Champaign; IL.

CHAPTER SIX

The structure of language and its axiomatic-logical nature

6.1 Introduction

In this chapter, we summarize some of contemporary philosophical concepts on linguistics to highlight the main theories on the structure of language opposing to ours. They are conceived essentially as (Araújo, 2004, p. 20):

(i) a linguistic exchange that is publicly accessible, by reality (objective world);

(ii) the evaluation of the world by the mind through sensations, memory and experience (subjective world); and.

(iii) signification process constituted by the expression, content, and referent in which "the value of the sign depends on whether it is related to a previous fact" (Araújo, 2004, p. 20) (in this last case, language provides a meaning that adds a value uniting the two worlds, objective and subjective, through the symbols).

It is essential that language is something mediating between reality and the mind which acts in the process of signification and depends on a system of linguistic symbols and signs coded through employment rules (Araújo, 2004, pp. 9–10).

The axiomatic-logical description of language that we propose in this book is used to specify the particularities of natural language. For this, in addition to the practice of linguistic theories that idealize and freeze mechanical aspects of language, we seek to investigate what is the characteristic of the dynamic process of the latter, within a context, that interferes with the construction of meaning. We seek to see language as a functioning system, subject to change. If we describe the displaced language of a dynamic system of meaning formation, we are led to resort to linguistic procedures that do not cover all their functioning. As a result, we pursue a new perspective to explain how these two aspects—dynamic and mechanistic—are covered in

The Natural Language for Artificial Intelligence
https://doi.org/10.1016/B978-0-12-824118-9.00002-3

language. The language, as a whole, needs to be studied and viewed under a different way from what we are used to finding in linguistic theories. Along with the rules of language, there is a transversal system, which groups certain operating conditions that are updated within specific practices. This cannot be ignored when trying to reproduce the natural language to the machine learning: There is a subjective essence that is recognized in meaningful socially accepted practices. This heterogeneity of natural language must be replicated in artificial intelligence (AI) so that the latter is less ambiguous.

6.2 The science of linguistics

There are linguists who defend language as an objective process of representing things, dependent on the exclusive and sovereign relation of reason, which excludes the context to culminate in pure Kantian a priori forms (Fig. 13). On the other hand, there are empiricists who claim that there is no sovereign mind or reason, but a subjective linguistic functioning that leads to knowledge of things (Araújo, 2004, pp. 27–28, see Fig. 14). At a certain moment in history, linguistics, to establish itself as a science, started to deal with the conventional "langue" with its rules of syntax, leaving aside the "parole," which was seen as a real obstacle for the linguists due to having its reference outside the language (contextual reference). Saussure (1916) founded linguistics under the assumptions that signs are related to each other and are not related to reality (Fig. 15). This led to a problematic consequence: Structural linguistics is forced to abandon the reference problem to preserve the scientific character of linguistics itself (Araújo, 2004, p. 28).

6.3 The new concept for natural language

The concept of natural language to which we associate the universal structure of language is broader than that of the science of linguistics

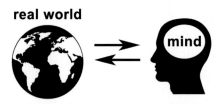

Fig. 13 Some linguistic theories conceive language as an objective process, as a relation of reason.

real world

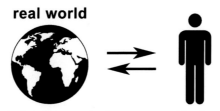

Fig. 14 Other linguistic theories conceive language as subjective process, as an assessment of the world by the mind through sensations, memory, and experience (subjective world).

(Saussure, 1916) because we agree that the language sign system does not automatically assign meaning (although some linguistic theories consider it so) and, therefore language should be considered only within its social context.

Nevertheless, there is consensus that language is a particularly complex process. If we limit ourselves to natural language—that is, the language characterized as a human phenomenon that goes beyond the linguistic-structural one advocated by Saussure—we argue that the complexity stems from the fact that there is a mixture of biological systems (axiomatic principles of natural language) and a symbolic system (logical structure of conventional language with its grammatical rules). We should explain here that "biological" means something that is evolving with the featuring properties of birth and death, as occurs in nature in all biological species. Natural language is considered the whole phenomenon that results from cognitive processes, among which is a conventional language symbolization process that "imprints" a mental representation associated with a value/meaning, as clearly described in Perlovksy and Kozma (2007). The complexity is mainly due to the existence of large number of unknown parameters influencing the whole language process. However, beyond its complexity, natural language presents regularity (syntactic restrictions, semantic and pragmatic objectives, discourse, etc.), and that regularity can be modeled mathematically as it is

conventional language as a set of signs

Fig. 15 Saussure structural model: Signs are related to each other and are not related to reality (deal with "langue" and leave aside "parole"). Saussure describes language as a set of rules that govern writing; while this book considers language as encompassing the complex natural intelligence system that plays an important role in the construction of subjectivity.

done for a dynamic system (Elman, 1995; Kelso and Tognoli, 2007; Thelen, 1988). In fact, according to Elman,

> *The rules are not operations on symbols, but [are] incorporated in the dynamics of the systems, a dynamic that allows the movement from certain regions to others and hinders other transitions.*
>
> **(Elman, 1995, p. 196).**

Following Elman, language operates according to a system of its own (incorporation) and not according to an external operation. Thus we can consider it a biological phenomenon in action and AI would be considered as the movement dependent on a machine learning system. In this sense natural language is not a static structure but a biological structure that is always moving from some regions (input organs of human body) to others, on a path until it reaches a central processor located in the brain. In any case, although it is difficult to understand the idea of the language as a physical dynamical system, we can easily agree with Elman that it is not a static structure. In particular the incorporation of mathematical rules into the dynamics of symbols configures a mental operation that aims to contextualize the math rules, so that they acquire a value of representation, a meaning. It is important to highlight that this is one of the main goals of this book, that is, to provide an overview of how scientific fields uses language as a means of expressing ideas, to facilitate the work of the AI expert in the contextualization of mathematical rules to the dynamics of symbols in each specific discipline.

In our opinion the "contextualization of mathematical rules" means that the natural language should be understood as the union of a repository of facts about individual words, added to the structural rules of language organization.

6.3.1 Parameters influencing the whole language process

The natural language understood as a biological cognition system works as a synchronized process to unite two different fronts: The axiomatic resource of language (i.e., input signals through auditory, tactile, and visual subsystems, which, being biological phenomena, is translated by us as a set of axiomatic principles, that is, unquestionable truths universally valid). On the other hand, the front linked to the logical resource of language (i.e., a set of rules that restrict how the words can be combined to form sentences or, better saying, the grammar rules that influence information production) (Elman, 1995, p.197; Monte-Serrat and Belgacem, 2017).

Natural language also encompasses a nonlogical resource (which will not be discussed further in this paper)—the unconscious—which has a different sequence from the logical one that we are used to in conventional language. Lacanian psychoanalysts have a negative interest in the grammar of conventional language to access the functioning of the structure of the unconscious (Arrivé, 2000, pp. 9–10).

6.3.2 The logical and the biological fronts of language

Conventional language (logical resource of language) learning has a transformative role for the individual.

> *The acquisition of literacy transforms the human brain. By reviewing studies of illiterate subjects, we propose specific hypotheses on how the functions of core brain systems are partially reoriented or 'recycled' when learning to read. Literacy acquisition improves early visual processing and reorganizes the ventral occipitotemporal pathway: Responses to written characters are increased in the left occipito-temporal sulcus, whereas responses to faces shift towards the right hemisphere. Literacy also modifies phonological coding and strengthens the functional and anatomical link between phonemic and graphemic representations. Literacy acquisition therefore provides a remarkable example of how the brain reorganizes to accommodate a novel cultural skill.*
>
> **(Dehaene, et al., 2015, n.p.).**

The logical front of language interferes with natural language, organizing the senses produced by the latter through the subsystems of auditory, visual, olfactory, tactile input and others, giving them a logical sequence "if P then Q." This process takes place within the central system of the cognition located within the brain. We assume that mental representation (or cognitive representation) constitutes a hypothetical internal cognitive symbol that represents external reality (Morgan, 2014). The logical sequence—that the rules of conventional language impose on our impressions of the world—organizes information making it intelligible to us (Perlovksy and Kozma, 2007). Therefore the organization of sensory information comes from an external system, from idealized rules that establish how a sentence should be uttered, or how should we understand a phenomenon for example. These learning rules come from otherness (Lacan, 1949; Wallon, 1995), from living with other human beings who communicate with us. Only later, when we become literate, will we learn the idealized rules (Monte-Serrat, 2019; White, 1991; Wallon, 1995) that command the construction of meaning through our conventional language. Thus the idealized grammatical rules interfere with our perception of reality (which occurs through the cognitive system of biological essence) (Monte-Serrat, 2013, 2017, 2018, 2019; White, 1991). If we write a sentence "I believe in God," that sentence is a written idealization that would correspond to something that maybe I am feeling (written things do not mean that they necessarily correspond to the reality we experience). My real belief in God is a biological experience and my cognitive system identifies it as a real experience I am living at a given moment, making it intelligible/conscious.

Then, we can assume that we have grammatical rules (conceived as conventional language) and, on the other hand, we have the biological phenomenon of cognition that makes the world we experience intelligible/conscious for us. In short, we can say that both language fronts—biological and logical—impose meaning on the experiences we live. The biological front uses sensory systems to send messages to the brain; the logical front constitutes a learning process that imposes a meaning previously determined by the grammatical rules (this meaning will not necessarily be in accordance with the reality we experience, it detaches itself from the context through writing, for example) (Monte-Serrat, 2019). The cognitive system takes care of the two processes of signification, mixing the sense from the sensory systems and the sense from the logical chain of ideas processed by the prefrontal lobe mainly (Perlovksy and Kozma, 2007). The sensations obtained through the input sensory subsystems pass through the brain, where there is a process of transforming the sensations experienced into a mental representation (once represented mentally, the sensation is transformed into an information) (Morgan, 2014). In this way, the brain associates a reality (experienced or idealized) with a meaning that is related to it.

6.4 The universal structure of language

To define the universal structure of natural language as a dynamic system (and not static and predictable as conventional language is), we need to think of language as a system of edges that connect the nodes of a two-front network:

(i) Language is a set of links (edges) between ideas (nodes) in our mind;
(ii) Language is a set of links (borders) existing in human beings (nodes) that interact (through subsystems such as olfactory, tactile, auditory, and visual) with the real world (Perlovksy and Kozma, 2007).

This comprehensive concept is crucial to understanding the structural and dynamic properties of language. This universal (axiomatic-logical) structure thus defined can be used to redesign the mechanisms of language based on the algorithms developed by AI. It allows in detecting previously unknown clusters in real networks, making AI intuitive like natural language: The latter has an axiomatic nature for integrating living organism that reacts to the real world, so it is unpredictable/unknown; and, at the same time, it is predictable in its conventional (logical) feature regulated by grammatical rules.

Natural language is also real, in the sense that it depends on input and output sensory subsystems. The dynamics of natural language constitutes a network that makes connections between the real world (through sensory subsystems) and the mind (cognitive system that integrates these sensations into a mental representation) building the meaning, that is, establishing a correspondence (networking) between what resides in our mind and the real world.

This process starts from the conception of the human being, in the very beginning of his life and it develops until reaching more complex levels (this complexity is not static, it always increases due to brain plasticity) (Carter, 2012). In childhood the human being is already able to connect ideas in the mind with the real world (Carter, 2012).

An important system in this connection is memory (Kozma, 2007) and even dreaming we are already in a network, interacting with the sensations that we collect from the real world and forming meaning through an exchange between heterogenous categories to produce networks under certain preferential attachments toward more optimal effects (Levine, 2007), although the dreams are only for ourselves and we do not need to share them with others. In an awake state, this interaction with the real world takes place through a more complex system for interacting with others and, therefore we need a more complex language that integrates a logical chain (Zhang, 2016; Gandy, 1988; Del-Moral-Hernandez, 2007; Charlton and Andras, 2007). This integration, that we call language's symbolization process, occurs within memory: Memories potentially may increase the adaptedness of a system by increasing its complexity, and therefore the potential closeness of "match" between the system's model of the environment and the (infinitely complex) environment itself (Charlton and Andras, 2007, p. 330).

6.5 Time and language

Along with the reflection on the axiomatic character of natural language (as it is a process of a living organism), we need to make considerations about the conception of time. Dynamic systems have "dependence on time," so we need to say which conception of time is related to natural language and which conception of time is related to conventional language.

Although the concept of time is difficult to grasp, we can describe it as a biological perception, as a fleeting reality, with a "before" and "after" that merges into the human phenomenon (Gonord, 2001). On the other hand, the interference of the grammatical rules with our thinking, ordering it, has the function of selecting, classifying and expressing aspects of the experience to determine which aspects of each experience should be expressed (Boas, 1938; Whorf, 1942); giving a direction to the formation of meaning because in this case there is an overlap of the expression rules on the experience (there is a "how" to express an experience) (Monte-Serrat, 2013, 2017). The interference of grammatical categories has a previous given time (Monte-Serrat, 2017) and leads to semantic information (Jakobson, 1990, 2010).

Both natural and conventional language is time-dependent. In natural language, time is probabilistic, unpredictable, and susceptible to contextual changes. On the other hand, in conventional language, time is deterministic, distinguished between "before and after," "antecedent and consequent," therefore in a deterministic order we have "if P, then Q," where P comes first and Q follows. If we are thinking of a probabilistic order, we mean that P and Q are independent, and if P and Q are independent, and "if P" does not mean automatically "then, Q." In short: In natural language sometime Q follows P; and in conventional language Q always follows P. For instance, we can see unpredictability instead of determinism in the phrase: "Rothschild treated me just like an equal, 'famillionaire'" (Freud, 1963, pp. 18–19, our highlight). It was expected (predicted) to be stated "familiar," but the enunciator of the sentence, who was so excited by the host's wealth, enunciated a mixture of "familiar" and "millionaire" making the unexpected "famillionaire."

In conventional language, time is predictable due to the grammatical logical reasoning (if P, then Q), which presents a hypothesis that anticipates the meaning, that is, the meaning is formed independently of the context, following the rules only.

According to Whorf (1942, n.p. our highlight), "the linguistic order embraces all symbolism, all symbolic processes, all processes of reference and of logic," turning the mind in the "'great slayer' of real [...] words and speech are not the same thing. As we shall see, the patterns of sentence structure that guide words are more important than the words." It is in this sense that Whorf (1942) conceives the conventional language system as an "organization [that imposes] from outside the narrow circle of the personal consciousness, making of that consciousness a mere puppet whose linguistic maneuverings are held in unsensed and unbreakable bonds of pattern," overriding and controlling the lexation and sentences "as equations and functions." In this way, we affirm that conventional language imposes an ideal dynamic in reasoning, with an ideal timing (given by the formula "if P, then Q"), making it out of step with the biological time in which human beings perceive the world with their sensory subsystems (probability dependent). Thus the "conventional" language is classified in two axes (Jakobson, 1990, 2010): Syntagmatic axis "x" and paradigmatic axis "y," carrying an ideal temporalization (hypothetical) of the axis "x."

Thinking of "natural" language as a system dependent on a living organism, with an axiomatic character, it carries the temporalization in the probability vector (z axis) (Monte-Serrat, 2017) (Fig. 16).

Concluding, we assume that natural language is a neurocognitive (axiomatic) process merged with some convention (conventional language) as a system of symbols that depends on the syntax (logic) of grammatical rules determining how the subject should express his ideas. Therefore we call this model the axiomatic-logical structure of the language and this structure is universal with respect to individuals, cultural context, and disciplines. It is with a focus on this universal characteristic of natural language—split into axiomatic and logical aspects—that we will see how the use of language differs in the various branches of science and disciplines.

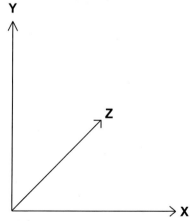

Fig.16 Simulation of natural language with the probability vector "z" between metonymic axis "x" and metaphoric axis "y" (Monte-Serrat, 2017, p. 165).

References

Araújo, I., 2004. Do signo ao discurso. Introdução à filosofia da linguagem. Parábola Editorial, São Paulo.

Arrivé, M., 2000. Lacan Gramático. Ágora III (2), 9–40. jul/dez.

Boas, F., 1938. Language. In: General Anthropology. International Periodical for the Languages, Literature, Boston.

Carter, R., 2012. O livro do cérebro. Jones F. (trad.), Ed. Agir, Rio de Janeiro (1949).

Charlton, B., Andras, P., 2007. Complex biological memory conceptualized as an abstract communication system: human long term memories grow in complexity during sleep and undergo selection while awake. In: Perlovsky, L., Kozma, R. (Eds.), Neurodynamics of Cognition and Consciousness. Springer-Verlag, Berlin, Heidelberg, pp. 325–340.

Dehaene, S., Cohen, L., Morais, J., Kolinsky, R., 2015. Illiterate to literate: behavioral and cerebral changes induced by reading acquisition. Nat. Rev. Neurosci. 16, 234–244.

Del-Moral-Hernandez, E., 2007. Recursive nodes with rich dynamics as modeling tools for cognitive functions. In: Perlovsky, L., Kozma, R. (Eds.), Neurodynamics of Cognition and Consciousness. Springer-Verlag, Berlin, Heidelberg.

Elman, J., 1995. Language as a dynamical system. In: Port, R., van Gelder, T. (Eds.), Mind as Motion: Explorations in the Dynamics Cognition. Massachusetts Institute of Technology, Cambridge, MA.

Freud, S., 1963. Jokes and their Relation to the Unconscious. Norton, New York.

Gandy, R., 1988. The confluence of ideas in 1936. In: Herken, R. (Ed.), The Universal Turing Machine. Kammerer & Unverzagt, Berlin.

Gonord, A., 2001. Le temps. GF Flammarion, France.

Jakobson, R., 1990. Two aspects of language and two types of aphasic disturbances. In: Language. Harvard University Press, Cambridge, pp. 115–133.

Jakobson, R., 2010. Linguística e Comunicação. Bliknstein, I. e Paes, J. (trad.), Ed. Cultrix, São Paulo.

Kelso, J.A., Tognoli, E., 2007. Toward a complementary neuroscience: metastable coordination dynamics of the brain. In: Perlovsky, L., Kozma, R. (Eds.), Neurodynamics of Cognition and Consciousness. Springer-Verlag, Berlin, Heidelberg.

Kozma, R., 2007. Neurodynamics of intentional behavior generation. In: Perlovsky, L., Kozma, R. (Eds.), Neurodynamics of Cognition and Consciousness. Springer-Verlag, Berlin, Heidelberg.

Lacan, J., 1949. Le stade du mirroir comme formateur de la function du Je telle qu'elle nous est révélée dans l'experiénce psychanalytique. In: Revue Française de Psychanalyse, France, Octobre 1949. Taylor & Francis, France, pp. 449–455.

Levine, D.S., 2007. Rule changing and selection via continuous simulated annealing. In: Perlovsky, L., Kozma, R. (Eds.), Neurodynamics of Cognition and Consciousness. Springer-Verlag, Berlin, Heidelberg.

Monte-Serrat, D., 2013. Literacy and Juridical Discourse, USP-RP 2013. Thesis guided by Tfouni, L. Retrieved from http://www.teses.usp.br/teses/disponiveis/59/59137/tde-14032013-104350/. (Accessed 28 July 2020).

Monte-Serrat, D., 2017. Neurolinguistics, language, and time: investigating the verbal art in its amplitude. Int. J. Percept. Public Health 1 (3), 162–171.

Monte-Serrat, D., 2018. Inclusion in linguistic education: neurolinguistics, language, and subject. In: Psycholinguistics and Cognition in Language Processing. IGI-Global.com.

Monte-Serrat, D., 2019. A fala idealizada pela escrita. In: Lorenzatti, M., Bowman, M. (Eds.), Educación de Jóvenes y Adultos. Ed. UniRio, Córdoba, Argentina, pp. 35–52.

Monte-Serrat, D., Belgacem, F., 2017. Subject and time movement in the virtual reality. Int. J. Res. Methodol. Soc. Sci. 3 (3), 19.

Morgan, A., 2014. Representations gone mental. Synthese 191 (2), 213–244.

Perlovksy, L., Kozma, R. (Eds.), 2007. Neurodynamics of Cognition and Consciousness. Springer-Verlag, Berlin Heidelberg.

Saussure, F., 1916. In: Bally, C., Sechehaye, A. (Eds.), Cours de linguistique Générale, third ed. Payot, Paris.

Thelen, E., 1988. Dynamical approaches to the development of behavior. Kelso, JA; Mandell, M.; Shlesinger, M. (orgs.), In: Dynamic Patterns in Complex Systems. World Scientific, Singapore, pp. 348–369.

Wallon, H., 1995. As origens do caráter na criança. Pinto, H. (trad.), Nova Alexandria, São Paulo.

White, H., 1991. O valor da narratividade na representação da realidade. Jobin, J. (trad.), Instituto de Letras da UFF, Niterói.

Whorf, B., 1942. Language, mind and reality. In: Theosophist. JSTOR, Madras, India. January and April.

Zhang, W., 2016. A supplement to self-organization theory of dreaming. Front. Psychol. 7, 332.

CHAPTER SEVEN

Maintaining a "questing eye" at the natural language synchronization function to improve artificial intelligence

7.1 The axiomatic-logical structure of natural language

Before analyzing the functioning of language in the context of various fields of science and disciplines (Chapter 9), it is necessary to deconstruct those fundamental parameters of language that enable us to see it as something that works both with some independence from the individual users and/or independently of specific innate properties that are deeply rooted in the biological nature of man.

Considering language as a comprehensive phenomenon, it is seen as a structured entity that allows us to interpret the reality around or improve our interaction with it. Any interaction that our body has with the exterior context, it receives input information that is transformed into mental representations, which, in their turn, can be understood as evaluations related to things, such as consistency, accuracy, appropriateness, and truth (Collins, 1987; Dennett, 1987; Gibson, 1966). The human cognitive system interprets reality through the symbolization process: There are external input stimuli (reality in which the individual lives) that are correlated, through the neurocognitive system, to mental representations (which can be understood as mental objects with semantic properties) (Collins, 1987; Dennett, 1987; Gibson, 1966).

The concept of natural language with which we work in this book provides inputs from the context and from the set of signs of conventional language. The central cognitive system, at some point, "translates" the stimuli of contextual reality into the signs of conventional language. Mathematically speaking, conventional language (logical aspect of language) establishes relationships to those stimuli (axiomatic aspect of language).

The Natural Language for Artificial Intelligence
https://doi.org/10.1016/B978-0-12-824118-9.00007-2

In every sphere of life, there are unexpected connections between apparently unrelated disciplines with the concepts and methods of using language to describe and interpret the phenomena. Our focus in this chapter is to make an approach of the essence that governs the functioning of natural language which is a human phenomenon to understand: (1) how the meaning is constructed; (2) and what are the particularities of the scientific functioning of language that could bring benefits for the improvement of filters for deep learning or of an appropriate learning design for machine learning. Our suggestions are based on the polysemic characteristic of human language that is still a problem for machine language while the meaning is mathematically constructed. Our comments on the meaning construction aim to show ways for artificial intelligence (AI) to reach the ability to circumvent the ambiguity found in human language, so that the machine learning processes are brought closer to the intuitive processes of human cognition.

AI is represented by different algorithms attempting to reproduce human behavior. If we understand that human language is comprehensive that it is dynamic because it is produced by living beings and follows a logical chain (axiomatic-logical structure of the language we have developed so far), the way to relate the outside world to computer codes and algorithms will be more intuitive and, as a consequence, will be less ambiguous. Thus AI can take advantage of the axiomatic-logical structure of the language, bringing specific characteristics of the natural language to its own algorithms, which are computer codes. In this way, language cannot be understood in a hermetically closed way; we could say that the logic of the computer would be similar to the logic of the functioning of the natural language when the axiomatic-logical structure of the latter is replicated to the machine becoming the most natural component of both languages, natural and artificial.

A feature of language as the central axiomatic-logical mechanism that cannot be left out is the role of synchronization of the interpretive process into a contextualized meaning. A "questing eye" must be maintained in its role of connecting several interdependent subsystems, making comparisons between objects, to allow deciding whether two objects are the same or not. We define synchronization as a process of selecting the equivalent objects from a set of different objects by a functional or relational comparison (see Section 7.3.1). Interpretation is the brain activity which assigns to a mental object a finite set of other objects, so that the first one is synchronized by a finite set of equivalent ones. The most important is that the synchronization is a map between elements which also considers the time dependence, in the sense that two things that are equivalent today could not be the same in another time. Therefore the synchronization is a time-dependent comparison between objects and the resulting interpretation is time dependent too. We assume that the work of interpretation is carried out by language and goes far beyond the elementary processes of reading, speaking, and writing. We need language to calculate a movement, to interpret something we are seeing, or to decide our behavior in front of an unexpected event.

7.2 The mechanistic theory of language revealing the intelligent sequence of sensing and moving to a mental representation: The intelligence is putting the sequence

Let us now shortly remind about the fundamental concepts of mechanical philosophy. According to the Newton principles of mechanics, there is a dualism in the interpretation of the physical reality where movement (that is the observation of a phenomenon-reality) is due to some external sources (abstract causality). In other words, we can compare (synchronize) the reality (world and effect) to some sets of objects (forces, cause, and causalities). The interpretation of this comparison (synchronization) is defined as mechanical motion (movement). According to Aristotle, this comparison is somehow different but is still a comparison between causality (forces, abstraction, and mind) and effect (world and reality). The interpretation (signification) is described in philosophy as mechanical theory.

In this sense, language might be defined as a mechanical process that unites varied and simultaneous functions of the brain, giving a comprehensive view to compose a phenomenon that is perceived as an abstraction, as a representation in individual consciousness. The language, as a mechanical (signification) process, which is linking cause (mind and abstract) and effect (world and reality) plays a major role in human intelligence if accepted as a unit self-consistent body of life interaction. The movement of the brain is the signification (comparison and synchronization) process that unites the formation of patterns in which the sum of the latter does not correspond to the final product (Perlovsky and Kozma, 2007; Kelso and Tognoli, 2007).

We propose a founding axiomatic concept of natural language (as a live system) that is challenging due to the difficulty of understanding its multiple attributes, acting in a dualism in interpretation: The linguistic system makes the physical reality (which involves the movement of a natural phenomenon triggered by external sources/causality) synchronize with a mental phenomenon that results in a meaning (interpretation/correlation/abstraction). This complexity occurs because natural language encompasses several attributes that work in harmony so that the individual can learn to perform a complex range of tasks in an optimized way.

7.3 "Pure observation" of natural language's principle of periodicity

This topic is dedicated to questioning not a theory, but the pure observation of the essential aspect of language: Synchronization. The principle of periodicity underlies language and is present in other phenomena of nature; it is a way to explain language in a large context. Vibration and pulsation are present in the physiological processes exhibiting periodicity, which creates the flowing form of language. Synchronization reveals the hidden nature of language, unveiling the very principle through which stimuli coalesce in meaning.

Although there is a lot of written material about linguistics, we need to strive to penetrate more deeply the superficial level of what language appears, in order not to evaluate as being cause what is just an effect of underlying linguistic processes. We believe that this book, with a meticulous presentation and acute observation of natural language, is the most appropriate way to articulate a new conceptual basis on language that may well be fundamental in other scientific fields, including AI and cognitive computing.

Understanding language extrapolates the implications of the theories we already know. Attention to synchronization leads us to confront two spectra: That of a standardized formation on the one hand, and dynamic processes on the other. Both are supported by essential periodicity. Linguistic theory despises speech. We understand that it must integrate the concept of language as a pole of its dynamic kinetic process—vibration should be understood as periodicity—capable of provoking the creation of a standardized mental representation (for this, probably neurons should have a periodic activity at low frequencies and some isolated spikes at high frequency). The holistic view of language seeks to observe how axiomatic and logical fronts behave in the formation of meaning: Axiom (dynamics of stimuli) and logic (logical chain) are implicated in the whole (construction of meaning). The periodic field must be considered fundamental for both aspects (axiomatic-logical) of natural language. If we abstract and separate them, the whole ceases to exist.

The conception of language must be concentrated in unity so as not to be distracted by the behavior of the parties: Its two characteristics, axiomatic and logical, appear as one thing; they are inconceivable without one another. If axiomatic feature is abstracted, the whole of natural language ceases to exist and gives way to the conventional language, which is nothing more than a set of rules, an idealization of what language "should" be, which leads to the replication of a "frozen" or decontextualized meaning. On the other hand, if the logical feature is set aside, biological stimuli do not take on a logical meaning; in this case we would have "shapes" of meaning, but we would not be able to explain them logically. Perhaps, these "shapes" of meaning can be associated with what Lacan calls the unconscious organized "as" language. Lacan (1970) associates the unconscious with a different structure from logical reasoning; the negative interest in the latter gives access to the functioning of the former's structure (Arrivé, 2000, pp. 9–10). We can infer from these ideas that the relationship between both aspects of language would be as following: The axiomatic aspect would be associated with stimuli from oscillators giving rise to structural "forms" of the unconscious, which disagree with the "forms" of language in the logical sense. At some point, axiomatic "forms" align with logical "forms," acquiring meaning, reaching human consciousness.

In short, the idea of natural language must be thought of as the way in which our physical body processes and, at the same time, interprets stimuli. Stimuli can assume axiomatic "forms," which underlie the "forms" of logical reasoning. Two results of language functioning can be achieved: (1) the axiom animating the logical aspect, which results in the construction of meaning according to the context (in this case the axiomatic "form" would immediately alter the interpretation of the phenomena being observed— there is transformation of an element); (2) the axiom detaches itself from the logical aspect, resulting in the last one building a sense separate from contextual reality, giving rise to the idealized, abstract sense (there is fixation of an element).

7.3.1 Organization and periodicity

Nature, animated or inanimate, brings evidence of periodic systems, which show repeated and continuous changes from one set of conditions to another (Jenny, 2001, p. 17). This occurs both in systematized and standardized elements and in processes and series of events (op. cit.). Systems of circulation and respiration, or even nervous system are physiological examples controlled by natural periods or rhythms, whose impulses occur in series and can be described as frequencies. In the systematized structures we find repetitive patterns: "Indeed, there is something of a periodic nature in the very concept of a tissue" (Jenny, 2001, p. 17).

The principle of organization is repeated in the segments affecting an entire system. The tissues are not homogeneous masses and continue to develop in a regular sequence of alternating polar phases. This periodicity is also found in the oscillatory phenomena of language (Jenny, 2001, p. 18). Periodicity is revealed as a systematic and universal character in a wide range of phenomena.

Jenny (2001, p. 19) explained that the particles that make up nature exhibit a behavior similar to a wave will show what may be the process of forming mental representation, when our brain accommodates serial structures (which could come from logical reasoning) to real acoustic waves within the periodic dynamics of language. In this case, the language would be accommodating elements of a polyperiodic character, making rhythms of the conventional language and vibrations coming from the sensory systems interpenetrate. We can consider that periodicity is constitutive of the nature of language; without periodicity, language would not exist.

> Solar physics is another field in which oscillatory and wave processes are prominent. Our mental picture of the sun can accommodate serial structures, actual acoustic waves, plasma oscillations, turbulences, tendencies to recurrence of many kinds, periodic dynamics, etc. Moreover, many of the systems we have mentioned are polyperiodic in character. The rhythms and vibrations interpenetrate. But in every case periodicity is constitutive of their nature; without periodicity they would not exist at all.
>
> [...] it might be said without hesitation that the systems available to our experience are essentially periodic and that phenomena appear to be periodic throughout. However different the objects concerned, however different their causes and functional mechanisms, they have in common rhythmicity, oscillation and seriality.
>
> **(Jenny, 2001, p. 19).**

The fact that we consider language as a process that includes rhythms and wave processes, does not yet lead to a conclusion about the role of vibrations. What would be the function of neural impulses or mechanical or chemical factors that interfere with the language process? What would be the most essential nature of the sign (conceived as the encounter of the signifier with the signified through mental processes)? Is it the result of a concentration of vastly complex processes of mechanical oscillations in the auditory and optical systems included in a periodicity that corresponds to the pulse frequencies of the brain regions responsible for the language functioning?

The axiomatic-logical concept of language must be observed in such a way that we do not deconstruct it in a periodic and rhythmic process or detached from the complexities of the context. But it must be studied in its own environment with its specific empirical effects. This prevents us from idealizing language to see it as an effect of vibrations (which can occur in a real vibrating field or without it).

Jenny (2001) theorized about cymatics, conceived as the study of the vibratory movement that makes the powder of some substances (thrown on glass, copper, wood, steel, cardboard, and earthenware plate) move, as soon as the plate is stimulated by the vibrations of the sound, from the antinodes to the nodal lines, forming figures that, in turn, allowed to establish the experimental principles of acoustics. This rotational effect forming centers appears systematically throughout the vibratory field.

> Indeed, these currents, centers of rotation, revolving heaps with influent streams and connecting flows must actually be expected, and the material occupying the field will indicate the vibrational pattern prevailing there. There can be no doubt about the occurrence of these formations. It is obvious that all these processes (interference, flows, rotation) could be more appropriately documented by cinematography; photographs can only stimulate the mind into grasping these processes imaginatively.
>
> **(Jenny, 2001, p. 26).**

In the case of experiments with liquid, Jenny (2001, pp. 27–28) observed that while the tone impulse persisted, the liquid and viscous masses remained in a position under antigravity effect. If the vibration stopped, the masses slipped under the force of gravity.

Jenny (2001, p. 29) draws attention to the difference between before and after the movement. For him "the actuating is, as it were, opposed to the actuated, the creating to the created" and asks what happens before separation of fibers (op. cit.).

> This draws attention to the fact that the patterns taking shape must be understood in terms of their environment, that patterns in general are, as it were, an expression of the movement and energizing process. One might speak of a creans/creatum relationship. Thus, there are many conditions under which the mind might be said to be directed to the environment, to the circumambient space, to the field from which space lattices, networks, etc. take their rise in the first place. In other words: Observation of organized patterns and the milieu creating them raises questions as

to the processes incidental and precedent to the formation of such patterns [...]
What happens before fibers, fibrils and crystals are separated out?
(Jenny, 2001, pp. 29–30).

This questioning is appropriate to the use of natural language. What happens when it is separated from its context? The periodicity experienced in the axiomatic aspect must present a corresponding periodicity in the logical aspect, to align with it. It is understood that grammar rules, with punctuation, for example, are an attempt to reproduce the phenomenon of a periodicity linked to the axiomatic aspect of language, in which the oscillation works in a dynamic context. The punctuation determined by the grammar rules are intended to simulate a context.

From the large number of periodic phenomena one can observe those in which no real vibration is involved. Some examples of these phenomena involve processes in the field of chemical reactions (Jenny, 2001, p. 85). The result is not a uniform diffusion, but periodic or rhythmic, in the case of chemical reactions, alternating precipitation zones with free precipitation zones. Thus the characteristics of the two standards can be seen side by side and compared.

In terms of human language, our eardrum is a membrane that vibrates with pressure waves (sound), these pressure waves are encoded by the mechanisms of the inner ear and processed by the brain. Here comes the whole question of the neural network that discriminates a signal (a valid, logical sound that we can call language, music, etc.) of a noise. The structure of the ear is the same for all individuals, but the processing can be totally different. What is noise to one can be a signal to another. There are certain aspects of processing that are universal, harmonic frequencies for example. We are different but not so much, although we have different software, the hardware is the same. We are equal and unique at the same time. We could think that language accommodates the rhythm with the vibration of stimuli coming from sound waves. The effects of vibration are different. It is necessary to keep in mind the pulsating or oscillating rhythm that will form an organized pattern. The speech sound would be dispersed according to a concentration gradient, under a process that would involve periodic dynamics occurring in a pulse pattern inspired by the grammatical rules of conventional language (that simulate a context); or it would follow a vibrational pattern according to oscillations inspired by biological phenomena of the human body. So, the language flows, but it is actually flowing according to patterns and rhythms. According to Jenny (2001, p. 103), pulsations come from vibration, which produces a multiplicity of effects. Periodicity "is inherent in them, it lies in their nature to be rhythmic, whether in form, in configuration, in movement or as a play of forces" (op. cit.).

> [...] the waves are a kind of middle category; they are the periodic element par excellence. But here again it must be noted that it is the essential character of the waves, their characteristic periodicity, that is the basic causative factor throughout.
>
> **(Jenny, 2001, p. 111).**

Jenny (2001, p. 63) observed the action of the human voice in various materials in various media. For this, he developed a device called tonoscope, through which an experimenter can speak without any intermediate electroacoustic unit.

> Thus, vibrations are imparted to a diaphragm on which sand, powder, or a liquid are placed as indicators. Speaking, actually, produces on this diaphragm figures which correspond, as it were, to the sound spectrum of a vowel. [...] The pattern is characteristic not only of the sound but also the pitch of the speech or song. The indicator material and the nature of the diaphragm are, of course, also determinative factors. However, given the same conditions for the experiment, the figure is a specific one.
>
> **(Jenny, 2001, p. 63).**

In an experiment on the dynamic-kinetic phenomenon in lycopodium powder under the influence of vibration, Jenny (2001, pp. 74/78) observed that there is no chaos, but an order in the dynamic pattern: "The streams of powder move in a significant manner [...] the powder must be imagined to be streaming along at a great rale in the visible forms, but exactly in the pattern and direction imposed by the vibration."

Some of the observed effects are:

> These vibratory effects are:
> The creation of forms, formations.
> The creation of figures
> Patterned areas
> Circulation
> Constancy of the material in a system
> Pulsation
> Rotation
> Interference
> Seesaw effect
> Correlation
> Integration effect
> Individuation
> Conjoining and disjoining of a single mass

Dynamics of eruption
Dynamics of current flow, etc.
This list shows that vibration produces a great diversity of effects. Vibration is polyergic and many of its effects are specific. It is not our intention to order or ana-lyze these categories but rather — in accordance with the empirical method adopted — to leave the whole complex of phenomena as it is, with this category, now that category dominating. But it is through this generative and sustaining vibrational field that the entire complex comes into being, and this complex whole is omnipresent. There is no parcelation, no patchwork: On the contrary what appears to be a detail is utterly integrated with the generative action and merely acquires the semblance of an individual, of an individualized quasi-existence, the semblance of individuality.

(Jenny, 2001, p. 74).

Language is not static as linguistic science wants. It goes through a transition until it reaches the norms of conventional language, but we cannot ignore the state of natural language that was taken as a starting point.

It is evident that there is a polarity between natural language and conventional language: In poetry, for example, although we work with metric-dependent rigid writing, there is, on the other hand, an ever-changing, fluid language. These two aspects of language present, on the one hand, the organized forms and patterns and, on the other, the movement and the dynamics. The "whole" of language in poetry is supported by this oscillation: The manifestation of an intellect that is understood as a moving entity.

Jenny's (2001) discovery of cymatics involves a spectrum of phenomena, which

can be approximately described in the following terms: Figures, organized patterns, texture, wave processes in the narrow sense, turbulences, kinetics, dynamics. These terms are not conceptual pigeon-holes: They do not package reality. They are derived from empirical perception.

(Jenny, 2001, p. 111).

In a moving world "shapes and patterns appear simultaneously, whatever the kinetics and dynamics, the cymatic spectrum is omnipresent and manifests itself consistently everywhere as the basic triadic phenomenon" (Jenny, 2001, p. 114).

Concluding this topic on the phenomenon of periodicity in language, we saw that meaning results from processes that are constantly changing, interconnected and interpenetrated. A concept of language as a fixed process (conventional language) is inevitably linked to dynamic processes of natural language, which work toward unity. In the next topic, research is reported in neuroscience in which some structural elements of the language process can be observed, showing it as a dynamic system capable of harboring axiomatic and logical features.

References

Arrivé, M., 2000. Lacan Gramático. Ágora III (2), 9–40. jul/dez.

Collins, A., 1987. The Nature of Mental Things. Notre Dame University Press, Notre Dame, IN.

Dennett, D., 1987. The Intentional Stance. The MIT Press, Cambridge, MA.

Gibson, J., 1966. The Senses Considered as Perceptual Systems. Houghton Mifflin, Boston, MA.

Jenny, H., 2001. 1967; 1974, Cymatics: A Study of Wave Phenomena and Vibration. Compilation of vol. 1, 1967, The Structure and Dynamics of Waves and Vibrations; and vol. 2, 1974, Wave Phenomena, Vibrational Effects and Harmonic Oscillations With Their Structure, Kinetics and Dynamics. Volk, J. (org.). Newmarket, New Hampshire. Revised Edition.

Kelso, J.A., Tognoli, E., 2007. Toward a complementary neuroscience: metastable coordination dynamics of the brain. In: Perlovsky, L., Kozma, R. (Eds.), Neurodynamics of Cognition and Consciousness. Springer-Verlag, Berlin, Heidelberg.

Lacan, J., 1970. Radiophonie. Seuil, Paris.

Perlovsky, L., Kozma, R. (Eds.), 2007. Neurodynamics of Cognition and Consciousness. Springer-Verlag, Berlin, Heidelberg.

CHAPTER EIGHT

Natural language and its universal structure

8.1 Introduction

The linguistic process of the living organism—which coordinates and synchronizes the information until it results in the operation of mental representation perceived as an abstraction—has a behavior that "does the most with the least," that is, it "expands the dimension of the processors with the least expense possible energy, achieving preservation excellence" (Gangopadhyay et al., 2020). The activation of neurons in the natural intelligence depends on a process that connects certain conditions—among them we highlight the eight topics described in this chapter—which trigger the transmission of information, creating a communication channel that configures natural language as a living and dynamic phenomenon, linking cause and effect in a self-consistent interaction.

Gangopadhyay and Chakrabartty (2018) propose a growth transforming neuron (GT) model that reconciles dynamic and peak neuronal responses as derived directly from a network objective or functional energy. In this case, the authors (op. cit.) propose a structure in which the coupled neurons display memory, even though they are under different initial conditions. Gangopadhyay and Chakrabartty (2018) remake a peak neural network to propose the visualization of neuronal activity in relation to a network hyperplane (and not to individual neurons). This geometric interpretation given by the authors is close to the reality of the human cognitive system which, in its dynamic neural network, responds to different stimuli.

These studies (Gangopadhyay and Chakrabartty, 2018; Gangopadhyay et al., 2020) were cited to argue that the cognitive system and language should be explored in their complexity, considering their varied elements.

How a combination suits the situational context to provide an answer (output) is still a mystery of human intelligence. We place some bets with eight attributes that we believe are fundamental for the functioning of

The Natural Language for Artificial Intelligence
https://doi.org/10.1016/B978-0-12-824118-9.00013-8

natural language. They express how the brain deals with the collection and interpretation of information from the world during a temporal duration (as a dynamic, nonstatic system) in a path (ranging from the stimulus in the nervous system until it becomes information), to obtain an optimized result, which does not correspond to the total number of elements involved. Therefore we define natural language as one that meets the following resources:

(1) It is a central axiomatic-logical mechanism;

(2) it synchronizes the functioning of the brain;

(3) in all closed human neural architecture linked to blood flow;

(4) it runs through several interdependent connection systems;

(5) it performs interpretation/mediation between real, symbolic, and imaginary kingdoms;

(6) it has the ability of overlapping the functioning of reading, speaking, and writing;

(7) it is working as a central mechanical process that interconnects/calculates movements, images, behavior, decisions, uniting these varied and simultaneous functions; and

(8) to, finally, compose a phenomenon that is perceived by the human being as an abstraction or a representation.

Each point is explained in the following sections.

8.2 Language is a central axiomatic-logical mechanism

The axiomatic-logical characteristic of language has to do with its two faces: The building process of the meaning by the cognitive system as a comprehensive process; and, on the other hand, the information previously given by the structure of the language as a convention. Both elements become a mechanism that gives a specialized organization to the sparse brain connections engendering an increasing order of instances within a dynamical system so to be integrated in a meaning to configure a persuasion, an information, an understanding, and so on.

The universal principles (axioms) of the natural language operate as the basis for the logical deductions that follow. According to Pinker (1994), the meaning construction depends on the constraints imposed by the inputs of the logical mechanism given by the language as a convention: "Naming an object involves recognizing it, looking up its entry in the mental dictionary, accessing its pronunciation, articulating it, and perhaps also monitoring the output for errors by listening to it" (Pinker, 1994, pp. 323–324). He states that words are tied together in order (Pinker, 1994, p. 312). This logical sequence in the construction of meaning is coordinated by Broca's area, "involved in the anticipations and predictions that define the syntactic structures of [...] linguistic expression" (Turner and Ioannides, 2009, p. 161). We believe that this logical sequence centralizes, synchronizes the cognitive system through the rules of language as a convention, during its input signals, providing values previously given to the auditory and visual systems of individuals, which will join with other subsystems to integrate sensations.

The axiomatic-logical basis of natural language can be mathematically represented with low values of similarity for less conscious states; and for more conscious states, such as perceptions, cognitions, and concrete decisions, the description can be made by concrete models of high values of similarity (which are better adapted to the input signals) (Perlovksy and Kozma, 2007, p. 2). The neurodynamic process changes from a chaotic and vague dynamic (unconscious state) to a logical dynamic (mechanism) that evolves using a cycle of action and perception motivated by the model of increasing clarity (similarity value presented) as the cognitive cycle progresses (op. cit.). According to Perlovksy and Kozma (2007, p. 83), "dynamic logic is a convergent process. It converts to the maximum of similarity and, therefore, satisfies the instinct of knowledge."

> If likelihood is used as similarity, parameter values are estimated efficiently (that is, in most cases, parameters cannot be better learned using any other procedure) [...] it is proven that the similarity measure increases at each iteration. The psychological interpretation is that the knowledge instinct is satisfied at each step: a NMF [Neural Modeling Fields] system with dynamic logic enjoys learning. [...] the fundamental property of dynamic logic is evolution from vague, uncertain, fuzzy, unconscious states to more crisp, certain, conscious states.
>
> **(Perlovksy and Kozma, 2007, p. 84).**

We understand the "knowledge instinct" as a principle of dialectics, in which there is a search for "the most economical and reasonable reconciliation of information and apparently contradictory attitudes" (Manzo, 1992, n.p.). Gangopadhyay et al. (2020), in their turn—who work with individual models of neurons connected through synapses, from the bottom up, to form large-scale neural networks—would explain that the aforementioned information reconciliation would occur through physical processes of nature, with a tendency to self-optimize for a state of minimal energy.

8.3 Language synchronizes the functioning of the brain

Synchronization means that we can compare different phenomena to decide who comes first and put an order between them so that one of them might be considered the first. The understanding of a sentence does not depend only on the arrange given by the grammar (in this case, the sentence would be virtually opaque), but it also depends on semantic information, which is recovered from a complex chain of inference (Pinker, 1994, pp. 224–226).

Memory, in this case, would function as a cross-reference, increasing the efficiency of meaning formation. Understanding, therefore, requires the integration of fragments collected from a sentence, for example. A list of facts in a trivia column needs to be organized, synchronized, in a complex network to become understanding. When a series of facts occurs successively, as in a dialogue or in a text, the language must be structured so that the listener can place each fact in an existing structure (Pinker, 1994, p. 227).

In terms of cognition, synchronization is made possible by the fact that the response of each neuron is connected to the rest of the network (Gangopadhyay et al. 2020) under a kernelized coupling. In this way, natural intelligence works with the definition of a nonlinear limit for each neuron, which offers a dynamic and specific hyperplane stimulus to give occasion to intuitive interpretations about various dynamics (Gangopadhyay et al. 2020). This is a general approach given by Gangopadhyay et al. (2020) to design machine learning (ML) algorithms that simulate biological neural dynamics. The energetic function proposed by the authors (Gangopadhyay et al., 2020) covers all neurons in the network, establishing synchrony and allowing easier and more effective training of neurons hidden in deep networks.

According to Kozma (2007, p. 130), neural assemblies in the brain have dynamics of cognition based on the form of sequences of oscillatory patterns that are seen as intermittent representations of generalized symbol systems computed by the brain. The cognitive system synchronizes perceptual experiences into meaningful and understandable pieces of concepts that will be accessed during the selection of future actions and decisions (Kozma, 2007, p. 131).

8.4 Language is in all closed human neural architecture linked to blood flow

The cortex was found to be responsible for higher cognition and that its different parts are associated with different functions, paving the way for mapping the human brain (Huettel et al., 1973). The development of functional magnetic resonance imaging (fMRI)—a noninvasive technique that measures changes in blood oxygenation over time—has become the dominant technique in cognitive neuroscience to measure the change in blood oxygenation levels after the activity of neurons in a certain region of the brain (Huettel et al., 1973).

> *The fundamental element of information processing in the human brain is the neuron. Neurons have two primary roles, integration and signaling, which rely on changes in cell membrane potential and the release of neurotransmitters. While the integrative and signaling activities themselves do not require external sources of energy, the restoration of ionic concentration gradients following these activities does require an energy supply. The primary metabolites supplied to active neurons are glucose and oxygen, which together are important for the synthesis of ATP. These metabolites are supplied via the vascular system. The main components of the vascular system are arteries, capillaries, and veins, each present at different spatial scales. Changes within the vascular system in response to neuronal activity may occur in brain areas far from the neuronal activity, initiated in part by flowcontrolling substances released by neurons into the extracellular space, or by direct influences from neurons or nearby glial cells. Neurons may directly alter flow in pial arteries, arterioles, and capillaries, but it is unknown whether such effects have consequences for fMRI measurements. A major consequence of the vascular response to neuronal activity is the arterial supply of oxygenated hemoglobin, from which oxygen is extracted in the capillaries. These changes in the local concentration of deoxygenated hemoglobin provide the basis for fMRI.*
>
> **(Huettel et al., 1973, p. 190).**

Cerebral blood flow is related to the levels of neuronal activity (Huettel et al., 1973). The latter is therefore investigated indirectly through vasodilation, a relevant process for interpreting fMRI signals or for detecting motor and cognitive decline. Progress in imaging technologies makes it possible to relate blood flow and oxygenation to the functioning of language, allowing to detect which brain regions that are linked to language.

The neuronal context then follows oxygenation patterns. The lack of oxygen in specific areas affects some human abilities. fMRI allows to observe the integration between the circulatory and respiratory systems: where there is more neuronal activity there will also be greater blood flow: "A typical neuroimaging study relates changes related to stimuli and tasks to changes in neural activity of a patient try to discern which regions of the brain underlie a specific type of processing and how those regions do their work" (Gernsbacher and Kaschak, 2014).

Understanding neurovascular function (or its dysfunction in the disease) alone is not sufficient to accurately explain dynamic and spatially distributed processes of vasodilation.

This topic does not deeply develop the relationship between blood flow and language, but only draws the reader's attention to the importance of brain irrigation for the structure of language. Magnetic resonance imaging (fMRI) makes it possible to identify, indirectly through the intensity of the blood oxygen level dependence (BOLD), reflex changes in the cognitive system when there are changes in language factors such as, for example, metrics (i.e., accent) (Beaver and Zeevat, 2007; von Fintel, 2008; Simons, 2003); frequency modulation in relation to tone (Domaneschi and Di Paola, 2018). In such cases, the meaning production can be tested by the BOLD during an MRI scan. These discoveries illuminate aspects of the functioning of natural language—which requires integration of semantic information, memory, and management of inconsistencies in relation to interpretation—in understanding the meaning dependent on existing mental representations. According to Dietrich et al. (2019, with due differences of perspective), the cognitive processing effort corresponds to the level of representational steps adopted to reach a final interpretation and, for tasks suggested to the subject in which the proposal is acceptable, there is a corresponding successful formation of meaning. In the latter case, according to the authors (Dietrich et al., 2019), there is a type of accommodation evidenced by a lower BOLD index.

8.5 Language runs through several interdependent connection systems

Conventional language imposes logical reasoning that results in patterns of mental coordination and causes stability in neurodynamics (Perlovksy and Kozma, 2007, p. 3). Perlovksy and Kozma (2007, p. 3) report that there is "experimental evidence of the formation of a global cortical neurocognitive state" in which the "cortex consists of a large number of areas profusely interconnected by long-range pathways in a complex topological structure" that each cortical area exhibits a "unique pattern of interconnectivity with other cortical areas" suggesting that "cortical monitoring and integrative functions are the result of cooperative interaction among many distributed areas, and not the sole property of any one area or small group of areas."

Kelso and Tognoli (2007, p. 39) report that cognitive activity reveals a subtle interaction of two forces: "The tendency of the components to couple together and the tendency of the components to express their intrinsic independent behavior" reconciling "the well-known tendencies of specialized brain regions to express their autonomy (segregation) and the tendencies for those regions to work together as a synergy (integration)." For the authors (op. cit.), this interaction would be a principle of brain function, it would be a "fact that arises as a result of the observed self-organizing nature of both brain and behavior."

The neural activation fields have an interaction mechanism between adjacent systems with signals from bottom to top and top to bottom as input and output of a processing level (Perlovksy and Kozma, 2007, p. 78). Kozma (2007) relates that there is a connectionism in the brain that organizes it into macroscopic spatiotemporal patterns that control behavior.

Gangopadhyay et al. (2020) propose a neuron model that combines the different response characteristics and dynamic properties of the human cognitive system. They suggest the adoption of a continuous time dynamic system to produce a special property of growth transformations that corresponds to the different sets of neuronal dynamics consistent with the dynamics reported in neurobiology.

The approach of Gangopadhyay et al. (2020) allows to dissociate fixed points from the energy of the neural network, from the nature and shape of the neural responses and from the peak and neural dynamics statistics, independently controlling and optimizing each of these properties, adjusting them for variables local and/or global. In this way, the authors (op. cit.) understand that there is the same ideal solution applied to widely different shooting patterns in the network. This understanding, in our opinion, reinforces the idea of the existence of a universal language structure connecting different systems.

8.6 Language performs interpretation/mediation between real, symbolic, and imaginary kingdoms

The element that makes the connection/mediation between the human mind and the world is language, which can process the symbolization of the outside world in various parts of the brain (Damasio, 2012).

Wallon (1995) stated that the development of the language symbolic function is linked to the intellectual progress of the human being. To move from sensorimotor intelligence to intelligence at the symbolic level, social life is an essential element: The human environment plays a constituent role in language and emotion (Lacan, 1949; Padilha, 2000; Monte-Serrat, 2018). The symbolic function "involves building a bridge between the physical and mental worlds," it involves consciousness (Carter, 2012, p. 174). Neurolinguistics experts (Damasio, 2012; Vieira et al. 2011; Sacks, 1986) state that if there is any brain damage in a certain region, some cognitive skills are affected. They add that there is no specific language organ, but there are generic cognitive modules with the potential to become language processors. This network of interdependence makes language a complex gift.

There is an interrelation between brain, language, and body: It is one thing to mentally understand a difficult movement; executing this movement is another challenge, which requires the integration between body and brain (Monte-Serrat, 2018; Bergson, 1911). Natural language is a complex process in which information/meaning is not a modular category but is an operation distributed in different areas of the brain involved in the construction of meaning, using the body for this task.

To have an idea of how the formation of meaning occurs in body-brain integration, we have the example of people with cerebral dysfunction (body) which reflects on the complexity of information processing (people with aphasia). Aphasia, for example, alters more than one language level, as this affection consists of a disintegration of language in both aspects, syntactic (grammar) and semantic (sociohistorical) (Benveniste, 1966; Jakobson, 1975, 1990, 2010). Aphasic people have language difficulties, such as word search, sentence malformation, inability to relate a word to a daily activity (Jakobson, 1990).

The language belongs to the symbolic dimension which has an effect on the human being that is not of the order of the image but depends on the "dialectic of representation," that is, on the "intervention of a dissociation" (Lacan, 1949) that is not interior to the individual. It brings a unity from the outside to the inside (symbolic, abstract, representing something that comes from the real dimension). This process mixes reality with the subject, blending what is for him an object of perception as something that exists in himself, and not something external to him (Bairrão, 2001, p. 12).

The imaginary dimension of the natural language has the role of representing something that is not present. "The prefix 're-' imports the substitution value into the term. Something that was present and is no longer represented" (Marin, 1993, pp. 11 et 17). It is under this re-presentation that all motion or motor performance is related to the brain's Math process, which calculates real actions or facts transforming them in a kind of code that we call symbolization process.

According to Perlovksy and Kozma (2007, p. 90), "the hierarchical structure of the mind is not a separate mechanism independent of the instinct of knowledge." Abstract models are cultural constructs and cannot be perceived directly from the world, they are symbolic due to accumulation in cultures about which the individual speaks with other members of society, in mutual understanding.

Turner and Ioannides (2009, p. 171) state that "our brains are made to take the imprint of experience," thus "it can become very difficult to disentangle nature from nurture" while talking about "forming a neural imprint corresponding to a particular skill" of the brain areas as the most appropriate to some tasks.

The functioning of language depends on a logical movement in the process of construction of meanings in which the linguistic order embraces symbolic processes, transforming the mind into the belief that the patterns of sentence structure are more important than the words themselves that anticipate interpretation. At the same time, the language mechanism can present paradoxes and inaccuracies, which bring a kind of refutation to that standard functioning. This second mechanism establishes contradiction and is essential to show that the complex dynamics of body space has a role in the work of interpreting language, integrating knowledge, and experimentation with external elements such as touch, smell, sight, hearing, movement, and orientation.

8.7 Language has the ability of overlapping the functioning of reading, speaking, and writing

The brain has a complex pattern of functioning that integrates, within its own system, psychological and physiological components (Zhang, 2016). This integration can be observed through image tests that show overlapping lines of different time scales corresponding to the different changes in the language that organizes neural activity. It is in this sense that language, as a system, can superimpose the functioning of reading, speaking, and writing. There is a neurodynamic of consciousness whose signals evolve from vague and unconscious states to more concrete and conscious states until behavioral decision-making is reached (Perlovksy and Kozma, 2007, p. 1).

Natural language has an unlimited combinatorial nature: "Smaller elements can be combined into larger structures based on a grammatical system, resulting in a hierarchy of linguistic units such as words, sentences, and phrases" (Ding et al., 2016, p. 158). These hierarchical linguistic structures have their limits built internally during the understanding (interpretation). The cortical activity of speech is accompanied by different time scales indicating a hierarchy of neural processing schedules underlying the internal construction of speech based on the grammar of the hierarchical linguistic structure.

The electroencephalogram (EEG) provides the precise moment of neural activity; the sequence of mental operations; the recording of mixtures of all brain activities arising from different networks. This kind of examination tracks different electrical potentials between the electrodes. One of the prerequisites for the EEG test is the aligned and synchronized activity: "Brains do not work with digital numbers, rather they operate using a sequence of amplitude-modulated (AM) patterns of activity, which are observed in EEG, MEG, and fMRI measurements" (Kozma, 2007, p. 157).

8.8 Language is working as a central mechanical process that interconnects/calculates movements, images, behavior, decisions, uniting these varied and simultaneous functions

The embodied language poses the challenge of unified understanding to arrive at an understanding that stems from three sources of empirical data or validation: The data from ordinary experiments on brain and behavior, are seen objectively; the data from subjective experience, seen within ourselves; and the data we get from systematically testing the functional capabilities of our models/designs when applied to complex tasks, as in engineering (Werbos, 2007, p. 124).

To understand the language incorporated in a living organism means to understand it as a central mechanical process that unites various functions simultaneously. The unified apprehension made by the embedded language derives from three validating data sources: Data from common experiments on brain and behavior (viewed objectively); the data of subjective experience (seen within ourselves); and the data we obtain by systematically testing functional features when applied to complex tasks (Werbos, 2007, p. 124).

The brain makes unexpected connections between apparently unrelated areas, following criteria based on the axiomatic aspect of natural language.

There are also connections made under logical reasoning, which operate according to symbolic and logical operations to be performed. According to Kozma (2007), brain dynamics reaches notable achievements as abstraction of the essentials of figures of complex, unknown, and unpredictable origins; as generalization about examples of recurring objects; as reliable attribution to classes that lead to appropriate actions, and as planning of future actions based on past experiences and constant updating through the learning process (Kozma 2007, p. 139).

The functioning of language in its intriguing integrative function is intuitive in nature and does not follow rules of conventional language, overlapping with the latter to maintain coherence. In the semantic or narrative processing, experiment tasks are required from various regions of the brain (classical language areas, but not only them):

> *[Pulvermuller] He presented a theory of word structure in the brain in which it is asserted that words are Hebbian cell assemblies that link orthographic, phonological, and meaning-specific information. For instance, Pulvermuller proposes that "vision words" have distributed representations that include temporal regions (phonological word-form representation) as well as areas in the occipital lobe (semantic information), whereas motor words (such as verbs) have representations that span temporal regions as well as frontal areas in and around the motor cortices. Evidence from ERP studies, neuropsychological case studies, and behavioral studies are cited in support of this hypothesis [...].*
> **(Gernsbacher and Kaschak, 2014).**

Werbos (2007, p. 110) states that the individual is able to learn to perform a complex range of tasks in an optimized manner, rather, there is an optimization principle in the human brain to deal with spatial complexity to do choices that produce the best results. It is intelligence or it is learning process of how to make a better choice, according to the author (op cit., p. 111). The brain translates the options into a Mathematics of a different order in which values and relationships are not in an ordinal relationship to evaluate what results are "better" than other results, and this operation demands all the attributes of what we propose as being the universal structure of natural language.

When we speak of discrete "goals" or "intentions," we are not talking about the organism's long-term values. Instead, we are talking about subobjectives or tactical values, which aim to produce better findings or results. The utility function that defines what is "best" is the foundation of the system as a whole (Werbos, 2007, p. 111): The brain learns the "symmetries of the universe" exploiting them through a "reverberatory generalization" or a "multiple gating" (Werbos, 2007, p. 122), which are learning principles of symmetry for an approach based on principles of spatial complexity. According to the author (Werbos, 2007, pp. 126; 129) our brain operates approximately as a system called optimal power flow that optimizes the entire system as one large system, proposing parameters of the decision to made and integrating results much better from independent components working separately on their own (it should be mentioned that that system cannot handle the complexity of the possible developments foresight).

8.9 Language to finally compose a phenomenon that is perceived by the human being as an abstraction or a representation

The brain, through natural language considered as a central mechanical process, has the capacity to understand the variety in the form of unity. This task is performed by means of dynamic characteristics of the cognitive system whose result is the establishment of an "unexpected unity" between the phenomena that were observed separately (Gaufey, 1998, p. 17).

The time synchronization of the various aspects of natural language can reach a more comprehensive result in terms of the unification of different brain functions, for example, as in the music: Activity in different areas of the brain reflects the musical structure at different time scales; the auditory and motor areas closely follow the low-level, high-frequency musical structure. In contrast, the frontal areas contain a slower response, presumably playing a more integrating role. All results show that listening to music simultaneously involves distant areas of the brain cooperatively over time. This may be one of the reasons why music has such a profound impact on human beings (Turner and Ioannides, 2009, p. 171).

In conclusion to this topic on the aspects of the natural language, we must note that some attributes above can be partially found also in the "conventional" language, but it has different characteristics from what we call the axiomatic-logical structure of language. The synchronization (Section 8.3) in conventional language obeys the rules of logical reasoning, while the synchronization in the axiomatic aspect (living organism) depends on varied factors as explained earlier. The connection (Section 8.5) in natural language depends on the cognitive center unifying the inputs received by the human body; the connection, in conventional language, in its view, obeys an arboreal structure derived from logical reasoning (Pinker, 1994). As for Section 8.5, the mediation between real, symbolic, and imaginary is provided by the axiomatic character of natural language; conventional language, in turn, presents only the symbolic nature. The Section 8.7 refers only to the axiomatic character of natural language because, once incorporated into the living organism, it functions as the central mechanic process which interconnects input stimuli to movements, behavior, and decisions (output stimuli). As for the Section 8.8, abstraction and representation are phenomena mentally constructed by a living organism (axiomatic character of language) that are described by conventional language. As we have seen, our conception of natural language goes far beyond the concepts that linguists gave it. Under the concern of making linguistics a science, they left aside "parole" (speech) taking only "langue" (as conventional language dependent on grammatical rules) (Saussure, Chomsky). Even Jakobson (1990, 2010), who is concerned with neurophysiological aspects of language when describing the phenomenon of aphasia, fails to describe it comprehensively as we did it here. Our model of natural language is more comprehensive and is suitable to be classified as the universal structure of language.

All of these attributes function as optimization principles (axiomatic characteristic of natural language) for the individual to perform a complex range of tasks arising from spatial complexity (reality in which he interacts), to make choices (to interpret) that produce the best results (Werbos, 2007, p. 110 et seq.). The human brain translates options into mathematics of a different order, in which values and relationships are not in an ordinal relationship to assess which results are "better" than other ones. The individual develops tactical values designed to produce better results based on a utility function that defines what is "best" (Werbos, 2007, p. 111). In summary, through the eight attributes (axioms) of natural language, the brain learns the "symmetries of the universe," exploring them through a "reverberating generalization" or a "multiple gating" (Werbos, 2007, p. 122), which are principles of learning from symmetry groups as the basis for an approach on principles of spatial complexity.

The eight attributes of language—such as functioning of live organism (axiomatic) working in synchrony toward a reduction phenomenon that is perceived by the human being as an abstraction or a representation— reveal, for example, a lot of similarity with the way the convolutional neural networks (CNN) modules are designed. CNN analyzes the information under a comparison process learned from filters that are hand-engineered, to measure how two functions overlap as they roll together (from Latin "convolvere") (Goodfellow et al., 2016), and to reduce the spatial size of the convolved feature, decreasing the computational power required to process the data. Both, natural and machine language go toward dimensionality reduction.

On the other hand, we have the conventional language which also functions toward a conclusion/reduction (representation). Unlike natural language (axiomatic/living organism), conventional language organizes ideas starting from premises that stem from previously established grammatical rules (Monte-Serrat, 2017). In the case of natural language, stimuli from the world are organized by the cognitive system of an individual until reaching a conclusion (construction of meaning); in the case of conventional language, ideas are organized according to a sequence predetermined (Levitt, 1996) by grammatical rules established in the field of ideas (and not of realities experienced by the individual) (Monte-Serrat and Tfouni, 2012; Monte-Serrat, 2013; Araújo, 2004). The sequence of words comes from a conclusion "that is true if and only if the [text] contains representations of premises that are true" (Pinker, 1994, p. 67), combining the arrangements of symbols to produce intelligent deduction, interpretation. In this way, grammar is understood as a discrete combinatorial system.

A "finite number of discrete elements (in this case words) sampled, combined, and permuted to create larger structures (in this case, sentences) with properties that are quite distinct from those of their elements" (Pinker, 1994, p. 75). Grammar, according to Pinker (1994, p. 78) "specifies how words may combine to express meanings; that specification is independent of the particular meanings we typically convey or expect others to convey to us," and if we come across ungrammaticality, it would be a "consequence of our having a fixed code for interpreting sentences" (Pinker, 1994, p. 79).

The logical sequence of words or phrases determined by grammatical rules is transformed from chain to tree due to mixing with the human brain. This is what Pinker explains:

> The difference between the artificial combinatorial system we see in word-chain devices and the natural one we see in the human brain is summed up in a line from Joyce Kilmer poem: 'Only God can make a tree'. A sentence is not a chain but a tree. In a human grammar, words are grouped into phrases, like twigs joined in a branch. The phrase is given a name – a mental symbol – and little phrases can be joined into bigger ones.
>
> **(Pinker, 1994, p. 90).**

> [...] the labeled branches of a phrase structure tree act as an overreaching memory or plan for the whole sentence. This allows nested long-distance dependencies, like 'if...then' and 'either...or', to be handled with ease [...] [The] rules embed one

instance of a symbol inside another instance of the same symbol (here, a sentence inside a sentence), a neat trick – logicians call it 'recursion' – for generating an infinite number of structures. The pieces of the bigger sentence are held together, in order, as a set of branches growing out of a common node.

(Pinker, 1994, pp. 92–93).

Summarizing this topic, we can say that the dynamics of language reveals the intelligence in placing sequence in the elements to form the result. If we take as a basis the dynamics of natural language (with its axiomatic/living organism attributes), the result of the linguistic process—from input stimuli to becoming aware by the neurocognitive system—will be the mental representation printed in the mind. On the other hand, if we take the logical attribute of conventional language in isolation as a basis, the result will be the construction of a socially shared meaning, because it stems from socially shared grammatical rules. This dismemberment of mental representation and meaning had already been observed by Frege in 1892. According to the author (Frege, 1892), there is meaning, reference to a sign or representation. While the first two can be classified as common property to several individuals, representation is the subjective (individual) way of meaning something. For Frege (1892), intuition and representation are linked, so that two individuals can never effectively have the same representation of the same object.

8.10 Natural language and artificial intelligence: Symbolization process and resources

What I cannot create, I do not understand.

(Richard Feynman).

Artificial intelligence (AI) and ML had biological inspiration to imitate the human brain. Cognitive computing, in turn, is moving in that direction. In this book, we have dedicated space to explain how natural language works to collaborate for the improvement of AI.

So far, we showed how the structure of natural language collects stimuli and interprets them (inputs)—through symbolization process—revealing its immutable configuration so that AI is based on a similar one. In this topic, we are dedicated to bringing natural language and AI closer to the moment before the output. Just to remember, natural intelligence receives stimuli through subsystems until they reach the central cognitive system, as it is from there that decision-making (output) is produced.

Although AI initially focused on big goals, such as building machines that mimic the human brain, it has been perfected through cognitive computing that, based on neural learning networks, applies cognitive science knowledge to simulate human reasoning processes.

This characteristic of cognitive computing brings it closer to human cognition in the sense that both receive and store varied information: The cognitive system receives varied stimuli and transforms them into mental representations that will serve as a basis for decision-making; cognitive computing, in turn, covers several disciplines (such as ML, natural language processing, vision, and the human-computer interface) to cope with forming resources, which will be the starting point for the output.

In Chapter 7, we saw that the meaning-building process is important to improve filters for deep learning (DL) or ML, so that AI has the necessary conditions to reduce ambiguity. We saw that natural language involves periodicity and synchrony to connect several subsystems until the formation of meaning, that is, the mental representation of external reality. AI (cognitive computing in this case), in turn, to be able to perform foreseeing activities in specific domains, is based on ML which, with new learning methods, enables interaction with human being.

The idea of building a machine that imitates the human brain needs to be aligned with the synchronous functioning of the latter. Therefore it is observed that systems based on a set of rules and inferences are limited in the user interface. ML is a learning technique that has its origins in statistics and mathematical optimization. Multilayer neural networks associated with back propagation increased ML. The development of CNN Neural Convolutional networks, composed of several layers from which resources and classification are extracted, is the closest to the process of human mental representation, from our point of view. CNN divides the image into receptive fields and groups resources together, reducing dimensionality. This process maintains the most important information, resembling human mental representation, in which one has, mentally, the "generic" image of the object (fundamental characteristics of a chair, e.g., which allows us to recognize any chair).

With this introduction, we start to talk about the underlying structure of natural language, showing how it takes data from the real world. This is a task that interests ML, especially those of deep generative models. We will establish similarities between them to pave the way for AI to approach the intuitiveness of human cognition.

Bearing in mind the universal structure of language—axiomatic-logical: Axiom to build meaning as a living organism, and logic to construct meaning from abstract grammatical rules—we seek to explain why AI should benefit from this axiomatic-logical model. In this topic, we develop the strategy of articulating the symbolic process of mental representation of natural language to the process of resource formation carried out by AI, to expose, in the end, what we understand to be similarities between both.

Since "intelligence" is exactly the way in which the formation of meaning is organized, we look for arguments underlying the structure of natural language that can be applied to AI. As the machine language (sequence of instructions to be executed by the processor) is the result of a set of techniques that allow a system to automatically discover which representations must be extracted from reality data to classify them (AI), we seek, through structural knowledge about natural language, see how the machine can learn and what resources to use to perform a specific task.

Natural language involves cognition, or rather, the process that involves the individual's perception to interpret it, symbolizing it. According to de Chardin (1956, p. 39), the two external and internal faces of the world correspond (dialectical structure) in a such a way that they can move from one to the other, with the only condition of replacing "mechanical interaction" with "consciousness." We emphasize that the understanding of the world under a dialectical structure must be applied also to AI. This structure would serve as a basis for the reasoning procedure, establishing relationships of similarity between situations, uniting them (Perelman and Olbrechts-Tyteca, 1973; Pessoa, 2004): Cognitive function operates by associative property which is a "property of some binary operations" (Hungerford, 1974, p. 24).

The neurocognitive system works at some levels that correspond to the layers of the cortex, interconnecting a dense dynamic system formed by several specialized subsystems. It encompasses "subsystems with particular formal properties to do with their relationship with the primary system to which they are a subsystem" (Charlton and Andras, 2007, p. 334). Perlovsky and Kozma (2007, p. 3) report that there is the "experimental evidence of the formation of a global cortical neurocognitive state" in which the "cortex consists of a large number of areas profusely interconnected by long-range pathways" in a complex topological structure that each cortical area exhibits a "unique pattern of interconnectivity with other cortical areas" suggesting that "cortical monitoring and integrative functions are the result of cooperative interaction among many distributed areas, and not the sole property of any one area or small group of areas."

This way the memory works by making the interaction of subsystems in the functioning of the brain corresponds to DL system that works in a hierarchy of concepts, with many layers, by gathering knowledge from experience (Goodfellow et al., 2016; Nielsen, 2015). Both the human brain and DL must work with similar relationships and not with similar situations (Perelman and Olbrechts–Tyteca, 1973; Pessoa, 2004). DL is successful because the various modeling formalisms it presents reveal the basic structure of natural language. This is what will make it possible to establish a link between natural language and AI: The argument based on the structure common to natural and AI will allow to link realities at unequal levels, giving them a recognized connection (Perelman and Olbrechts-Tyteca, 1973; Pessoa, 2004).

The universal axiomatic-logical structure of natural language can be applied to a specific AI situation, helping to build a similar relationship between them. Both natural language and AI must be conceived as a system, that is, as a group of elements interacting forming a unified whole. Just as the natural language system is synchronized in the formation of meaning, the AI system is focused on the formation of resources.

The most important lesson to be learned from the behavior of natural language in this case is that its axiomatic-logical structure can absorb the stimuli of contextual reality placing them in a logical chain to give them meaning. Human cognition stores the main aspects of the observed elements and stores the structural data to be used in the construction of meaning.

An AI technique has been developed that is not restricted to just modeling data distribution. It is a model designed to directly learn the structure of the data. Instead of providing input and output variables, tasks are performed that combine probabilistic modeling and DL: This is the generative model (Fraccaro, 2018).

A generative model must be able to find the underlying structure and causal structures of the data to generate data. An example of a generative model is the Adversarial Generative Networks, which generate realistic images of faces from a learned data distribution (Fraccaro, 2018). Another model is the Variational Autoencoder (VAE) (op. cit.). These models learn the hidden structure of data distribution within the parameters of deep neural networks.

In the generative model, to give rise to a new data point, it is necessary first to obtain a sample, and then use it (Fraccaro, 2018). For this, a latent variable is used, which carries a conditional distribution for the data, called likelihood. So, in probabilistic terms, this variable can contain a hidden representation. This generates a compressed representation of the data, as if it were a bottleneck through which all the information must pass, necessary to generate the data. VAE offers an inference network (encoder) which allows calculating the parameters of the posterior approximation. Rather than forming a set of parameters for each data point, variational parameters are shared across all data points (Fraccaro, 2018).

Although generative modeling uses AI to produce a representation or abstraction of observed phenomena or target variables that can be calculated from observations, real-world data is not captured in a "neutral" way but is affected by the context (see Chapter 9). Showing what the axiomatic-logical structure of natural language is and how cognition works is not enough for AI to be intuitive like the human mind. In the generative modeling, the interference of the context (external reality) in the formation of meaning must also be considered. This is the purpose of Chapter 9: To show how natural language behaves in different contexts in the fields of science so that AI can be improved.

References

Araújo, I., 2004. Do Signo Ao Discurso. Introdução à Filosofia da Linguagem. Parábola Editorial, São Paulo.

Bairrão, J., 2001. A imaginação do outro: intersecções entre psicanálise e hierologia. Paideia 11 (20), 11–26.

Beaver, D., Zeevat, H., 2007. Accommodation. In: Ramchand, G., Reiss, C. (Eds.), Oxford Handbook of Linguistic Interfaces. University Press, Oxford, pp. 503–538.

Benveniste, E., 1966. Da subjetividade na linguagem. In: Problemas de Linguística Geral. vol. I. Cia. Ed. Nacional e Ed. da USP, São Paulo. Novak, M. e Neri, L. (trad.).

Bergson, H., 1911. Matter and Memory. George Allen and Unwin, London.

Carter, R., 2012. O livro do cérebro. Jones F. (trad.), Ed. Agir, Rio de Janeiro (1949).

Chardin, P., 1956. Tome I: Le phénomène Humain. Les Éditions du Seuil, Paris.

Charlton, B., Andras, P., 2007. Complex biological memory conceptualized as an abstract communication system: human long term memories grow in complexity during sleep and undergo selection while awake. In: Perlovsky, L., Kozma, R. (Eds.), Neurodynamics of Cognition and Consciousness. Springer-Verlag, Berlin, Heidelberg.

Damasio, A., 2012. O Erro de Descartes: Emoção, razão e o cérebro humano. Vicente, D. E Segurado, G. (trad.), third ed. Companhia das Letras, São Paulo.

Dietrich, S., Hertrich, I., Seibold, V., Rolke, B., 2019. Discourse management during speech perception: a functional magnetic resonance imaging (fMRI) study. Neuroimage 202, 116047. Elsevier.

Ding, N., Melloni, L., Zhang, H., Tian, X., Poeppel, D., 2016. Cortical tracking of hierarchical linguistic structures in connected speech. Nat. Neurosci. 19, 158–164.

Domaneschi, F., Di Paola, S., 2018. The processing costs of presupposition accommodation. J. Psycholinguist. Res. 47, 483–503. https://doi.org/10.1007/s10936-017-9534-7.

Fraccaro, M., 2018. Deep Latent Variable Models for Sequential Data. Technical University of Denmark, Kongens Lyngby.

Frege, G., 1892. Uber Sinn und Bedeutung. Z. Philos. Philos. Krit. 100, 20–25.

Gangopadhyay, A., Chakrabartty, S., 2018. Spiking, bursting, and population dynamics in a network of growth transform neurons. IEEE Trans. Neural Netw. Learn. Syst. 29, 2379–2391. https://doi.org/10.1109/TNNLS.2017.2695171.

Gangopadhyay, A., Mehta, D., Chakrabartty, S., 2020. A spiking neuron and population model based on the growth transform dynamical system. Front. Neurosci. 14, 425.

Gaufey, G., 1998. El lazo especular. Un estudio traversero de la unidad imaginaria. Leguizamón, G. (trad.), Edelp SA, Argentina.

Gernsbacher, M., Kaschak, M., 2014. Neuroimaging studies of language production and comprehension. US National Library of Medicine, National Institute of Health.

Goodfellow, I., Bengio, Y., Courville, A., 2016. Deep Learning. MIT Press, Cambridge, MA.

Huettel, S., Song, A., McCarthy, G., 1973. Functional Magnetic Resonance Imaging. MIT Press, Cambridge, MA, USA.

Hungerford, T., 1974. Algebra. Springer Ed.

Jakobson, R., 1975. Les règles des dégâts grammaticaux. Kristeva, J., Milner, J.C. et Ruwet, N., (org.), In: Langue, discours, société. Seuil, Paris, pp. 11–25.

Jakobson, R., 1990. Two aspects of language and two types of aphasic disturbances. In: Language. Harvard University Press, Cambridge, pp. 115–133.

Jakobson, R., 2010. Linguística e Comunicação. Bliknstein, I. e Paes, J. (Trad.), Ed. Cultrix, São Paulo.

Kelso, J.A., Tognoli, E., 2007. Toward a complementary neuroscience: metastable coordination dynamics of the brain. In: Perlovsky, L., Kozma, R. (Eds.), Neurodynamics of Cognition and Consciousness. Springer-Verlag, Berlin, Heidelberg.

Kozma, R., 2007. Neurodynamics of intentional behavior generation. In: Perlovsky, L., Kozma, R. (Eds.), Neurodynamics of Cognition and Consciousness. Springer-Verlag, Berlin, Heidelberg.

Lacan, J., 1949. Le stade du mirroir comme formateur de la function du Je telle qu'elle nous est révélée dans l'experiénce psychanalytique. In: Revue Française de Psychanalyse, France. Presses Universitaires de France, pp. 449–455. Octobre.

Levitt, N., 1996. Mathematics as stepchild of contemporary culture. In: Gross, P., Levitt, N., Lewis, M. (Eds.), The Flight From Science and Reason. Annals of the New York Academy of Sciences.

Manzo, A., 1992. Dialectical Thinking: A Generative Approach to Critical/Creative Thinking. Eric, Institute of Education Sciences. December.

Marin, L., 1993. Des Pouvoirs de l'image: Gloses. Éd. du Seuil, Paris.

Monte-Serrat, D., 2013. Literacy and Juridical Discourse, USP-RP 2013. Thesis Guided by Tfouni, L. Retrieved from http://www.teses.usp.br/teses/disponiveis/59/59137/tde-14032013-104350/. (Accessed 28 July 2020).

Monte-Serrat, D., 2017. Neurolinguistics, language, and time: investigating the verbal art in its amplitude. Int. J. Percept. Public Health 1 (3).

Monte-Serrat, D., 2018. Inclusion in linguistic education: neurolinguistics, language, and subject. In: Psycholinguistics and Cognition in Language Processing. IGI-Global.com.

Monte-Serrat, D., Tfouni, L., 2012. Efeitos ideológicos da gramática do discurso do Direito. Silva, D. (Org.), In: Revista Cadernos de Linguagem e Sociedade. vol. 13,1. Ed. Thesaurus UnB, Brasilia, pp. 11–19. March.

Nielsen, M., 2015. Neural Networks and Deep Learning. Determination Press.

Padilha, A., 2000. Bianca. O ser simbólico: Para além dos limites da deficiência mental. PhD thesis, Faculty of Education, UNICAMP, Brazil.

Perelman, C., Olbrechts-Tyteca, L., 1973. The New Rhetoric: Treatise on Argumentation. Wilkninson, J. (transl), University of Notre Dame Press.

Perlovksy, L., Kozma, R. (Eds.), 2007. Neurodynamics of Cognition and Consciousness. Springer-Verlag, Berlin, Heidelberg.

Pessoa, M., 2004. A análise retórica de acordo com Perelmam. In: Linguagem em (Dis)curso - LemD, Tubarão, pp. 135–151. v. 4, n. 2, jan./jun.

Pinker, S., 1994. The Language Instinct. Harper-Collins Publishers Inc., New York.

Sacks, O., 1986. The Man Who Mistook his Wife for a Hat and Other Clinical Tales. Alfred A. Knopf, New York.

Simons, M., 2003. Presupposition and accommodation: understanding the stalnakerian picture. Philos. Stud. 112, 251–278. https://doi.org/10.1023/A:1023004203043.

Turner, R., Ioannides, A., 2009. Brain, Music and Musicality: Inferences From Neuroimaging. Oxford University Press, New York.

Vieira, A.C., Roazzi, A., Queiroga, B., Asfora, R., Valença, M., 2011. Afasias e Áreas Cerebrais: Argumentos prós e contras à perspectiva localizacionista. Psicol. Reflex. Crít. 24 (3), 588–596.

von Fintel, K., 2008. What is presupposition accommodation, again? Philos. Perspect. 22, 137–170. https://doi.org/10.1111/j.1520-8583.2008.00144.x.

Wallon, H., 1995. As Origens Do caráter na Criança. pinto, H. (Trad.). Nova Alexandria, São Paulo.

Werbos, P., 2007. Using ADP to understand and replicate brain intelligence: the next level design? In: Perlovsky, L., Kozma, R. (Eds.), Neurodynamics of Cognition and Consciousness. Springer-Verlag, Berlin, Heidelberg.

Zhang, W., 2016. A supplement to self-organization theory of dreaming. Front. Psychol. 7, 332.

CHAPTER NINE

Interdisciplinary paths for the construction of meaning: What natural language has to say for artificial intelligence?

9.1 Introduction

This chapter is dedicated to explaining an aspect of the functioning of natural language that cannot be ignored by artificial intelligence (AI): The interference of context in the meaning construction. The universal structure of language is axiomatic-logical. There is not much difficulty in applying the logical aspect of natural language in AI. There are obstacles to designing for the machine what would be the axiomatic aspect of language, as it is dynamic in the sense of flexibility according to the context. It is precisely this contextual adaptation that reduces the occurrence of ambiguity and increases the similarity with the intuitiveness of human cognition.

The "raison d'être" of this chapter is the interdisciplinary articulation of the study of language to expose the different ways of organizing the meaning construction in each science branch. It is intended, with this clarification, to indicate new directions in the research of intelligent systems to improve future research in AI because "intelligence" is exactly the "way" in which the formation of meaning is organized. It is in this sense that we look for arguments underlying the structure of natural language that can be applied to AI. The methodological approach of discourse analysis (Pêcheux, 1975, 1988) to the diversified scientific context aims to promote a cross-fertilization between natural language and AI, to better understand the structure of the living being language, to develop the machine language in an intuitive way. Deepening the understanding of how language is processed benefits and gives quality to research in improving AI.

It is believed that the greatest difficulty for AI is to know what resources should be extracted. The sciences install an order of discourse, a materiality

The Natural Language for Artificial Intelligence
https://doi.org/10.1016/B978-0-12-824118-9.00001-1

discursive distinct from the order of the language, which, however, imposes conditions for the functioning of the latter (Courtine, 2016, p. 14). In this case, our explanation of how the language is used in different contexts can help in the process of mapping and learning the representation of AI, to gather understanding of the experience and formally specify all the information necessary for the computer (Goodfellow et al., 2016; Nielsen, 2015).

Our wager on the universal structure of language and on the explanation of how language works in different branches of science brings strategies to the defy in the development of machine learning, ML. Simple ML algorithms depend on the process of representing the information provided, but it is necessary to know the way these representations are formed. Each information included in the ML representation is known as a resource (Goodfellow et al., 2016; Nielsen, 2015), which, in natural language, would correspond to the symbolization process. For this reason, knowledge on how natural language works in its symbolization process is the "map" that will give direction to new discoveries in AI. If AI resources do not correspond to natural language today, this is due to obstacles in the correct choice of those resources. This challenge can be overcome when we have an understanding of the structure and functioning of human language (natural language) so that they can be applied to the machine, allowing the latter to have a higher quality language in the performance of algorithms and neural networks. In the following topics, we present some ways of meaning construction in the fields of science through qualitative analysis and discuss the way this functioning can be useful for AI.

The natural language as a unified whole body must be understood in the form of synchronization between brain and body, which traces the path that takes the physical world to neurons and cells. In its turn, the AI seen in the perspective of a whole body must be able to trace a path that unites the text to the context, resembling the functioning of the natural language in its axiomatic (that refers to the reality of the world) and logic (abstraction and symbolization) features.

Many AI tasks depend on projecting the right set of resources to be extracted for a simple machine learning (ML) algorithm (Goodfellow et al., 2016; Nielsen, 2015). What resources should be extracted is hard work that involves mapping and learning AI representation, to gather knowledge of the experience that formally specifies all the information that the computer needs (Goodfellow et al., 2016; Nielsen, 2015).

Before looking at the branches of science, it is necessary to make it clear that there is no absolute way to measure the appropriateness of thought to reality (Monte-Serrat, 2017). This correlation is made through the application of some method or criterion, which provides a "correct" knowledge of reality. Each scientific branch has its method and it is only through the application of it that it will be possible to verify whether a fact or idea faithfully reflects reality.

The sciences deal with "truths" and it is these truths that interfere with the value criterion for the formation of meaning. "Value," "hierarchy," and "context" are key words for AI to be successful in its performance in the scientific fields. In the previous chapters, we explained "how" natural language builds meaning, which leaves us alert to the "value" criterion that in turn is linked to the "use" of language and to the constructed meaning. The criterion "hierarchy" in language also has its importance, since, as language is used in different disciplines, its structural elements undergo changes in the hierarchy, altering the viewer's opinion. "Value" and "hierarchy" are at the origin of the axiomatic-logical structure of language, making the constructed sense leaning toward one or the other solution and, thus acting in the determination of "how" natural language behaves in different contexts. The arguments for understanding the functioning of natural language start, then, from the intrinsic qualities of language, which are intended to be transported to the machine.

9.2 Social sciences

In this field of Science, human behavior and societies are studied. We discuss some aspects of Law, Literature, Psychology, Psychoanalysis, and Linguistics from a qualitative point of view (which means a discussion in their context) (Pêcheux, 1975, 1988) that can be useful for discovering the choice path of representation in the AI development. We adopted interdisciplinarity to consider the theoretical elements of these scientific fields in a joint and exemplary manner to persuade the AI specialists, while working with natural language processes, inspiring them in the discovery of new algorithms that can be applied to AI.

9.2.1 Law

Taking as a starting point the axiomatic-logical structure of language as the guiding thread of our analysis, it can be said that Law is more prone to the logical characteristic of language, due to the prevalence of texts written in the standard form dictated by legal codes (Cornu, 2005; Monte-Serrat, 2013, 2014; Monte-Serrat and Tfouni, 2012). According to Cornu (2005), legal linguistics is a specialized language in which the law gives special meaning to certain words. In the field of Law, discourse is organized by means of sentences that communicate the law, which means that these sentences already have, in their origin, previous guidelines on their structure and style which make dominate the discourse of the law.

The discipline of Law is situated within universally logically stabilized societies to form a semantically "normal" world that, by not taking into account the existence of mistakes (Pêcheux, 1988, pp. 9, 30), instrumentalizes the processes of language and interpretation in such a way that, eventually, with previously defined criteria, it will target the intended final effects. These instrumentalized processes work under the disjunctive logic in which it is "impossible for a person to be single and married" (Pêcheux, 1988, p. 30). Whorf (1942) stresses the ways in which a person's thoughts are controlled by laws whose standards they are unaware of. There is a prohibition on interpretation other than that provided for by previously given logical propositions (Is the state of things A or non-A?) (Pêcheux, 1988, p. 31).

This is the primordial way of language functioning in the Law discipline, which makes possible "a construction of the physical reality as a process" (Pêcheux, 1988, p. 37). The writing of Law, according to Pêcheux (1988, p. 38), "does not interpret the real," but constructs the "physical real as a process." Law gives precedence to syllogistic reasoning, cleaning the language of supposed errors and lapses (Monte-Serrat and Tfouni, 2012; Monte-Serrat, 2013), which leads us to conclude that Law adopts the logical feature of language predominantly, making representation more abstract.

9.2.2 Literature

To make our presentation clear when explaining the axiomatic-logical structure of language, we consider, in an exaggerated way, that the language used in literature especially involves subjectivity and poetry, against the use of language in Law, where there is a concern to eliminate subjectivity (Monte-Serrat, 2013, 2014). Thus the axiomatic element of the language structure is more requested in Literature, whereas the logical element of language is more valued in Law (Monte-Serrat, 2017; Cornu, 2005).

Just to exemplify what we have just stated, we will use some excerpts from the work of James Joyce, a highly commented writer due to his practice of producing meaning from meaningless expressions or phrases. It will be demonstrated in these examples that the effect of meaning construction is due to the logical-axiomatic structure of language whether it is obvious or hidden. Although Joyce does not obey grammatical rules in his writing, he relies on this same logical structure of conventional language (Monte-Serrat, 2017) to create a new meaning. His success depends on removing the visibility of meaning from an invisible logical structure. According to Boas, grammar (as a logical structure) determines which aspects of experience "should" be expressed (Goldschmidt, 1959).

A relationship between hypothesis and conclusion to discover the truth is the mechanism of the rules that govern the conventional language to construct meanings (Monte-Serrat, 2017). A passive transformation in the sentence needs the previous application of a set of sentence structure rules (the logical structure we refer to). Chomsky (2001, p. 107) states that there are specific elements that determine the specific human language and there are general universal elements that are part of the organization of every human language and constitute the study of universal grammar. Whorf (1942) declares that "the linguistic order embraces all symbolism, all symbolic processes, all processes of reference and logic," turning the mind into the belief that "the patterns of sentence structure that guide words are more important than the words themselves."

Universal categories and relations of language are the basis of James Joyce's work for the writing of his special grammar in which he builds new meanings of syntax and restrictions on its structure that is apparently neglected. Joyce takes advantage of something that is outside of his discourse (such as grammatical rules, syntax) to, through the reader's deductive reasoning, build the effect of producing meaning, making the final sense come from certain postulates that are seen as evident truths or as obvious facts. This happens, for example, with the sequence of the days of the week—"All Moanday, Tearday, Wailsday, Thumpsday, Frightday, Shatterday"—with a sequence of lament, cry (moan for Moanday); tears (for Tearday); grieve and mourn (for Wailsday); beat or punch (for Thumpsday); horror and panic (for Frightday); finally, destruction or fracture (for Shatterday). Joyce also makes sense with a sentence constructed with one word. The meaning comes from the grammatical rules that previously establish what the meaning of the word will be due to the relationship/position of that word in the sentence: "Love loves to love love."

Kenshur (1996, p. 526) explains that the context of the century of lights imposes "the" way of building objective knowledge through the logical reasoning as general patterns of reasoning, with no reference to a particular meaning or context. This generalization is provided by the imposition of logical reasoning operated in the structure of conventional language; it is in this way that the language provides the prerequisites of the standard of writing and speech (Monte-Serrat, 2013; Levine, 2006, p. 71).

The grammar has a logical function in the sense of constructing reasoning over a conditional statement, so that the value of truth (true and false) depends on the truth values of P and Q in the logical expression "if P, then Q." In this case, Q must be true whenever P is true. "Statement P is called the conditional statement hypothesis and statement Q is called the conclusion of the conditional statement" (Sundstrom, 2019, p. 5).

James Joyce uses the same "if P then Q" logical structure to build meaning in his writings. The author starts from a grammar already existing in the language (if P) to write his ideas whose meanings only come from the dependence of the functioning of the language between hypothesis and conclusion, giving rise to new meanings. He manages to construct intelligible meanings of meaningless phrases that come from outside his discourse/text. In this case, he is based on deductive reasoning, making the final meaning come from certain postulates that are seen as evident truths or obvious facts of language. This obviousness comes from the universal axiomatic-logical structure.

9.2.3 Psychology and psychoanalysis

Psychology and Psychoanalysis deal with the "thoughts and acts of the human being as a subject of knowledge, law or conscience" (Roudinesco and Plon, 2006, p. 742). Language is important for these scientific areas because it gives access to the functioning of thought representations, which allows in its turn, the study of subjectivity (Pêcheux, 1975, p. 125). Due to the axiomatic-logical structure of language, it can be said that this same structure interferes with the functioning of the discursive process (writing and speaking) and, also, interferes with subjectivity (Monte-Serrat, 2014; Pêcheux, 1975; Haroche, 1992).

Psychoanalysis studies the role that language (understood as conventional language with its logical reasoning) has to do with the subject's point of view (understood at some point as the axiomatic feature of language), making him apprehend an "entirely rational" visual space (from outside), capable of purifying him of all subjectivity (Quinet, 2003, pp. 145–147). Psychoanalysis is concerned with the opposition of linguistic functioning—between those that have a logical sequence (designating conscious relations of the individual) and those that have no logical sequence (strictly linked to the structure of the unconscious). In the latter case, there would be a negative interest, by Psychoanalysis, in the logical structure of language, due to the understanding that the unconscious lives in language, the latter being structured by the totality of mistakes that remain in it (Arrivé, 2000). In this way, the interest in language lies in the relationship between error (in relation to its logical structure) and the structure of the unconscious (something that disagrees with language would reveal the truth of the subject) (Arrivé, 2000, p. 37).

9.2.4 Linguistics

Linguistics is the science that describes and analyzes specific languages (conventional languages), interfering with the process of how to think. Whorf (1942) points out that it is necessary to pay attention to the fact that "a person's thought forms are controlled by inexorable laws of patterns of which he is unaware" because "these patterns are the intricate systematizations not perceived by its authorship." Ferdinand de Saussure (1916, p. 97) dedicated himself to the static aspect of the language, in the sense of order and regularity and whose traditional grammar does not distinguish the written word from the spoken word (Saussure, 1916, p. 98).

Since speech is unpredictable and closely linked to subjectivity, it appears, according to Jakobson (1963, 1965, 1990, 2010, p. 27), that "private property, in the domain of language, does not exist: Everything is socialized" because communication depends on the diffusion of patterns (Jakobson, 1963, 1965, 1990, 2010, p. 30). It can be concluded that Jakobson did not consider the axiomatic aspect of language in the speech that is more linked to individuality (mental representation) and that its logical resource (common on writing) is more linked to the sharing of meanings (Frege, 1892).

Regarding (conventional) language, Jakobson (1963, 1965, 1990, 2010, pp. 34–35) states that it is governed by universal laws and houses a differential process of construction of meaning, that is, "only the existence of invariant elements allows to recognize the variations," "both in the sense level and in the sound level." Jakobson (1963, 1965, 1990, 2010, p. 43) is concerned with the fact that "the science of language passes in silence as if speech disorders have nothing to do with language." We can consider that the two aspects—axiomatic and logical—have always been linked to the study of the science of linguistics, which shows that they are rooted in the universal structure of language.

9.3 Natural sciences

Reading Perlovsky and Kozma's (2007) book on neurodynamics of cognition and consciousness leads us to recognize that language must be considered a unified whole, which involves perception and symbolization under an iterative process (trigger and reaction) that replaces mechanical interaction with consciousness. This process (already explained in Sections 3.6.3 and 3.6.4), carried out by language from the perspective of the Natural Sciences, establishes synchrony between brain and body, tracing the path that takes the physical world to neurons and cells. It encompasses both the concept of language as a convention (which depends on logical reasoning) and the concept of natural language (which has a biological aspect) involving at least eight attributes (see Chapter 8): (1) axiomatic-logical mechanism; (2) synchronizer mechanism; (3) linked to vascular and neuronal network dynamics; (4) interdependent process connector; (5) mediator of the real, symbolic, and imaginary realms; (6) intermittent synchronization cycle; (7) central process to join varied and simultaneous functions; and (8) to compose a mental representation.

The axiom and logic features of language in Natural Sciences work in their interdependence: The construction of meaning is coordinated by Broca's area "configured innately to be involved in the anticipations and predictions that define the syntactic structures of linguistic expression" (Turner and Ioannides, 2009, p. 161). The logical sequence is imposed on the cognitive system through the rules of language as a convention, and its input signals, with previously assigned values (meaning) to the individual auditory and visual systems, will join with the other subsystems to integrate the sensations (sense) (see Chapter 8).

In this case the language might be understood as a multilevel process working on self-similar invariant rules of scale. Language carries with it, at the same time: The chaotic neurodynamic characteristic of natural language and the dynamic logic linked to language as a convention. There is a connection in the brain that organizes language into macroscopic spatio-temporal patterns that control behavior (Kozma, 2007). The interference of language as a convention in the cognitive system can be recognized in several works by linguists such as those by Chomsky, Jakobson, Saussure, and Whorf already mentioned in this book (see Chapters 3 and 5). We wager that this interference has the function of organizing the formation of meaning through the symbolization process, that is, through a standard of operation by a universal structure (a whole phenomenon), which gives rise to the same linguistic characteristics/laws for different languages.

Taking the opposite path to that of the natural sciences, the science of Linguistics started from an epistemological rupture in the domains of knowledge (Auroux, 2017, p. 169):

> the Genevan author [Saussure] saw himself as the founder of the true linguistic 'science'. Before him, nothing scientific would have been done with regard to language [...] We quickly understood that this view of science did not correspond to its normal functioning.
>
> **(Auroux, 2017, p. 170).**

According to Auroux (2017, pp. 170–171), Saussure's stance of founding Linguistics as a science brought the following consequences: (1) the facts became "assertions dedicated to object domains and validated by empirical and formal recoverable protocols"; (2) knowledge about language becomes an invention and is discontinuous (corresponding to isolable inventions); (3) "new objects can appear in a knowledge domain or disappear from it; these phenomena may arise from the structure of the field, from a change of interest or from the emergence of new empirical data"; (4) language becomes part of a domain of knowledge with a rationality core, and is therefore subject to review; (5) assertions about language become "founded on the structure of a field of knowledge at a given moment [and] there is no need to be stable." Finally the fact that Linguistics is given the task of the study of language has detached the latter from its dynamic and complex context, transforming it into an invention that is not necessarily stable. With these premises, the AI must be more attentive to the axiological aspect of language and not only to its logical aspect (which is a characteristic of language as a convention).

The comprehensive concept of language (natural language) in the natural sciences encompasses the concept of language as a convention given by linguists in the social sciences, which considers language in and of itself. What does AI need to understand by "language"? It is necessary to conceive it as a whole phenomenon, uniting mind and body, as a dynamic and complex process that stems from social (collective) reality and that imposes itself on all individuals. The conventional language is opposed to speech in the Saussure's (1916) language conception. Natural language, however, takes speech into account, since the first consists of a system where everything is supported (Auroux, 2017, p. 177). The elements of the natural language (described in Chapter 8) must be considered as coexisting, forming a synchrony.

Saussure (1916) restricts (conventional) language under the binary conception of sign (signifier and signified). But the same Saussure (1916) affirms that the language is a set of differences and oppositions, it is form and not substance, in a way that the signs, by themselves, mean nothing. There is only sense marked by the deviation of meaning between one sign and the other, by the differences between them (Saussure, 1916). It is this characteristic that highlights the axiomatic feature of natural language, which interferes with the transformation and creation of the senses. Saussure (1916) argues that the distinction between sense and reference rests with the science of Semiology that the object never coincides with the signification, and this makes the conception of the sign (uniting signifier and signified) not univocal and stable (Auroux, 2017, p. 194). This discussion matters to AI, since, when designing machine learning, it must consider the sign's relative instability (given by conventional language). Therefore, AI must also consider the axiomatic aspect of natural language, which contributes to the understanding of language as a whole, subject to the formation of "value" resulting from the social context, which, in turn, will interfere with the constitution of meaning.

> [...] Saussure is a great scientist and author of multiple innovations, among which, some are of great invention. If it were necessary to evaluate them, I would undoubtedly choose to put the 'value' in the foreground, especially because the rest may well be deducted [...]. That this invention appears in a nucleus of rationality present in a very long series, not only sheds light on the normal process of the evolution of knowledge, but, above all, makes Saussure's surprising theoretical strength a difference in the very reality of the element [language].
>
> **(Auroux, 2017, p. 195).**

9.4 Formal sciences

There is considerable diversity among the views of the underlying mechanisms of language, with several fundamental assumptions about what counts as a cognitive process in each of the branches of Science and even in the field of the same science. Despite this variety, we can find a consensus on the fact that language is particularly complex and has a regularity (syntactic restrictions, semantic, and pragmatic objectives) (Jakobson, 1963, 1965, 1990, 2010; Saussure, 1916). In addition, it can be modeled as a dynamic system (Elman, 1995; Thelen, 1988), that is, its structure allows the rules (understood as the logical character of language that provides predictability in the formation of meaning) (Whorf, 1942; Monte-Serrat, 2017) to be incorporated into a system dynamics (that we assume to be its axiomatic feature taking into account human neurophysiology), which, for Elman (1995, p. 196) would allow the "movement from certain regions to others and hinder other transitions."

The "rules," referring to the structural organization of language, can be described in various ways within Formal Science. They can assume, for instance, the tree format to describe the "repository of facts about individual words and a set of rules that restrict the way these words can be combined to form sentences" (Elman, 1995, p. 197). Therefore these sentences, subject to grammatical rules (logic feature), can be built into higher-level structures or broken down into processes in the same way as branches along dimensions that reflect syntactic, orthographic, or phonological properties (op. cit., pp. 197–198). These language rules can take the form of Deep Learning or its subset, the Convolutional Neural Network (CNN) used to compare algorithms. Currently, preference has been given to CNNs because they are an integral technique measuring functions that overlap while they interact with more accuracy. Language rules can also be used to build or interpret corporeality in space in Formal Science. This is a resource commonly explored in Architecture to define shapes and space. The space built in three dimensions presents form and meaning from the sequential role that they have in the appropriation of that space: "we are led to interpret the purpose of space through its shape" (Eloy, 2012, p. 3). The discipline of Architecture uses spatial syntax as tool, which studies space through its abstract properties of a topological nature (in terms of its connections and not of its geometric properties); and shape grammar, which studies the geometry of the shapes that make up a given language (Eloy, 2012, p. 4). Also, in Architecture, as a formal science, we find the structure of universal language: Axiomatic, which comes from the relationship between spaces; and logic, which comes from the geometry rules of the shapes.

Formal sciences work with symbols. They describe natural language because the latter carries a complex symbolization process in its structure. What is most sought after in AI are ways of representing resource extraction in symbols. For this, it is necessary to understand "how" natural language captures the context in the formation of meaning.

We leave as suggestions (by way of example, knowing that we are not exhausting the possibilities of representing the natural language) in the

Section 9.4.1 some characteristics outlined by the theory of fractals that meet the following particularities of the axiomatic-logical feature of natural language: Complexity; periodicity/regularity; dynamic system modeling; movement from certain regions to others and hinder other transitions; structural organization in tree format; changes in dimension without losing characteristics; overlapping functions while the elements interact with more accuracy; showing or interpreting corporeality in space; encompassing spatial syntax in terms of its connections and not of its geometric properties.

9.4.1 New frontiers for the natural code of the brain

This topic is designed to place bets that broaden approaches to natural language as a dynamic system that goes from stimulus input to action, passed through a high-performance cognitive center. It remains a mystery "how" the input stimuli become mental information that gives rise to an output.

For this operation, a common element would be necessary, the existence of which would be proven both outside the human body and inside it, so that it serves as a "path" for the circulation of stimuli until they reach the central system of the human brain. Based on Mandelbrot's (1983) fractal theory, in which he conceptualizes theoretical fractional dimensions of the geometric patterns of nature, we bet on the fractal nature of natural language.

Mathematically speaking, the fractal involves enlarging or reducing its dimension while maintaining self-similarity, that is, it exhibits the same patterns in its unfolding (Fractal Foundation, 2011). An example of this process is replication in the same way at different scales (Menger sponge). This structure is interesting to bet on a fractal structure of language in which there may be an increase in the interaction (input) decreasing the volume until the information reaches the central cognitive system. Thus natural language, through its axiomatic and logical aspects, can interpret impressions and stimuli to which the body is exposed. This process would correspond to what Perlovsky and Kozma (2007, p. 83) describes as dynamic logic in a convergent process for maximum similarity.

The need for neuroscience to work with a single deep learning algorithm to solve many different tasks (Goodfellow et al., 2016, p. 15) leads to seeking a structure that does not rely on separate entities, but, on the contrary, works with a unitary phenomenon. Natural language, as described in Chapter 8, is synchronous and evolves into a confluent reality. The vibratory activity of speech is part of the linguistic phenomenon and cannot be neglected when trying to configure the language mathematically. In this case the characteristic of periodicity prevails (Jenny, 2001, p. 121) to establish configurations and patterns organized in several categories, transforming them into one and the same entity. This property of natural language also fits the fractal structure, which exhibits the characteristic of periodicity (Fractal Foundation, 2011; Delaney, 2017).

> *Since the various aspects of these phenomena are due to vibration, we are confronted with a spectrum which reveals patterned, figurate formations at one pole and kinetic-dynamic processes at the other, the whole being generated and sustained by its essential periodicity.*
>
> *[...]*
>
> *If we wish to describe this single entity, we can say this: There are always figurate and patterned elements in a vibrational process and a vibrational effect, but there are also kinetic and dynamic elements; the whole is of a periodic nature and it is this periodicity which generates and sustains everything. The three fields — the periodic as the fundamental field with the two poles of figure and dynamics — invariably appear as one. They are inconceivable without each other. It is quite out of the question to take away the one or the other; nothing can be abstracted without the whole ceasing to exist. We cannot therefore number them one, two, three, but can only say they are threefold in appearance and yet unitary; that they appear as one and yet are threefold.*
>
> ***(Jenny, 2001, p. 121).***

9.4.2 Understanding natural language as a threefold phenomenon

How to deal with language as an unfolding phenomenon? It involves morphology and dynamics giving occasion to forms, movements through its rhythmic, serial, and vibrational character. Morphology and language dynamics exist together in a unit verified in researches cited in Chapter 8. Therefore it is possible to speak of a universal algorithm as a generator of the natural language phenomenon, and not take it as a preconceived conceptual form.

The study of natural language as metamorphosis and variation, in our opinion, is possible through the theory of fractals, which accommodate real and virtual phenomena observed in simultaneous oscillation: on the one hand, a flexible and constantly changing structure can be found and, on the other hand, a stable and finite structure.

Several studies are offered equally convincing evidence in favor of one or another aspect of language. Accepting it as a phenomenon in constant transition is not comfortable due to the difficulty of describing something fluid, in a flux of constant change. We intend, in this chapter, to offer good foundations about what is really involved in the concept of natural language, mathematically speaking, to point out ways for new discoveries in AI.

The special arrangement of the axiomatic and logical aspects of language, that is, its semirigid structure, is the reason for the special position that periodicity occupies. The change in structure, to flexible or rigid, becomes more understandable when we accept natural language as a unified structure that suffers interference from values resulting from vibrations or pulsations, which will distort the structure, giving rise to new formations of meaning. This disturbance can be small, without interfering in the rigidity of the structure, or it can be turbulent, causing mutations of meaning. This is what we seek to explain mathematically in the following topics.

9.4.2.1 Relations and functions having different meaning mathematically and different roles in language

We resume what we said (Chapter 3) about the mechanism of language symbolization. This mechanism carries different operators designed to help the brain translate aspects of the physical world into information intelligible to the biological body. To explain this operation, we adapted Abrahan Moles' (1978) theory of information (see Section 3.6.4).

A mathematical possibility to explain language "translation of information" phenomenon would be in terms of "relations" and "functions," whose meanings are different. A simple explanation of this difference between them would be: Take an ordered pair represented as input and output. "Relationship" shows the liaison between input and output; while "function" shows a relationship that derives from an output for each input provided. It can be said that all functions are relationships, but not all relationships are functions (Fig. 17).

Function is a relationship that describes that there must be only one output for each entry. In the set of ordered pairs, function follows the rule that every value "x" must be associated with only one value "y." Our bet to describe the transmission of information under the axiomatic aspect of

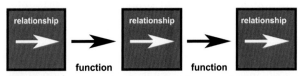

Fig. 17 The difference between relationship and function: "relationship" is the liaison between input and output, while "function" shows a link that derives from an output for each input provided.

language is that this transmission occurs through different functions, such as: Functions are intended to indicate constancy (Constant Function), identity (Identity Function); linearity (Linear Function); absolute value (Absolute Value Function); or inverse relation (Inverse Functions). In terms of relations, functions are classified into the following types:

One-to-one function or Injective function: A function $f: P \rightarrow Q$ is said to be One-to-One if for each element of P there is a distinct element of Q.

Many-to-one function: A function which maps two or more elements of P to the same element of set Q.

Onto Function or Surjective function: A function for which every element of set Q there is preimage in set P.

One-one and Onto function or Bijective function: The function f matches with each element of P with a discrete element of Q and every element of Q has a preimage in P.

Relation, in turn, is the subset of the Cartesian product, or simply, a bunch of points (ordered pairs). This aspect of the link for the transmission of information, in our opinion, is appropriate to the logical character of natural language. The relationships can be represented through sets, tables, XY-axis or through mapping diagram (Fig. 18).

The relations can be classified in: Empty relations; universal relations; identity relations; inverse relations; reflexive relations; symmetric relations; and transitive relations.

The axiomatic and logical aspects of language can be represented, respectively, by function and relation. The construction of meaning obeys processes that will establish either a random value, or a fixed value in the discursive chain. The reader can refer Chapter 3, in which the axes of language are discussed. Because it is a dynamic system, the natural language encompasses both the function (between one output and the next input) and the relation (between an input and output). In the Section 9.4.2.2, we explain that a transition between function and relation is possible, when the brain "translates" stimuli (axiomatic aspect) and places them into the logical chain, giving the meaning the quality of "fixed" in the discursive chain. We understand this transition possible under the assumption that natural language harbors fractal nature.

Mathematically speaking, the language exhibits the "discrete" and the "continuous" model. Function is a physical phenomenon (whose values vary in a certain interval) that depends on another physical phenomenon that also varies in another interval (continuous model). For example, let think about the meaning of a word within the discursive chain. Its value would

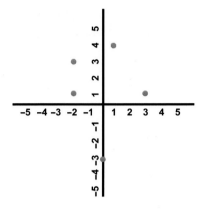

Relation in graphic

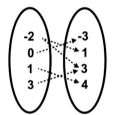

Relation in mapping diagram

x	y
-2	1
-2	3
0	-3
1	4
3	1

Relation in table

Fig. 18 Ways to represent the relationship mathematically.

correspond to several words within a spectrum, with some having a more distant value and others closer depending on the variables of the context in which it was stated. On the other hand, the value can be assessed according to fixed rules, as, for example, by dictionaries, which fix the meaning by assuming in advance a hypothetical situation, regardless of the context in which the word was uttered. In the latter case, we have a discrete model of possibilities for finding different meaning values. If, instead, we evaluate the context on an ongoing basis (context), we will have a corresponding meaning for each situation, updating the value found according to the context of the statement (continuous model).

9.4.2.2 The natural language related to fractal theory

Cognition or intelligence involves perception of the world and how the individual symbolizes and reacts to it. The understanding of the world is based on the axiomatic-logical structure of language, which, in turn, depends on interconnected cortex layers through a dense dynamic system formed by several specialized subsystems (such as the auditory, visual, olfactory, palatable and tactile that detect incoming signals, which follow a path toward the word outside) (see Chapter 8). Natural intelligence and natural language are treated as a multidisciplinary function that forms a unified whole (see Chapter 7). The natural language based on cognitive neuroscience exhibits the qualities of this unified whole, as there is synchrony between brain and body, tracing the path that takes the physical world to neurons and cells.

The brain's natural code, which makes the path between the physical world and neurons possible, is explored through language and its related mental representations. This code is considered by us as a central mechanism, with its principles of operation and periodicity. It cannot be interpreted just as a series of rules of syntax and grammar. There is much more to language than a simple mathematical modality of a set of concepts and tools used to model our inner life mechanisms. Certain mathematical concepts help to describe some of the language characteristics, but we must be aware that there is a synchronization process changing over time. This synchronization leads us to explore language as a dynamic system related to time (periodicity). All these reflections guide us to future investigations about what fractal systems would represent for natural language, making natural intelligence a perfectly determined structural reality that continually improves over time.

We suggest some characteristics of fractals that could be used to mathematically represent natural language, showing the "path" that takes the information from the external stimulus to the central cognitive system.

Fractals are mathematical concept for the study of continuous and non-differentiable functions, that is, they represent dimensions theoretical fractionals that describe geometric patterns of nature or processes over time. Fractals are shapes similar to the whole with varying degrees of self-similarity that can be found in images, structures and sounds, in nature, in technology, art, architecture, and others. Anyway, they are complex shapes that repeat

$$Z_{n+1} = z_n^2 + c$$

Fig. 19 Iteration repeating a simple process—inspired by Mandelbrot (1983). The new value of the variable Z is equal to the old value of Z, squared, plus a constant C.

details on different scales through the repetition of a simple process over and over.

1. Through this brief introduction to the fractals, we can connect them to the elements developed in Chapter 7 on periodicity in language. Jenny (2001, p. 103) states that periodicity is inherent to the nature of language, whether in rhythm, in form, in movement. Periodicity is also found in nature and in society. The recursive property of fractals, repeating processes with degrees of self-similarity, is important to think "how" language can transport fractal information from the external environment to the central cognitive system without modifying it. If fractal forms can be found outside and inside the human body, they can be the "bridge" to transmit stimuli to the cognitive system, where they are transformed into information. Some mathematical properties help to explain how this process occurs. Although there is an infinite diversity of fractal shapes and patterns, they are governed by universal rules. Among these rules we cite, by way of example, some that can shed light on the complex behavior of natural language (Fractal Foundation, 2011) (Fig. 19):

   1. Iterated Function Systems (IFS): Geometric fractals feature a repeated replacement process in which each iteration continues to repeat with twice as many copies of the original generator.
   2. Lindenmayer Systems (L-Systems): It is a simple language with iterative power to create plant structures. The initial condition is a straight vertical line (axiom "f") to which a rule is applied to form two new branches ($f=f [+f]\cdot[-f]$), one tilted to the right and one to the left. Then this rule is applied recursively creating the next iteration, and so on, creating the tree iterations.
   3. The Spiraling Rule: The spiraling rule is universal and is designed to explore the main valley that divides the "head" and "body" of the Mandelbrot set.
   4. The Branching Rule: It is the bifurcation property of fractals in which the symmetry folds from 2 to 4 arms to 8 to 16 arms, etc.
   5. Periodicity: It can increase by two for each element in the progression or, clockwise, a sequence of periodicities can be found.

6. Iteration: It is a characteristic of fractals that infinitely complex patterns can be created by repeating a simple process as, for example, in the repeated branches of a tree.

7. Complex Numbers: In the iteration, the destination of the starting points can be very different: The output of the equation can grow to infinity, it can shrink to a fixed value, or it can alternate steadily between two or more fixed values (Fractal Foundation, 2011). These fractal characteristics are adaptable to the axiomatic (variable values) and logic (fixed values) characteristics of natural language. They can be presented in a plane corresponding to an iterated equation in two-dimensions: Complex plane, with real x axis and imaginary y axis. A complex number combines a real and an imaginary number. If the iteration occurs within what would be the set of finite rules (fixed rules), the orbit converges to a finite value. If the iteration, on the other hand, happens outside the edge of the Mandelbrot set (variable rules), the orbits will diverge and spiral to infinity.

Fractals have sensitivity within the system, so that sudden and radical changes in the diagram, no matter how close the points may be, the orbits can have radically different results. This type of behavior demonstrates sensitivity to the initial conditions, which is a characteristic key in dynamic systems, based on fractals.

8. Iteration Artifacts: If a finite number of iterations are used, the resulting elements can consist of approximations of the object. There are sets that can serve as "Attraction Basins" ("Julia Virtual Sets" incorporated in the Mandelbrot set), changing the exponents and disturbing the initial value of Z and C. This iteration can very well be used in the articulation between axiomatic features and logic of natural language, interfering with the values that will constitute the senses. The set of C values generates connected Julia sets. Any initial C value inside the Mandelbrot Set creates a connected Julia Sets, any C value outside the Mandelbrot Set creates disconnected Julia Sets.

The Julia set is self-similar across all scales, while the Mandelbrot gains complexity as the scales change. In this case, we could establish a relationship between Julia sets with the logical aspect of language (which is based on fixed values); and Mandelbrot set could be related to the axiomatic aspect of language (based on variable values and gaining complexity). Both interact, as the Julia sets can be found incorporated into the Mandelbrot set, in the form of Julia's virtual sets. This aspect is intriguing, as it resembles the real (Mandelbrot set) and virtual (Julia set) characteristics of natural language.

Natural language also features tender spots "close to the edge" between Mandelbrot set and Julia set. As the constitution of meaning approaches the edge, the virtual part (Julia set) begins to look like the real part (Mandelbrot set). Elements of the Mandelbrot (1983) (infinite) set can also be found that will never appear in the Julia (finite) sets. These similarities in behavior with language should be further investigated, as it turns out that the meaning constituted by the fixed rules of language is ideal and, at any time, may be different (Pêcheux, 1975), as, for example, in the witz, in the joke, in the poetry.

9. Basins of Attraction: Julia sets are based on the identical equation to the Mandelbrot set, with the difference that, instead of examining the fate of all initial C values (as done in the Mandelbrot set), only one value is chosen for C and we see what happens with the different Z values. For the Julia connected sets (within the Mandelbrot set), all the initial Z values will remain finite. Julia Set in this case works as a "Basin of Attraction" because the value of Z is attracted to a stable and finite orbit.

   Julia virtual sets incorporated in the Mandelbrot set generate strange phenomena, since being virtual, it resembles a real Julia Set from the corresponding point in the entire Mandelbrot Set. However, Julia set is only assembled from parts of the Mandelbrot set arranged in the form of a Julia set. This phenomenon can be found in writing, which is set up to reproduce speech, but it is only organized as if it were a speech, and in fact it is virtual, just looking like the real speech.

10. Perturbation: The change in the normal functioning of a system reveals characteristics of that same functioning. A pendulum whose balance is disturbed will return to its original position. If it is in a state of instability, the disturbance will bring it down. Changes in the Mandelbrot set can result in large differences, breaking up, for example, in small disconnected islands, preserving or not the initial symmetry.

11. Universality: The same iconic form of the infinitely complex Mandelbrot set is found in the patterns created by many other mathematical equations. This is the phenomenon of Mandelbrot's universality.

12. Chaos: In mathematics chaos is exciting. Fractals reflect the chaos theory as they present a transition between order and disorder. From this perspective, we can say that the natural language system is chaotic, because, under the conditions of conventional language (subject to rules), language behaves in a predictable way, but when least expected, this

behavior becomes unpredictable, irregular (when there is the unexpected of language, according to Pêcheux, 1975). And, after a few iterations, it can converge to stability/predictability again.

Chaos theory approaches dynamic systems with caution because although it recognizes stability, it admits that small changes in the system can lead to unpredictable results.

13. The Butterfly effect in fractal theory is related to the curse of dimensionality. The origin of the difference ends up being taken as a rounding error. Such a small difference would appear to be insignificant, but instead of disappearing, the error in going from iteration to iteration leads to a result that is totally different from the original answer. This phenomenon is called Sensitivity to Initial Conditions and appears near the edge of the Mandelbrot Set (see item 7 of this list). Any error in measuring initial conditions will be amplified through the iterations.

9.5 Conclusion

The common basis for the functioning of the cognitive system has access to various information and, at the same time, integrates information that supposedly makes sense "outside" that set. It is important to know this mechanism of the cognitive system in relation to the scientific branches to replicate it in the machine, so that the latter learns "how" to obtain data: If we present to it a finite set of examples within the context of a science, it will capture the path of reasoning (semantics and intentionality). Information, resulting from the universal language algorithm, be it natural or artificial language, leads us to believe that "consciousness" or decision-making arises from the execution of this algorithm. Better explaining: Decision-making depends less on the elements that make up the language and depends more on "how" these elements are combined, within a specific context, at the time of execution (output) (Monte-Serrat, 2020). This factor of contextualizing the output reduces misunderstandings in well-defined areas of interest, as are the cases listed in this chapter in each of the scientific branches.

References

Arrivé, M., 2000. Lacan Gramático. In: Ágora. vol. III, pp. 9–40. n. 2, jul/dez.

Auroux, S., 2017. Que peut dire un historien des sciences sur Saussure? Université Paris Diderot, Paris. Paris 7 et Centre National de la Recherche, CNRS. *In* Entremeios: Revista de Estudos do Discurso. Brasil. v. 15, jul-dez.

Chomsky, N., 2001. Le langage et la pensée. Coll. Petite Bibliothèque Payot. Payot-Rivages, Paris.

Cornu, G., 2005. Linguistique juridique. Monschrestien L.G.D.J, Paris.

Courtine, J., 2016. Definição de orientações teóricas e construção de procedimentos em Análise do Discurso. In: Souza, F., Silva, M. (Eds.), Policromias, Junho 2016, pp. 14–35. Ano 1.

Delaney, T., 2017. Mandelbrot set: periodicity of secondary and subsequent bulbs as multiples of their parent bulbs. In: Mathematics Stack Exchange. 2017-07-15. Retrieved from https://math.stackexchange.com/q/2346867. (Accessed 14 August 2020).

Elman, J., 1995. Language as a dynamical system. In: Port, R., van Gelder, T. (Eds.), Mind as Motion: Explorations in the Dynamics Cognition. Massachusetts Institute of Technology, Cambridge, MA.

Eloy, S., 2012. Ferramentas de apoio à análise da geometria do espaço arquitetónico: Sintaxe especial e gramáticas de forma. In: Boletim da Aproged. vol. 29. Viana, V., Porto, pp. 3–14. Portugal.

Fractal Foundation, 2011. Fractals: Math, Science, Art, and Sketchpad. Fractal Foundation, Albuquerque. November 2011. Retrieved from https://fractalfoundation.org/OFC/OFC-1-0.html. (Accessed 28 June 2020).

Frege, G., 1892. Uber Sinn und Bedeutung. Zeitschrift für Philosophie und philosophische kritik 100, 20–25.

Goldschmidt, W., 1959. Boas' view of grammatical meaning (org.). In: Goldschmidt, W. (Ed.), The Anthropology of Franz Boas. American Anthropologist. v. 61, n. 5, part 2, October 1959.

Goodfellow, I., Bengio, Y., Courville, A., 2016. Deep Learning. MIT Press, Cambridge, MA.

Haroche, C., 1992. Fazer dizer, querer dizer. São Paulo, Hucitec.

Jakobson, R., 1963. Essais de linguistique générale. Les Éditions de Minuit, Paris.

Jakobson, R., 1965. À la recherche de l'essence du langage. In: Diogène. vol. 51. Gallimard, Paris.

Jakobson, R., 1990. Two aspects of language and two types of aphasic disturbances. In: Language. 1990. Harvard University Press, Cambridge, pp. 115–133.

Jakobson, R., 2010. Linguística e Comunicação. Bliknstein, I. e Paes, J. (trad.), Ed. Cultrix, São Paulo.

Jenny, H., 2001. Cymatics: A Study of Wave Phenomena and Vibration. Compilation of V. 1, 1967, the Structure and Dynamics of Waves and Vibrations; and v. 2, 1974, Wave Phenomena, Vibrational Effects and Harmonic Oscillations with their Structure, Kinetics and Dynamics. Volk, J. (Org.). Newmarket, New Hampshire, USA. Revised Edition (1967; 1974).

Kenshur, O., 1996. Doubt, certainty, faith and ideology. In: Gross, P., Levitt, N., Lewis, M. (Eds.), The Flight from Science and Reason. Annals of the New York Academy of Sciences.

Kozma, R., 2007. Neurodynamics of intentional behavior generation. In: Perlovsky, L., Kozma, R. (Eds.), Neurodynamics of Cognition and Consciousness. Springer-Verlag, Berlin, Heidelberg.

Levine, R., 2006. Geography of Time. Oneworld, Oxford.

Mandelbrot, B., 1983. The Fractal Geometry of Nature. Macmillan.

Moles, A., 1978. Théorie de l'information et perceptionesthétique. Flamarion, Paris. Portuguese version Cunha, H. (transl.). Rio de Janeiro: Ed Tempo Brasileiro Ltda.

Monte-Serrat, D., 2013. Literacy and Juridical Discourse, USP-RP 2013. Thesis guided by Tfouni, L. Retrieved from http://www.teses.usp.br/teses/disponiveis/59/59137/tde-14032013-104350. (Accessed 28 July 2020).

Monte-Serrat, D., 2014. A questão do sujeito: Perspectivas da análise do discurso, do letramento e da psicanálise lacaniana. Ed. Pedro e João, São Carlos.

Monte-Serrat, D., 2017. Neurolinguistics, language, and time: Investigating the verbal art in its amplitude. Int. J. Perceptions Public Health 1 (3).

Monte-Serrat, D., 2020. Post-Doctoral Research on Linguistic Theoretical Frameworks for Dealing with Semantic Treebanks in the Context of Abstract Meaning Representation at Computing and Mathematics Department of Faculty of Philosophy, Sciences and Letters of Ribeirao Preto. University of Sao Paulo, FFCLRP-USP, Brazil. Supervisor Prof. Dr. Evandro Eduardo Seron Ruiz.

Monte-Serrat, D., Tfouni, L., 2012. Efeitos ideológicos da gramática do discurso do Direito (Org.). In: Silva, D. (Ed.), Revista Cadernos de Linguagem e Sociedade. Ed. Thesaurus UnB, Brasília, pp. 11–19. v. 13, 1. Mar 2012.

Nielsen, M., 2015. Neural Networks and Deep Learning. Determination Press.

Pêcheux, M., 1975. Les vérités de La Palice. Linguistique, sémantique, philosophie (Théorie). Maspero, Paris.

Pêcheux, M., 1988. Discourse: Structure or Event. Illinois University Press.

Perlovsky, L., Kozma, R. (Eds.), 2007. Neurodynamics of Cognition and Consciousness. Springer-Verlag, Berlin, Heidelberg.

Quinet, A., 2003. Le plus de regard: Destins de la pulsion scopique. Étude psychanalytique. Ed. du Champ lacanien, Paris.

Roudinesco, E., Plon, M., 2006. Dictionnaire de la psychanalyse. Fayard, Paris.

Saussure, F., 1916. In: Bally, C., Sechehaye, A. (Eds.), Cours de linguistique Générale, third ed. Payot, Paris.

Sundstrom, T., 2019. Mathematical Reasoning. Writing and Proof. Version 2.1. Grand Valley State University, California.

Thelen, E., 1988. Dynamical approaches to the development of behavior (orgs.). In: Kelso, J. A., Mandell, M., Shlesinger, M. (Eds.), Dynamic Patterns in Complex Systems. World Scientific, Singapore, pp. 348–369.

Turner, R., Ioannides, A., 2009. Brain, Music and Musicality: Inferences from Neuroimaging. Oxford University Press, New York.

Whorf, B., 1942. Language, mind, and reality. In: Theosophist. Madras, India. January and April.

CHAPTER TEN

The natural language for artificial intelligence

Science is more than a body of knowledge; it is a way of thinking.
(Carl Sagan, The Demon-Haunted World).

10.1 Introduction

We have been raising questions about natural and artificial languages. In this topic, we bring some practical examples of applying some suggestions already outlined. However, before addressing the main points to be observed by artificial intelligence (AI) to reproduce natural language, we make some reflections on the nature of the narrative, as those involve knowledge that needs to be told through the latter. How to translate "knowing" into "telling"? Understanding the characteristics of natural language to be transported to artificial language is not enough. We also need to be aware that the structure, by which meaning is built, needs to be "assimilable," molded to human experience. In short: There is a value in telling the knowledge (narrativity) so that it represents reality.

An example to argue about the difficulty offered by "telling something" is in the following sentences. The construction of meaning is not a simple matter. It involves guidance of another order that needs to be considered by the machine learning technician. In the following sequence,

In our direction we deliver what we promise

When we take power we will do the impossible so that
End privileged situations
We will in no way allow
Our children have insufficient training
We will fulfill our purposes even though
Didactic resources have been exhausted
We will exercise teaching until
Understand now that
We are the new direction

The Natural Language for Artificial Intelligence
https://doi.org/10.1016/B978-0-12-824118-9.00011-4

if we read those phrases following from the beginning to the end, we have the sense of ethical principles being defended. On the other hand, if we read them from the end to the starting phrase, we have a meaning opposite to moral principles. Although the phrases are the same, opposite ethical meanings are formed according to the direction given to the reading. This is just an example of linguistics to show that the formation of meaning is linked to the concept of value, which comes from another instance.

In the field of mathematics, we cite as an example Whitehead and Russell's (1910) work, "Principia Mathematica," that inspired contemporary formal theory. The authors propose the concept of axioms as something intended to be believed, or at least to be accepted as plausible hypotheses concerning the world. Their work (Whitehead and Russell, 1910) mentions a theory about symbols manipulation according to rules of grammar, introducing the notion of "truth-values" and the "assertion of truth." This work aimed to analyze the ideas and methods of mathematical logic and to minimize the use of axioms and rules of inference; to express mathematical propositions in symbolic logic; and to resolve paradoxes, which motivated "type theory" (which adopts grammatical restrictions in formulas). "Principia Mathematica" (Whitehead and Russell, 1910) makes it clear that there is a syntax of formalism, although the work does not accurately describe this syntax. We want to highlight with this quote is that mathematical interpretation is regulated by principles presented in terms of "truth values." There are impositions of notions of "truth" and "falsehood," removing the arbitrariness of symbols. In short, the "Principia Mathematica" (op. cit.) theory specifies "how" symbols behave based on grammar theory. It also assigns "values," providing a model for specifying the interpretation of what the formulas are saying, such as, for example, regulating the interpretation of equations by first determining calculating what is in parentheses and then calculating what is in brackets.

The crucial point of our discussion about those issues is that.

> *far from being a code among many that culture can use to endow the experience with meaning, the narrative is [...], a human universal, on the basis of which transcultural messages about the nature of a shared reality can be transmitted [...] the narrative constantly replaces the meaning of the pure and simple copy of the events reported.*
> **(White, 1991, p. 5).**

Narrative becomes a problem for AI when machine learning is to be shaped, to be given the form of real or fictional events. How can these events be shown to have formal consistency? It is necessary to pay attention to the fact that the narrative (as telling the knowledge about something) is mediated and arbitrated to represent the event; the character of narrativity "presupposes a notion of reality in which 'true' is identified with 'the real'" (White, 1991, p. 10). "Events must not only be recorded within the chronological framework of their original occurrence, but also narrated, that is, revealed as having a structure, an order of meaning, which they do not have as a mere sequence" (op. cit., p. 9).

To justify the crucial importance of "relationship" in the construction of meaning, we can think about the frustrating effects of the disturbance on the narrative. There is a need for a "structure of relationships by which the events, contained in the register, are invested with meanings as parts of an integrated whole" (White, 1991, p. 13).

AI is looking for completeness and continuity in an order of events. Adapting White's teaching (1991, p. 13, highlighted by the author) to the content of this chapter, we can say that the most intuitive and realistic expectation of natural language to be transferred to machine learning resides more in a "'substance' [that] operates before in the domain of memory than in the […] 'imaginary'."

White (1991, p. 14) makes it clear that there is something that interferes with the narrative, giving it an image of continuity, coherence, and meaning:

> Every narrative, no matter how 'complete' it may seem, is built on a series of events that could have been included but left out; this is true for both imaginary and realistic narratives. And this consideration allows us to ask what kind of notion of reality authorizes the construction of a narrative record of reality in which continuity, instead of discontinuity, governs the articulation of the discourse.

The regularity found in the speeches of the different disciplines is a notion constructed and invested with significance, so that the narrative of the respective contents acquires a certain order or form, as taught by Hegel (1956, p. 60, highlights given by the author):

> In our language the term 'History' unites the objective with the subjective side, and denotes quite as much the 'historia rerum gestarum', as the 'res gestae' themselves; on the other hand it comprehends not less what has 'happened', than the 'narration' of what has happened. This union of the two meanings we must regard as of a higher order than mere outward accident; we must suppose historical narrations to have appeared contemporaneously with historical deeds and events. It is an internal vital principle common to both that produces them synchronously.

We can infer from Hegel's clarification that there is a "subject of his own" that supplies the ability to make scientific records of the disciplines; rather, there is a "proper method" to make this record in such a way that the event lends itself to narrative representation. It is in this sense that the content of the scientific areas is presented not as an object of remembrance but is presented based on a specific method of producing discourse. The scientism of each branch of science comes with its own narrativity, there is a matter of legitimacy that cannot be ignored by AI when applied to the various disciplines.

The narrative given by the machine cannot take general instead of specific values as a principle. When it comes to branches of science, it is about legitimacy, authority over a specific content to be produced or interpreted. The more awareness the machine learning technician has, assuming that there is a system behind the formation of the senses, the more successful AI will have in representing reality. The development of the machine's intelligence has to do with the focus given to it by previous human action. The events to be narrated by the intelligence, whether real or imaginary, will acquire an identifying meaning with their scientific context, with their source. This meaning was nonexistent while these events constituted a mere sequence. Here lies the axiomatic-logical character of language, be it natural or artificial: The logical feature puts it in an intelligible sequence, but it is the axiomatic feature that works the context to establish values in the construction of meaning. It is in this sense that cognitive computing comes closer to human intuition: Instead of focusing on a unique set of technologies, it aggregates several such as machine learning, natural language processing, sight and human–computer interface. In our opinion, to get closer to human intuition, cognitive computing must absorb the contextual values of the branches of science (see Chapter 9).

The machine design technician must conduct his work in such a way that AI registers the ability to analyze events with the same type of "purpose," which must be implied in the sequence of machine learning. In this way the amount of information can be aggregated in sequences in an intuitive and meaningful way, resembling natural language. AI will, therefore, be successful in substituting one meaning for another, in such a way that the latter is organized into meaningful chains arranged according to a principle (legitimate for production and interpretation) by which "difference" is translated into similarity (taken as a topic common to all referents in a given scientific branch). This common topic, which serves as a reference, has a value that overlaps the narrative by functioning as a central principle that organizes meaning in a certain way. AI—after being molded with predictive learning methods within a discipline—will be able to reproduce a "realistic" (portraying reality) and "narrative" sense (legitimized in the discipline in which it is used, in the sense that it was added to it a discernment).

It is because there are differences between scientific fields that it is necessary to narrativize in a legitimate way. When AI registers data within a narrative "order," this brings authenticity to its narrative. Better said, in this way the machine, when recording data, does so in a "desirable" manner, in accordance with the formal coherence processes of the respective discipline; the machine records "within a narrative order," producing an expected meaning. The result of regularity, order and coherence that comes from this strategy results in less human mediation, presenting an aspect of completeness, in the demand for meaning, so desired by cognitive computing.

This brings us closer to the demand for intuitive meaning in which the machine evaluates events/data by their significance, filling in gaps to organize the narrative/interpretation according to the structure of the discipline in which the events/data are inserted. The machine becomes able to "read" the value of meaning as long as those events/data belong to an "order" of existence. The ambiguity and failure of AI occurs when this identification is not transmitted to the machine system, preventing it from attesting to reality with the expected property.

A given event or data, when interpreted by AI, will have that interpretation moved from one discipline to another. The tracking of this displacement is also narrativity/interpretation made by the machine. This brings more clarity to the issue of the value attributed to AI in relation to representations of reality: Science has transformed the act of interpreting or understanding into a paradigm in which reality presents itself. Scientism transformed the interpretation of the context into a preestablished value so that the discourse or narrative of a certain "real" event must point out its objectivity, its coherence and integrity already determined by the scientific branch, anticipating, in this way, its interpretation. Therein lies the success of AI in interpreting "properly."

To get the most out of from the knowledge of the natural language structure focusing on applying AI by discarding noisy activations to obtain maximum value, it is suggested to move toward a reduction in dimensionality of information. "The intelligence can be defined as 'the use of knowledge to restrict search'" (Beeson, 1988, p. 211). It is this intelligence that outlines the interaction between man and machine making it possible when we work on the very structure (simplest form) of language: Its axiomatic-logical structure. We recommend the following steps: (1) knowing the structure of natural language; (2) recognizing that a certain meaning and function come from a relationship; (3) applying the representation property of natural language in AI: Value is constituted by relations and differences; (4) knowing the fundamentals of the structure that best combines the elements of natural language to be put into practice in programming the machine learning, that is, to know the structure of the universal algorithm of natural language, well defined in steps or instructions.

10.2 Knowing the structure of natural language

Knowing the universal structure of natural language (seen in the previous chapters) is the fundamental step to develop AI making it more intuitive and less ambiguous. We have already described the two basic aspects of language that must be considered: Its axiomatic and logical features. Why should we learn about this? Because AI involves "intelligence," which means "how to organize." To know how we should organize the machine so that it reproduces or interprets natural language, we must know how the latter organizes itself and must try to replicate that in the machine. The universal structure of language basically houses two processes of meaning construction: One that is dependent on relations between elements, and another that is dependent on previously established rules (grammar rules). The existence of this universal structure constitutes the invariant element that allows recognizing variations in language (in any branch of science or in any kind of conventional language, that is, Italian, Russian, Portuguese, English, etc.), be it linear or spatial, arising from image, sound, or sign. There will be contextual situations that will primarily require axiomatic character, and other situations in which the logical character of language overlaps. Both operate together on dynamic systems. We consider that the two aspects—axiomatic and logical—have always been linked to the study of language because they are rooted in its structure.

10.3 Recognizing that a certain meaning and function come from a relationship

After understanding "how" natural language works, to use it in the construction of meaning or in the interpretation of data, it needs to be replicated. AI organizes this construction of meaning or analysis. For this, we propose another reflection: That the meaning does not come from the number of repetitions, but from "how" relationships happen to form it. That is what we explain in this topic. The "decomposition" of a sentence, image or space into simpler elements must consider the relationship existent between the analyzed elements. On the other hand, in the "construction" of meaning it is important to emphasize that each element will acquire a specific meaning and function according to the combination/relationship with other elements; it is their articulation that brings the specification, the meaning.

We learn this from Saussure (1916, p. 140). He (op. cit.) states that the characteristic of the linguistic institution is precisely to maintain the parallelism between the phonic elements and the psychic elements. If they are observed separately, they may have a negative value. As they are considered as a whole, they will generate a positive order that is expressed through a system of values in the neural connection. When both elements are confused, there is no more talk of difference: Value and unity start to correspond to a certain concept/meaning. According to Saussure (1916, p. 140): The characters of the unit are confused with the unit itself in a paradoxical character in which the unit is expressed in the opposition of terms—"Simple terms result from a set of relationships. Language is, so to speak, an algebra that would only have complex elements" (Saussure, 1916, p. 141).

The antagonistic structure that we propose between axiom and logic elements of the natural language corresponds to Saussure's (1916, p. 141) view on language, which "everywhere and always, that same balance of complex terms […] conditions each other […] To put this another way, language is a form and not a substance." The author (Saussure, 1916, p. 145) recognizes that there is no categorical limit between these two elements, and this is because both factors contribute—in proportions impossible to determine—to the production of meaning. This conflicting structure of language can be observed both in its micro perspective (that is described by Saussure), and in its macro perspective, under the interdisciplinary view (explored in Chapter 9). It can be deduced that the axiomatic-logical phenomenon of language is present in the language structure itself, whatever its dimension has been seen.

According to Ferdinand de Saussure (1916) language is conceived as a system of signs. The separation he (Saussure, 1916) proposes of the sign into signifier (sounds or speech marks) and signified (concept or idea behind the sign); and his idea of classifying "langue" (conventions that makes utterances understandable) separately from "parole" (individual utterances) can be extended to other signs than language. The author (Saussure, 1916, p. 132 and following) states that, the representation property of an idea is linked to the value of words. Value is one of the elements that make up meaning/signification. Signification, in turn, is the result of a relationship between signifier and signified:

> *Even outside the language, all values seem to be governed by this paradoxical principle. They are always constituted: 1- by a 'dissimilar' thing, susceptible of being 'exchanged' for something whose value remains to be determined; 2- by 'similar' things, which can be 'compared' to the thing whose value is at stake.*
>
> **(Saussure, 1916, p. 134, author highlight).**

In this section, we propose an extension of linguistic theory (Saussure, 1916; Chomsky, 2001; Pinker, 1994) in the sense that we remain with the logical perspective of language understood as a grammar which contains a finite system of rules that infinitely generates many properly related structures. To that perspective, we add the axiomatic character of language encompassing principles that relate (dynamically) those abstract logical structures to certain mental representations (neurophysiological phenomena) for the meaning formation. Our bet on the constitution of the senses in language is as follows: The exchange for something "different" (given by the neurophysiological system of the human body) resulting in the axiomatic way of constructing meaning; and the exchange for something "similar" (previously provided by grammatical rules/binary choice true or false), resulting in the logical way of constructing meaning. In the first case, instead of causing an inert choice between two values (binary choice), there is a movement. This movement is carried out by checking the sense through the axiological system, which moves away from the combinations anticipated by the logical system and presents possibilities of meaning (Monte-Serrat et al., 2017).

The logical-axiomatic structure of the language underlying the use of signs (whether numbers, images, letters, and movements) has the function of establishing relationships linking signifier and signified according to the principles and values of each scientific field. Values emanate from the system.

With regard to the logical aspect of language, one can take as a starting point what Saussure proposes in the sense that values correspond to concepts that they are purely differential, defined not positively by their content, but negatively by their relations with other terms of the system (Saussure, 1916, p. 136). In this case, the "value is constituted only by relations and differences with other terms of the language [...] what matters are the differences, because they are what lead to meaning" (Saussure, 1916, pp. 136–137).

When we relate the construction of meaning to the axiomatic structure of language, other aspects must be evaluated regarding the arbitrary and differential (Saussure, 1916, p. 137) qualities of language, harboring differentiation operations in which the value is questioned to construct meaning.

In this case, the values assumed as meaning cease to operate only by reciprocal opposition within a defined system (Saussure, 1916, p. 139), that is, not only does the logical aspect of language come into operation, but other means of producing the sense. In the latter case, the relation that gives rise to sense does not depend only on rules of abstract structures but also on axiomatic structures linked to certain mental representations of sound and meaning (sign = signifier + meaning) (Saussure, 1916, p. 133), which are constituted of elements that belong to the concept of language in its comprehensive concept (axiomatic-logical) we propose here. It does not matter if the idea is expressed in numbers or words: The "relationship" between them is more important for the formation of value (meaning).

10.4 Applying the representation property of natural language in AI: Value is constituted only by relations and differences

Representation property is the keyword for AI to build its learning algorithm to repeat patterns in new data, condensing the latter into an invariant. Natural language is the inspiring model for providing the universal algorithm that houses representation property aiming to generalize the execution of a set of factors of variation without leaning toward the "curse of dimensionality." This property found in cognitive computing moves away from simple distribution and closer to the ability to identify the data of interest, recognizing patterns, causal structures, and making correlations.

As explained in Chapters 4 and 5, the representation property can be applied to the form of deep learning (DL) whose several layers of neural network operate to reduce the information to simpler elements. It can also be applied to the convolutional neural network (CNN) used to compare algorithms and measure functions that overlap while interacting. Another application of representation property can help to interpret corporeality in three-dimensional space. The most important element of these applications is in "how" to make them. We emphasize that form and meaning are constructed from the sequential role they play, that is, the relationship between elements is what builds meaning. This gives to language a profound and timeless reality that goes beyond any special construction. If in the construction of meaning by the machine, or in the analysis of the data made by it, we are aware that the connections are more important than the properties of the evaluated elements, then we will be closer to the intuition of natural language. The axiomatic-logical structure of the latter provides relation operations that consider various factors shaping the context, associating them with logical rules, that is, placing them into a logical sequence that gives them meaning. If the base is only in the logical sequence, the analyzed elements would detach from the context, which would lead to ambiguity or noise in the algorithm.

Another example of representation property applied to AI is our conceptual suggestion for applying the abstract meaning representation (AMR) theory (Banarescu et al., 2013) in which, since the theoretical foundations of AMR have limitations in the semantic representation of the target for some language phenomena, failing to establish a universal quantifier. We suggest that the notion of meaning should have linguistic treatment considering the comprehensive concept of language that we propose: The axiomatic–logical structure. This universal structure of language allows guiding the conceptions related to AI in the sense of assisting the construction of a sembank in such a way that it is combined with the logical meaning of the entire sentence. That is, it is proposed that the meaning of the sembank is constructed "in relation to," so that principles could be established in the theory of AMR that could be extended to sembanks in other languages (since they are principles closely linked to the logical–universal axiomatic of language). In 2020, our proposal in an ongoing, research at the Department of Computing and Mathematics of Faculty of Philosophy, Sciences and Letters at Ribeirao Preto, University of Sao Paulo, supervised by Professor Dr. Evandro Eduardo Seron Ruiz, is that the sembank is based on a combinatorial rule present in the universal structure of language that is repeated indefinitely, providing a comprehensive database forming basic NLP resources. These suggestions may improve the accuracy of meaning formation and may facilitate statistical analysis, presenting a better result for the generation of natural language, the NLG. In this way, we believe that the construction of meaning becomes more contextualized and unambiguous.

From the observation of how CNNs work and how we propose the functioning of the AMR theory, we can conclude that not only must the construction of meaning be relational, but interpretation must also follow this technique. Therefore a quantitative analysis carries with it an error range, as it ignores the context (the relationships between the elements). This does not happen in qualitative analysis, because it is done "in relation to" the context. This is the lesson we can draw from the application of natural language to machine language.

Just as the value of any word is determined by the elements that surround it (Saussure, 1916, p. 135), DL models will bring more advantages in specific tasks if they design resources with a specific branch of Science in mind, in which they seek to discover the representation for a task. In this way, the learned representations will produce much better results.

Although the contribution of DL through its useful tools for processing large amounts of data and making useful predictions in scientific fields (Goodfellow et al., 2016; Nielsen, 2015), it is recommended that the element "value," combined with a corresponding relationship between systems, should be considered previously as incorporated in a mapping of multilayer perceptrons so that the neural layers are more densely connected (producing nonlinear inputs and outputs). DL is already recognized as crucial to technology by the size of the reference data sets. The DL algorithm, when considering the axiomatic-logical structure of language, would give greater density to the performance of neural relations, which would bring AI closer to the intuition of natural language.

10.4.1 Representation property application on convolutional neural networks

Convolution is successful in interpretation because it works with inputs of varying length and is based on three important aspects of machine learning: Sparse interactions, parameter sharing, and equivalence of representations. These three aspects contribute to reducing the ambiguity of information because it is formed "in relation to" a context.

Fig. 20 shows an example of a two-dimensional convolutional network core in which the first argument (function x, input, which corresponds to a multidimensional array of data) and the second argument (function w, kernel, which corresponds to a multidimensional array of parameters) are restricted to output only to positions where the kernel is entirely within the image, called "valid" convolution in some contexts. The *arrow boxes* indicate how the upper left element is formed in relation to the nucleus in the corresponding upper left region. In machine learning applications, the input of the first (multidimensional array of data) and the second (multidimensional array of parameters) is readjusted by a learning algorithm (Goodfellow et al., 2016, pp. 327–330). CNNs are a good example of effectively incorporating domain knowledge into the network architecture:

Natural images have many statistical properties that are 'invariant to translation'. For example, a photo of a cat remains a photo of a cat if it is translated one pixel to the right. 'CNNs take this property into account' by sharing parameters across multiple image locations. The same feature

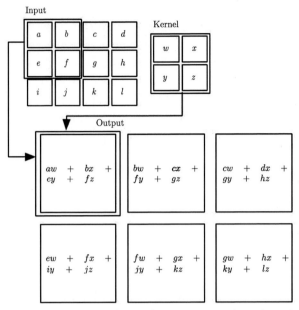

Fig. 20 Example of two-dimensional convolution. *Arrows* indicate how the element in the upper left corner is formed by the kernel match. *(Based on Chapter 9, Convolutional Networks. In Goodfellow, I., Bengio, Y., Courville, A., 2016. Deep Learning. MIT Press, Cambridge, MA, p. 334, with permission from Elsevier.)*

> *(a hidden unit with the same weights) is computed over different locations in the input. This means that we can find a cat with the same cat detector whether the cat appears at column i or column i + 1 [...].*
> *Parameter sharing has allowed CNNs to dramatically lower the number of unique model parameters and to significantly increase network sizes without requiring a corresponding increase in training data.*
>   **(Goodfellow et al., 2016, p. 254, our highlight).**

For graphical demonstration of sparse connectivity (Fig. 21 of convolutional network), it is observed that units in the deepest layers can indirectly interact with a larger portion of the entrance. This relationship allows the network to efficiently describe complicated interactions between many variables from simple blocks that describe only separate interactions.

The architecture design represented in Fig. 21 makes pairs of layers connect, without losing a pattern described initially. Each unit in an input layer connects to a subset of units in the output layer. This strategy gradually reduces the number of connections, while also reducing the number of parameters and the amount of computation.

Another example are the continuation methods which add strategies that facilitate optimization by choosing starting points that will guarantee

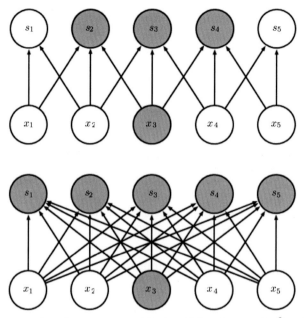

Fig. 21 Representation of sparse connectivity in which an input unit, x^3, and the output units in "s" are affected by this unit. In the case of "s" originating from the matrix multiplication, all outputs are affected by x^3. *(Based on Chapter 9, Convolutional Networks. In Goodfellow, I., Bengio, Y., Courville, A., 2016. Deep Learning. MIT Press, Cambridge, MA, p. 336, with permission from Elsevier.)*

well-behaved regions of space. These methods build a series of objective functions on the same parameters and have been successful (Goodfellow et al., 2016, p. 327; Mobahi and Fisher, 2015).

10.4.2 Representation property application on natural language inference

Inference in natural language (Natural Language Inference (NLI)) works with an asymmetric representation property recognizing the premise (P) and hypothesis (H). The paraphrase establishes equivalence between premise and hypothesis (hypothesis can start from the premise or premise can start from the hypothesis) (Pinheiro, 2010). The content justifies the list of concepts, and it is not necessary to make a formal calculation to determine the validity of the inferences.

In NLI the deduction is not formal, as the Hypothesis (H) is not necessarily inferred in a logically strict way from the Premise (P). According to

MacCartney (2008), we also have informal reasoning in NLI as we can see in the example that follows:

(P) Many airlines surveyed saw costs increase even after adjusting for inflation.

(H) Some survey companies reported rising costs.

In these phrases, there is informal reasoning because once the inference would be considered valid by an ordinary person, who would see the costs to increase, it does not necessarily imply "reporting" the cost increase. It is plausible that airlines companies have been silent about rising costs, for example.

NLI is taken as synonym of Recognizing Textual Entailment. The last one was implemented by Stanford University, in 2015, as a corpus with 570 thousand pairs of premises and notes in natural language elaborated by humans with three classes of implication (3-way) (Bowman et al., 2015). The corpus also contains syntactic trees with pairs of premises (P) and hypotheses (H). Each human annotator received a sentence set out in the description of an image and should write three others forming three annotated pairs, one with a list of implications, one with contradiction and another neutral. Each set of three annotated pairs was evaluated by five people. The pairs that obtained an agreement of the notes for a minimum number of three evaluators were incorporated into the corpus as the gold standard, the rest were discarded.

On the other hand, the recognition of the meaning in a text through computational processes is a challenging task due mainly to the ambiguity, informality, and knowledge of the implicit world found in natural language, making it difficult to create computational models for interpretation of linguistic expressions. Although faced with so many challenges posed by grammar (such as changing from active to passive voice; adjective removal; co-reference; knowledge of the world, which demands contextualization of time, place, kinship, etc.), it is possible to observe that a lexical similarity model has been successful. According to MacCartney (2008) the "bag-of-words" model reached an accuracy of 63%, which is a good assessment compared with other models with more sophisticated approaches. Even though this model is not perfect for reducing ambiguity, it takes an interesting approach that gathers indicators which can measure distance, number of synonyms/antonyms, number of words in common, chosen manually to represent P and H. This relationship is translated into a machine learning algorithm to obtain an implication relationship. A fundamental limitation of this approach is the need to manually define the attributes and not knowing how these definitions were established.

Our model focuses on giving this task to the machine, putting together the simplest and most fundamental relationships such as implication, contradiction, and compatibility, making the machine learn to apply them to words, sentences and texts, having the tree as a structure (from the branches to the trunk and from trunk to branches) so that (1) instead of Premise and Hypothesis, we have the connection between Antecedent and Consequent; (2) the shorter the trunk distance, the greater the similarity; and (3) lexical knowledge is described through a relationship between words that fits the tree structure.

Therefore, we seek to show the importance of finding and writing down basic values for the relationships between words or phrases to establish a model that can be used as a cross-validation standard. It is believed that this strategy helps to obtain greater precision regarding the adjustment of a particle to the interaction with other words of the sentence, for example, reducing ambiguity and noise in the meaning construction.

10.5 Suggestions for the universal language algorithm
10.5.1 Introduction

Before making a detailed description of the key elements of the universal natural language algorithm, we would like to make a few points to clarify the content of this topic.

The first one is alerting the reader to the concept of language to be used. If we work with the concept of conventional language with its norms, the algorithm will lead to ambiguity. To make AI reach human intuitiveness, we suggest the use of the comprehensive concept of natural language, which reveals the characteristic of synchrony connecting several interdependent subsystems and consists of a dynamic system exhibiting periodicity. In natural language, the signification process unites the formation of patterns so that the sum of the latter does not correspond to the final product.

An important element to be considered also is the way in which natural language organizes information taken from context to build meaning. This happens due to a dynamic process that unites logical reasoning with the body and the social context. This occurs to the fact that the mind is relational and works according to a functional hierarchy to build the process of understanding. Thus the criteria of "value" and "hierarchy" (relations) arising from the context interfere in the origin of the logical-axiomatic structure of language. Rhythm, form, and movement are also considered as elements of natural language that act in the construction of meaning, which leads us to bet on new research directions to include fractal theory in the description of the universal structure of natural language. The fractal structure is adapted to the axiomatic (tree) and logic (chain) characteristics of language.

Another important aspect to be taken into consideration is that AI seeks to replicate qualities of natural language to map the learning of AI representation. Since AI, because it is "intelligence," seeks the "way" that natural language constructs meaning, it is in search of a structure common to both. The existence of this structure, therefore, highlights exactly the point of overlap between AI and natural language.

We arrive, therefore, at a structured thread in the functioning of language that guarantees coherence between reality and truth: The axiomatic-logical structure, which gives language, be it natural or artificial, an ethereal characteristic.

This generic formula gives AI strategies on how resources should be used to perform specific tasks, as the information sought is provided "in relation to" a context. This universal algorithm has the advantage of generalizing the collection and execution of a set of more specific underlying factors, preventing the curse of dimensionality. Our universal model, therefore, specifies a generalized function (representational capacity of the model) in the universal algorithm, which will serve to be applied to specific cases. Finally, we provide an algorithmic core so that computational methods can generalize the execution of a set of factors.

10.5.2 Comments on the universal language algorithm

Natural language has several elements that interact with each other and, therefore, it can be described by a set of variables referring to each of its basic elements, which makes its study challenging.

The modeling of the systems that make up natural language in a broad sense, as conceived in this book, is constructed in such a way that the equation that represents the formation of meaning must correspond to the dynamics of all its elements. For this, we describe a sketch of the interaction between two basic elements in the formation of meaning—the one that represents the axiomatic step; and the one that represents the logical step. From this sketch, programmers are expected to decode this description and modify it in such a way that it is refined and appropriate to the program with which they are working.

This topic focuses only on the first step in the use of the model that we are proposing, conceiving it with the universality feature as it contains the essence of language in the construction of meaning, even before other complex elements have been added to the linguistic phenomenon (this more complex stage is not discussed here, as it is up to each researcher, in his specific area, the dedication to the language particular elements to carry out his studies to a successful conclusion).

We make it clear, then, that there is a hierarchy in the linguistic structure, although natural language does not establish limits for it. Ding et al. (2016) identified a neural hierarchy corresponding to time scales for speech processing, placing these scales as something underlying the basic structure of language (the authors identify grammar as a base, but our study points out that this base goes beyond grammar, covering the logical structure of language).

In "El Toro" (1945) Picasso developed a deconstruction process that we use here to illustrate how we arrived at the universal algorithm of language in a way that corresponds to something ethereal (Fig. 22).

Fig. 22 Picasso's "El toro" (1945) represents the process of deconstructing a bull's drawing until he reaches the simplest features, which identify the animal and excise the complex features. We use this work of art as a metaphor for the process of deconstructing language in this book until we reach its universal elements.

The language's universal algorithm is the result obtained after we "dissected" the concept of language throughout all the chapters of this book. We move back and forth, from finished to sketch in each chapter progressively, removing and simplifying some concepts related to natural language, until we reach this chapter, whose purpose is to close the essential elements of language, whether spoken, written, image, or symbol.

In the following paragraphs, we mention some language characteristics throughout the explanation of constructing the universal algorithm, aware that we do not cover all the elements related to the natural language due to its complexity. Our task is "erasing" some aspects to "highlight" those which we understand to be the essential "lines" that leave language outlined with regard to the meaning construction, reducing it, finally, to an algorithm description that maintains the qualities that really represent language. In comparative terms to Picasso's work, we closed the essential elements in a depiction that reduces language to the bull in line drawing. We removed the most complex areas of the language to leave the basic "lines" that characterize its fundamental elements, relations, and functions, reducing it to the simple "outline" of an algorithm delineation, carefully done through the development of each chapter of this book, capturing the essence universal use of natural language in an algorithm as concise as possible.

The language "installs" the meaning. Before language, there is no idea or meaning. In similar words, we can say that without the fundamental algorithm, there is no language. This algorithm establishes the intermediation of elements of different orders to compose the language in a meaningful way. The universal algorithm, therefore, brings together elements, placing them in relation, combining them in units that fix an idea to a certain thing or reality: It is a "form" that produces meaning and not a substance in itself (Saussure, 1916). The value that is established in the algorithmic relationship can be constituted: (1) or by a "dissimilar thing, susceptible of being exchanged for something whose value remains to be determined" (this operation is essentially axiomatic in the terms defined in this book); (2) or by "similar things that can be compared with the one whose value is at stake" (this operation is essentially logical in the terms defined in this book) (Saussure, 1916, p. 134).

Having made the above considerations, we proceed to describe the essential elements of the universal natural language algorithm with their respective relations.

The language universal algorithm is conceived as a universal structure of natural intelligence. It is therefore an abstraction, something ethereal that determines "how" natural language (in a broad sense) operates the complex biological systems (ranging from the entrance of the stimulus into the human body until the moment when it is "translated" or deciphered as such by individual) relating them to logical elements, to enter a chain of meaning (consisting of a latent structure of human cognition charged with operating the categorization of stimuli that reach it) (Lenneberg, 1967). This dynamic functioning of axiomatic and logical functions of the linguistic system carries sensory and conceptual representations (Dretske, 1995; Pitt, 2020), distinguishing experiences and thoughts.

Mathematical models of language structured in conventional language are easily found. The difference with our model is that we consider the complexities of natural language in a broad sense in the search for the elementary parameters that characterize it. In this way, our model adjusts nonlinear model (axiomatic aspect of language) to linear model (logical aspect of language). The first represents the influence of external factors and can be related to specific interactions. The description of the dynamics between the two models by means of an algorithm shows how much the nonlinear aspect influences the linear aspect of language, which can lead from coexistence to the cancellation of information (XOR).

XOR gate consists of a digital logic gate with two or more inputs and an output to perform the exclusive disjunction. The name is "gate OR exclusive" because only when one of the entries is true, the output will be true. If both entries are true, the output is false. Also, when both entries are false, the output to the XOR port will be false:

If input $A = 0$ and $B = 0$, output is 0
If input $A = 0$ and $B = 1$, output is 1
If input $A = 1$ and $B = 0$, output is 1
If input $A = 1$ and $B = 1$, output is 0

Our model unites the formation of patterns, so that the sum of the latter does not correspond to the final product. In this demonstration, we are working with opposite ends to make the result more evident according to the "information" results table, showing that there is only "value" under the conditions in which there is an XOR (and/or) relationship between the two models this way:

0–0 (There is a logical chain but there is no information, better saying, there is no context to match the construction of meaning—for example, Chomsky's (1957) "Colorless green ideas sleep furiously").

0–1 (There is information based on probability, prioritizing the logical aspect as the only way to reach the information, disregarding the context brought by the axiomatic aspect).

1–0 (There is information, but this stands out from the value previously given by the logical aspect, installing the subjective perspective in the construction of information arising from the axiomatic aspect).

1–1 (There is no information because there is no logical chain—Lacan (1970) associates the unconscious with a different structure from logical reasoning; the negative interest in the latter gives access to the functioning of the former's structure) (Arrivé, 2000, pp. 9–10).

The relationship defined by the XOR gate is adequate to the fact that the axiomatic and logical characteristics of language are inconceivable separately from each other. If the axiomatic trait is abstracted, all natural language ceases to exist and gives way to conventional language, which is nothing more than a set of rules, an idealization of what language "should" be, which leads to the replication of a "frozen" or decontextualized meaning (that we call here the absence of information as it is built by natural language) which often leads to ambiguity. If the logical feature is ignored, there may be a chain, but the meaning is not constructed.

The XOR logic operation used to arrive at the "true logical value" which we call "information" explains the relationship between the axiomatic and logical characteristics of natural language. Between the input of the stimulus in the human body and the output in the form of action/decision-making, this operation is located. The axiomatic aspect does not stand out from the logical aspect, on the contrary, the "process" of sense formation needs both to form a "value" (information) that houses an image/sound/sensation evaluated semantically, relating the content of thought to a perceptive experience. Natural intelligence establishes an unsuspected unity between phenomena that we observe separately (Gaufey, 1998, p. 17), articulating the three registers (reality, the symbolic, and the imaginary) (Quinet, 2003) when inscribing together awareness and meaning.

According to Moles (1978, p. 98), what marks the intelligibility of a message is the predictability of the rules that contribute to defining a repertoire. In the case of written language, it would be the predictability brought by grammatical rules; in the case of fMRI, these would be the interpretability rules for the signals captured. There is an "order" in the development of the message that extrapolates the temporal or spatial series of the message itself, printing a prediction, a degree of coherence, a rate of regularity, which makes a statistical "link" between the past and the future, between the what happened in the axiomatic scope of natural language and what will happen in time. It is this correlation that establishes meaning, that gives "value," and this is not restricted to signs.

The essence of the universal language algorithm is in the relationship between the axiomatic feature and the logical feature, since the natural language is dynamic and its factors change all the time. It is in this way that language is linked to the concept of "value," that is, to a "system of equivalence between different things and orders" that "determines nothing outside the momentary state of its terms" (Saussure, 1916, pp. 95–96).

It is within this axiomatic-logical relationship that the dynamic system of natural language becomes able to replace one element with another with an equivalent value within the symbolization process, balancing both elements according to certain rules, causing the identity of the thing to be confused with value and vice versa (Saussure, 1916, p. 128).

To counteract this function of natural language, we remember that Chomsky's theory (1957) idealizes language only in its logical aspect, attributing to the human being the idealized competence to produce and understand sentences. This theoretical attitude neglects specific actions of natural language, reducing it to an infinite set of phrases, in which creativity would be governed by rules. The relational structure of natural language, in turn, is described in the works of Foucault (1963, 1966, 1969, 1971) and Pêcheux (1975, 1988) because they consider the context.

We can affirm, then, that not only do the rules confer identity, but also the other element of the XOR relationship produces value effectively: The axiomatic aspect of natural language serves as a support for the logical aspect (which is incorporeal) to be established by constituting meaning and value in the chain of differences and similarities.

To explain the XOR relationship between axiom and logic in the linguistic chain, we bet on the fractal feature of natural language in the production of value/meaning. This explains why the complexity of language is based on some hidden logical-mathematical rules to guide research practice. The relationship XOR leads to a preferable solution over another and the argumentation on fractal characteristics provides a robust foundation both at the formal level in the creation of a sequence of structured symbols and at a higher level in the creation of meaning by later interpretation of the symbols. Both in the creation of the sequence of symbols and in the subsequent interpretation of the symbols, there is a hidden layer of assembly that is characterized by the fractal nature.

It is possible to observe the XOR relationship in the dynamics of natural language through the fractal characteristic that the language presents in a formal sequence, making the phenomenon of ambiguity evident, that is, the value of a word or phrase is changed only because the term or neighboring context has changed. This is what can be seen in the following example: I saw a man on a hill with a flag. The interpretation, depending on the situational context, can unfold in the following sentences: (1) There's a man on a hill, and I'm watching him with my flag; (2) There's a man on a hill, who I'm seeing, and he has a flag; (3) There's a man, and he's on a hill that also has a flag on it; (4) I'm on a hill, and I saw a man carrying a flag; (5) There's a man on a hill, and I'm sawing him with a flag. The contextual situation (axiomatic characteristic of language) establishes the conditions of truth that will make sentences intelligible, resolving ambiguity.

The universal algorithm that we propose is in line with Jakobson's (1990, 2010, p. 35) statement that "all linguistic meaning is differential." The axiomatic aspect of natural language provides contextual meaning, but, as the author states (Jakobson, 1990, 2010, p. 35) "only the existence of invariant elements allows to recognize variations," that is, only the logical aspect of language allows to recognize the variations presented by the axiomatic feature.

If we collect all elements of a sentence as an algebraic set, we can assume as invariant each element representative of the partition by classes of the set, that we can also call categories. All elements of a class are characterized by the characteristic of referring to the same subject/object. For instance, given the sentence:

$S =$ "There's a man on a hill, and I'm watching him with my flag"

we have the following classes:

$A = \{$a man, him$\}$—this class contains all elements referring to the invariant concept of "man"

$B = \{$a hill$\}$—this class refers to the concept of "hill"

$C = \{$I'm, my$\}$ this class contains all elements referring to the concept "me"

$D = \{$flag$\}$ this class refers to the concept "flag"

$E = \{$there's, on, and, watching, with$\}$ this class represents the axiomatic character of language, contextualizing the other elements through action and connectives.

As we can see the union of this classes gives the full set (sentence)

$$A \cup B \cup C \cup D \cup E = S$$

While the classes are pairwise disjoint, being

$$A \cap B = \varnothing, \ A \cap C = \varnothing, \ B \cap C = \varnothing, \ldots$$

We have the *axiomatic feature* when the invariant are merged with axioms to form self-consistent expression which reveals their contextualization, for instance, as follows:

"There's a man" $= E \cdot A$, "on a hill" $= E \cdot B$,

"I'm watching a hill" $= C \cdot E \cdot B$, "a man on a hill" $= A \cdot E \cdot B$.

Obviously, not all axiomatic construction are allowed because they must fulfill some the rules of *logical feature*, for example,

"a man on a hill" $= A \cdot E \cdot B$—logical construction.

"a hill on a man" $= B \cdot E \cdot A$—unlogical construction.

Let us now take the sentence S and write it as a combination of the classes:

"There's a man on a hill, and I'm watching him with my flag" $= S = E \cdot A \cdot B \cdot E \cdot C \cdot E \cdot A \cdot E \cdot C \cdot D$

There's	a man	on	a hill	and	I'm	watching	him	with	my flag
E	A	E	B	E	C	E	A	E	C	D

As previously shown, the partition in classes gives a formal recursive structure in the sense that some elements of a class are repeated, so that the invariants of the language (i.e., the classes or categories) are recursively written. This recurrence looks somehow like a random distribution or better as a fractal due to the recurrence of some patterns. This can be interpreted as a fractal nature of the language even if for the moment it is restricted only to a formal sequence of symbols. We will see that the fractal nature can also be seen in the higher level of interpretation of the natural language that is language as meaning creation. In other words, we have to separate the fractal nature as previously shown which characterizes a formal sequence of symbols from the higher level of language interpretation, which is also a fractal-like. Indeed, language is not a simple sequence of symbols but it is also a creative process of signification, that is, creation of meaning. We will show that also in the creation of meaning there is a recurrent process that can be interpreted as a fractal construction. To single out a more structured recurrence law, we need to remind some basic concepts on recursion in the language process.

Recursion, taken as a language process, must be considered as a fundamental step in the meaning construction. It represents a function, algorithm, or sequence of instructions that returns to the beginning of itself becoming part of the definition of that same function, algorithm, or sequence, until it detects that some condition has been satisfied (Rouse, 2020). The linguistic ability of the human being is related to the characteristic of recursion, present in the universal conception of language offered in this book. Recursion can be understood as the typical method to upload information and to process the information to give a reasonable interpretation of the incoming data. This model can be called a "learning machine" inherent both to the axiomatic aspect and to the logical aspect of the universal structure of language. The human cognitive system uses recursion rules for both axiomatic and logical inputs to perform its learning function.

For instance, a child, in the early stages of his life, has a simple cognitive functioning, but after many recursions, his knowledge gains complexity. Each step of the recursion can be seen as a scaling process where at each step (scale) many more details are added to improve the interpretation of the language or the meaning formation. For example, Fig. 23 illustrates a rough image at the first step (Fig. 23, top left), then at the second step some more details about colors and edges (Fig. 23, top right), and then at the third step some more clear details about the contours (Fig. 23, bottom left), until we are able to recover the full details of the image (Fig. 23 bottom right). At each step of the reconstruction of the image in our mind, we add some more details, by going back to the information we already have and by adding some more details. Of course in a prompt mind the four steps of the process leading to the reconstruction of Fig. 23 are nearly coinciding and we do not realize the nanoseconds separating all steps, while in some special conditions when our mind become slow (drunkenness, drugs addiction, or night vision), it takes some time to reconstruct the real image by some flashing inputs or even we fail at all (for instance in some brain diseases or at an advanced age).

In between the reconstruction steps, there is an upgrading from one scale of knowledge to an improved scale of knowledge where we add details to the previous image, we send back to our brain to process the updated information and if we are unsatisfied we add more details and so on until we have satisfactory results.

From the broad concept of language (axiomatic-logical structure), it can be said that linguistic differences or improvement result from the recursive process of cognition. In this way, we quickly discuss the relativistic theory of language. Although this subject is in disuse, it is worth the effort to relate linguistic relativity to the recursion characteristic of natural language, which interferes in the range of cognitive processes. We agree with Boas

Fig. 23 Deconvolution image of the bottom right shows how a recursive process by wavelets provides an improvement of information.

(Seuren, 1998) as to emphasize the equal value of all cultures and languages, attributing to them the equivalent capacity to express the same content, since language is shaped by the state of culture (Boas, 1911). We understand that the recursive process of language supports the principle that the structure of a language affects the worldview or cognition of its speakers. This phenomenon was defended by Whorf (1956) (he adopted the principle of linguistic relativity to affirm that language influences thought), Sapir (1929) (who claimed that language affects thought), and Vygotsky (1934) (which stated that the development of concepts in children was influenced by structures given in language).

Another way to approach recursion in the meaning formation through natural language (broad concept adopted in this book) is taking into account the scales (Fig. 23 in the image's analysis by scales). This concept is widely used in the so-called wavelet analysis, known as a frequency analysis technique for, among other purposes, compressing, and building data (Bishop et al., 2020). In the image of the tree (Fig. 24), going from the bottom right corner to the top left corner, it is possible to observe some more details at each scale (recurrence), going from an image without many outlines to an image rich in details. The recursive process in language provokes meaning creation (output) as consequence of a process in which experience and the learning machine (hidden layer of recursion) help to add more and more details.

The algorithm presented by us in this book is a combination of the essence that characterizes natural language for the purpose of organizing the high-level programming practices that represent language in AI. The operational principle of the heart of natural language is being exposed in this chapter through the description of an algorithm intended for human reading. For this reason, no details are given for the machine to read the algorithm. Our task is to indicate to the interested reader the way in which the universal algorithm establishes a highly specific connectivity between the

Fig. 24 From bottom right to top left reflects a recursive process. *(Picture by @niko_photo. Unsplash photos.)*

properties of natural language, simultaneously processing symbols, movements, depth, temporality, colors, shapes, which is in line with research by Livingstone and Hubel (1984, 1988). The universal structure of the algorithm can be observed in the adjustment of extreme parameters of the face in researches that are based on distance between the eyes, mouth size, nose shape, etc. What is known about the capture of structural points of vision can be used in reflections on language, since the dimensional space is captured by the subsystems that will take stimuli to a central system where they are interpreted (there is only interpretation if there is language): Three face dimensions are translated into values that, when compared with fixed values, mark a significant modulation (the meaning is constructed).

In the creation of meaning through language, we can explicitly see the recursion and scales by analyzing the above text: "There's a man on a hill, and I'm watching him with my flag."

We have the meaning creation by recursion as given in Fig. 25:

So that we can write that the meaning creation, might be represented by the following equation

$$x_{n+1} = x_n + y_{n+1}$$

which is typical of fractals (a similar equation is also known as Mandelbrot equation).

The language recursion explained here: (1) responds to Brown and Lenneberg's (1954) criticism of Whorf's works, showing how the connection between a linguistic phenomenon and how a mental phenomenon occurs; (2) corroborates Brown and Lenneberg's (op. cit.) discovery that language gives rise to a particular cognitive structure. Finally, although conventional languages provide cognitive differences in native speakers, it cannot be denied that the recursive process of the universal structure of language strongly determines cognition and, therefore, the worldview. We refer the reader to Chapter 2 in which we establish that cognition (natural intelligence) is a dynamic process that becomes viable through language (logical–axiomatic structure).

10.5.3 Elements of the universal language algorithm

The fundamental contribution of this book is the description of an algorithm as a product of the discussion on natural language and AI made in the previous chapters through brainstorming, testing, analysis, and theory.

STEPS-SCALE	INFORMATION	INPUT	RECURSION
STEP 1	$x0 = $ A man	$y0 = 0$	
STEP 2	$x1 = $ There's a man	$y1 = $ there's	$x1=x0+y1$
STEP 3	$x2 = $ There's a man on a hill	$y2 = $ there's	$x2=x1+y2$
STEP 4	$x3 = $ There's a man on a hill and I am	$y3= $ I am	$x3=x2+y3$
STEP 5	$x4 = $ There's a man on a hill and I am watching	$y4= $ watching	$x4=x3+y4$
STEP 6	$x5 = $ There's a man on a hill and I am watching him	$y5= $ him	$x5=x4+y5$
STEP 7	$x6 = $ There's a man on a hill and I am watching him with	$y6= $ with	$x6=x5+y6$
STEP 8	$x7 = $ There's a man on a hill and I am watching him with my	$y7= $ my	$x7=x6+y7$
STEP 9	$x8 = $ There's a man on a hill and I am watching him with my flag	$y8= $ flag	$x8=x7+y8$

Fig. 25 Meaning creation by recurrent law.

We intend to clarify which are the steps of the operational principle of the universal natural language algorithm, whose value lies in solving problems of AI such as ambiguity and curse of dimensionality. We do not offer "the" algorithm to solve "a" problem here, but we offer the set of steps that describe its essence behind the implementation of a specific data structure or algorithm. Therefore, we present a narrative with a strong abstraction about which elements should be considered in the formation of an algorithm to be executed in AI, so that the latter, when using the conventions of language, can imitate natural language in the construction of meaning.

Our intention in this topic is to facilitate the reader's understanding of the description of the key principles of the universal natural language algorithm, outlining its structure before specific coding for solving a problem occurs. Thus programmers can understand how natural language behaves and replicate this behavior for AI, starting with the structured approach of the universal algorithm and then translating it into the programming language, modifying, and refining it to suit a specific situation.

"Language is a form and not a substance" (Saussure, 1916, p. 141). Following Saussure's teaching, we propose the universal language algorithm as this "form" that gives natural language a balance between its complex elements, so that it shares properties not only with conventional language and its words but also with the world and the extralinguistic values that permeate the discourse of art, mathematics, AI, architecture, functional magnetic resonance, and so on, no matter which symbol is used to pass on information, which consists of a linguistic phenomenon that expands in time and space as an underlying stream of meaning. We suggest, therefore, that the universal algorithm have, as minimum elements, the following:

1. Axiom feature. Fractal properties of language lies in its axiomatic feature. Like plants and animals, language is recursive in itself, presenting branched structures, which unfold into two or more similar smaller parts, organizing themselves by self-similar patterns that continue at various levels in the form of a logarithmic spiral taken by a recursive process: The representation of the axiomatic characteristic through the recursive property of fractals $(Z_{n+1} = Z_n^2 + C)$ (Mandelbrot, 1983) is suitable for language as a dynamic system by repeating processes with degrees of self-similarity capable of transporting fractal information from the external environment to the central cognitive system without modifying them (only the function value is changed). The substitution process takes place by iterating with the following initial condition: A vertical straight line (axiom "f") to which a rule is applied to form two new branches $(f=f[+f][-f])$ (Fractal Foundation, 2020), one tilted to the right and another to the left, maintaining connection with context.

The fractal is a basic form that reappears at different scales and is defined by a recursive process, generating self-similar structures at a specific scales that combine structural irregularity and consistency at the same time (Mandelbrot, 1983). Fractal forms explain the nature of dynamic systems and for this reason they constitute the basic structure of natural language.

2. Logical feature (set of rules) is incorporated into natural language through recursion to reproduce language cognitive behavior (following the rules and performing the steps creating the possibility of an endless loop): It covers probable knowledge "if P then Q," prioritizing logical reasoning as the only possible way of reaching reality (Kenshur, 1996), highlighting the meaning of a direct relationship with the context. The logical feature

of language, being part of the human mind (biological nature), assumes (incorporates) the fractal complexity of the recursive association of values (series), presenting a particular dimension as a result of elements that were not part of a linear system, that is, the stimuli received (input) can form the unconscious until the moment they "fall" into the linear system of logical reasoning to constitute meaning.

Both the axiomatic feature and the logical feature of the language work under the recursive process in the construction of meaning (each with its own features of particular variations). In the logical aspect, recursion is recognized by Pinker (1994), who admits it when observing the consequence of the lack of an upper limit on the length of the grammatical sentence, which makes a sentence incorporate instances of one category into another (Pullum and Scholz, 2010). There is no limit to the length of the reasoning chains allowing consequences of the consequences.

The role of logic in the universal structure of language is to operate a closure, inducing the mapping of each set of hypotheses to their set of consequences. The recursive cognitive system presents this closing operation.

The equation $(Z_{n+1} = Z_n^2 + C)$ (Mandelbrot, 1983) represents structural autosimilarity in the linguistic process that takes information from the input stimulus to the central cognitive system. This self-similarity is present not only in the axiomatic feature but also in the logical feature of language, in which words and phrases repeat basic models in all languages, regardless of the scientific paradigm used, be it Chomskian, matricial, or the Terrence Deacon's autonomism of language (Pareyon, 2007, p. 375).

3. Relationship between axiomatic and logical characteristics based on the digital logic gate XOR: Provides the formation of patterns in the language (information/truth) so that the sum of the latter does not correspond to the final product. There is information production (output as true) when only one of the entries is true (if input A = 0 and B = 1, output is 1; or if input A = 1 and B = 0, output is 1).

The linguistic complexity represented in the universal algorithm has formal consistency, which considers the different parameters (axiomatic and logical) under the dynamic process that, although it encompasses constant changes, guarantees consistency of the rules of meaning construction.

The link between axiomatic and logical features occurs in a functional way, involving processes of inhibition of excitation observed in biological models. The XOR relationship represents the way in which both features coordinate the core of the natural language algorithm, ensuring iterative order and structural consistency.

4. Representation property must be expressed in terms of relation (for logical characteristic) and function (for axiomatic characteristic): The generalized function integrates fixed value (for logical characteristic) and arbitrated value (for axiomatic characteristic). The function "maintains" the characteristics of the value in the dynamic system because "to evaluate a function we determine an output value for a corresponding input value" (Sousa, 2020).

The relationship of scalar regularity (or sequential development) composes the arrangements that become more and more complex (projecting signs in phonemes, phonemes in words, words in sentences, etc.; or projecting contents such as name-rule-correct-incorrect-concept-intention-understanding-communication, etc.) (Pareyon, 2007, p. 375).

The relationship can occur also in superficial regularity considering, for example, speech as a continuum with its contrasts of intentional and pragmatic patterns; or considering an image with its contrasts of colors or shadows. The universal structure of natural language is represented by the algorithm as a set of connected items whose final shape exposes an arrangement of stochastically structured irregular patterns.

These four topics configure the essence of language as a mechanical process designed to unite varied and simultaneous functions of the brain that make up an abstract phenomenon: Representation in individual consciousness.

Fig. 26 illustrates how the linguistic process of construction of meaning occurs, taking into account the axiomatic and logical aspects of natural language.

Fig. 26 identifies a neural hierarchy corresponding to the time scales for processing natural language. These scales are underlying the basic structure of language (axiomatic-logical structure), until reaching the construction of meaning. Before stimuli pass through this language structure, there is no idea or meaning. In comparative terms, we can say that without the fundamental algorithm there is no language. The four elements of the universal algorithm that we describe in this topic bring together elements, relating them in such a way that meaning is produced. The algorithmic structure that we describe is not a substance, but it is a form, the way that language works in the production of meaning, operating simultaneously the axiomatic aspects arising from the sensory subsystems of the human body and relating them to the logical aspects of conventional language, to put the information in a chain that makes sense.

The proposed algorithmic model deals with a mechanical process (meaning), which links cause (mind and abstract) and effect (world and

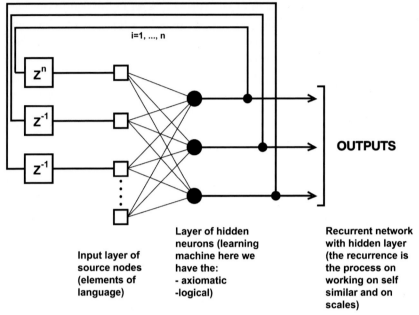

i=1, ..., n

Input layer of source nodes (elements of language)

Layer of hidden neurons (learning machine here we have the: - axiomatic -logical)

Recurrent network with hidden layer (the recurrence is the process on working on self similar and on scales)

Fig. 26 Language (in a broad sense) operates the complex biological systems (ranging from the entrance of the stimulus into the human body until the moment when it is "translated" or deciphered as such by individual) relating them to logical elements, to enter a chain of meaning. This structure adjusts nonlinear model (axiomatic aspect of language) to linear model (logical aspect of language). The first represents the influence of external factors and can be related to specific interactions. The description of the dynamics between the two models by means of an algorithm shows how much the nonlinear aspect influences the linear aspect of language, which can lead from coexistence to the cancellation of information (XOR).

reality) to play the role of a self-consistent unit of life interaction, the role of human intelligence.

The universal algorithm, as an elementary feature of natural language, is suitable for the conception of neuroscientists (Damasio, 2012; Vieira et al., 2011; Sacks, 1986) that there is no specific organ to process language, but there are generic cognitive modules (which we understand to be a generic algorithm) with the potential to process it.

The ethereal algorithm we propose should be followed by a high amount of numerical computation due to updating estimates of the solution through iterative process. It is not our goal to present a "formula" that provides a symbolic expression for the "correct" solution. The use of techniques related to AI goes beyond the application of algorithms. It is necessary to know "how" language works in its role of interpreting the world to adapt this functioning to the algorithm, as taught by Goodfellow et al. (2016):

A good machine learning practitioner also needs to know how to choose an algorithm for a particular application and how to monitor and respond to feedback obtained from experiments in order to improve a machine learning system. During day to day development of machine learning systems, practitioners need to decide whether to gather more data, increase or decrease model capacity, add or remove regularizing features, improve the optimization of a model, improve approximate inference in a model, or debug the software implementation of the model. All of these operations are at the very least time-consuming to try out, so it is important to be able to determine the right course of action rather than blindly guessing.

(Goodfellow et al., 2016, p. 423, our highlight).

In-depth knowledge of natural language shows that there is a standard structure for operations to find the value of the argument (maximize or minimize the function or apply the fixed function). The generalized function of the universal algorithm is adequate to represent a finite amount of memory. It is believed that the universal algorithm will help to overcome the challenge in performing computational mathematics, which needs to represent numbers and bit patterns. At the same time, it can be said that only the universal algorithm does not solve all questions of AI. This algorithm has the function of helping to determine goals and metrics of the operations to be performed. It is expected that the machine learning operator will also be able to make an appropriate diagnosis of the performance of the components and make changes to the algorithm so that it is better adapted to the specific discoveries of its instrumentation.

The universal algorithm makes itself intelligible from certain fundamental conditions of natural language taken in a broad sense. The content of natural language must be considered from the point of view of a system, that is, constituting a systematic unit in which the axiomatic characteristic is closely related to the logical characteristic. The axiomatic-logical feature constitutes an organic unit of natural language, whose products—art, knowledge, morals, techniques, and others—depend on this fundamental relationship of immediate and undifferentiated unity. We are referring, therefore, to a universal structure with a particular way of functioning, which reveals itself as the essence of a living and active superstructure that has plunged into its core indivisibility and interdependence between axiom and logic which work together to determine the production of meaning.

In conclusion the elaboration of a universal model that reproduces results of the linguistic system is of fundamental importance when the objective is to understand the structural mechanisms that lead this system to have determined behaviors. In addition, it reveals a pattern that can relate AI data in the same formalism. The application of this model to natural language and machine language reveals simple and singular aspects of natural intelligence that can be adjusted to AI, replicating, in the latter, a more realistic description of human language.

References

Arrivé, M., 2000. Lacan Gramático. In: Ágora. vol. III, pp. 9–40. n.2, jul/dez.

Banarescu, L., Bonial, C., Cai, S., Georgescu, M., Griffitt, K., Hermjakob, U., Knight, K., Kohen, P., Palmer, M., Schneider, N., 2013. Abstract meaning representation for sembanking. In: Proceedings of the 7th Linguistic Annotation Workshop & Interoperability with Discourse, Association for Computational Linguistics, Sofia, Bulgaria, 8–9 August 2013, pp. 178–186.

Beeson, M., 1988. Computerizing mathematics: logic and computation. In: Herken, R. (Ed.), The Universal Turing Machine. Kammerer & Unverzagt, Berlin.

Bishop, M., Brennan, W., Huo, D., Chi, Z., 2020. Spatial analysis and modeling in geomorphology. In: Reference Module in Earth Systems and Environmental Sciences. Elsevier. Science Direct.

Boas, F., 1911. Handbook of American Indian languages. In: 1. Bureau of American Ethnology, Bulletin 40. Government Print Office, Smithsonian Institute, Bureau of American Ethnology, Washington.

Bowman, S., Angeli, G., Potts, C., Manning, C., 2015. A large annotated corpus for learning natural language inference. In: Proceedings of the 2015 Conference on Empirical Methods in Natural Language Processing (EMNLP).

Brown, R., Lenneberg, E, 1954. A study in language and cognition. J. Abnorm. Soc. Psychol. 49 (3), 454.

Chomsky, N., 1957. Syntactic Structures. MIT Press, Cambridge, MA.

Chomsky, N., 2001. Le langage et la pensée. Coll. Petite Bibliothèque Payot. Payot-Rivages, Paris.

Damasio, A., 2012. O Erro de Descartes: emoção, razão e o cérebro humano, tradução Dora Vicente, Georgina Segurado, third ed. Companhia das Letras, São Paulo.

Ding, N., Melloni, L., Zhang, H., Tian, X., Poeppel, D., 2016. Cortical tracking of hierarchical linguistic structures in connected speech. In: Nature Neuroscience. v. 19, pp. 158–164.

Dretske, F., 1995. Naturalizing the Mind. The MIT Press, Cambridge, MA.

Foucault, M., 1963. Naissance de la Clinique. Presses Universitaires de France, Paris.

Foucault, M., 1966. Les mots et les choses. Gallimard, Paris.

Foucault, M., 1969. L'archéologie du savoir. Gallimard, Paris.

Foucault, M., 1971. L'ordre du Discours. Gallimard, Paris.

Fractal Foundation, 2020. https://fractalfoundation.org/. (Accessed 11 November 2020).

Gaufey, G., 1998. El lazo especular. Un estudio traversero de la unidad imaginaria, Leguizamón, G. (trad.). Edelp SA, Argentina.

Goodfellow, I., Bengio, Y., Courville, A., 2016. Deep Learning. MIT Press, Cambridge, MA.

Hegel, R., 1956. The Philosophy of History (J. Sibree, Trans.). Dover, New York.

Jakobson, R., 1990. Two aspects of language and two types of aphasic disturbances. In: Language. 1990. Harvard University Press, Cambridge, pp. 115–133.

Jakobson, R., 2010. Linguística e Comunicação. Bliknstein, I. e Paes, J. (trad.), Ed. Cultrix, São Paulo.

Kenshur, O., 1996. Doubt, certainty, faith and ideology. Gross, P., Levitt, N., Lewis, M. (Eds.), The Flight from Science and Reason, The New York Academy of Sciences, New York.

Lacan, J., 1970. Radiophonie. Seuil, Paris.

Lenneberg, E., 1967. Biological Foundations of Language. John Wiley and Sons, New York.

Livingstone, M., Hubel, D., 1984. Anatomy and physiology of a color system in the primate visual cortex. J. Neurosci. 4, 309–356.

Livingstone, M., Hubel, D., 1988. Do the relative mapping densities of the magno- and parvocellular systems vary with eccentricity? J. Neurosci. 8 (11), 4334–4339.

MacCartney, B., Galley, M., Manning, C., 2008. A phrase-based alignment model for natural language inference. Association for computational linguistics. In: Proceedings of EMNLP-08.

Mandelbrot, B., 1983. The Fractal Geometry of Nature. Macmillan.

Mobahi, H., Fisher, J., 2015. A theoretical analysis of optimization by Gaussian continuation. In: AAAI 2015, p. 327.

Moles, A., 1978. Théorie de l'information et perceptionesthétique. Flamarion, Paris. Portuguese version Cunha, H. (transl.). Rio de Janeiro: Ed Tempo Brasileiro Ltda.

Monte-Serrat, D., Belgacem, F., Maldonato, M., 2017. Decision making: the complexity of choice processes. Int. J. Res. Methodol. Soc. Sci. 3 (4). 22, Oct–Dec 2017.

Nielsen, M., 2015. Neural Networks and Deep Learning. Determination Press.

Pareyon, G., 2007. Fractal theory and language: the form of macrolinguistics. In: Form and Symmetry: Art and Science Buenos Aires Congress, pp. 374–377.

Pêcheux, M., 1975. Les vérités de La Palice. Linguistique, sémantique, philosophie (Théorie). Maspero, Paris.

Pêcheux, M., 1988. Discourse: Structure or Event. Illinois University Press.

Picasso, P., 1945. Le Taureau, State IV. Museum of Modern Art, New York.

Pinheiro, V., 2010. Um modelo semântico inferencialista para expressão e raciocínio em sistemas de linguagem natural. Tese (Doutorado)—Universidade Federal do Ceará, Brasil.

Pinker, S., 1994. The Language Instinct. Harper-Collins Publishers Inc., New York.

Pitt, D., 2020. Mental representation. In: The Stanford Encyclopedia of Philosophy. Stanford University, Spring Edition, Stanford, CA.

Pullum, G., Scholz, B., 2010. Recursion and the infinitude claim. In: Hulst, H. (Ed.), Recursion and Human Language. Walter de Gruyter.

Quinet, A., 2003. Le plus de regard: Destins de la pulsion scopique. Étude psychanalytique. Ed. du Champ lacanien, Paris.

Rouse, M., 2020. Recursion. In: Whatls.com, Tech Target. Retrieved from https://whatis. techtarget.com/definition/recursion. (Accessed 18 September 2020).

Sacks, O., 1986. The Man Who Mistook his Wife for a Hat and Other Clinical Tales. Alfred A. Knopf, New York.

Sapir, E., 1929. The status of linguistics as a science. In: Language. 5, pp. 207–214 (4).

Saussure, F., 1916. In: Bally, C., Sechehaye, A. (Eds.), Cours de linguistique Générale, third ed. Payot, Paris.

Seuren, P., 1998. Western Linguistics: An Historical Introduction. Wiley-Blackwell.

Sousa, J., 2020. Determine if a relation is a function. In: Lumen Learning Courses, College Algebra, Characteristics of Functions and Their Graphics. Retrieved from https:// courses.lumenlearning.com/wmopen-collegealgebra/chapter/introduction-characteristics-of-functions-and-their-graphs/. (Accessed 16 August 2020).

Vieira, A.C., Roazzi, A., Queiroga, B., Asfora, R., Valença, M., 2011. Afasias e Áreas Cerebrais: Argumentos Prós e Contras à Perspectiva Localizacionista. Psicologia: Reflexão e Crítica 24 (3), 588–596.

Vygotsky, L., 1934. Thought and Language. MIT Press, Cambridge, MA.

White, H., 1991. In: Jobin, J. (Ed.), O valor da narratividade na representação da realidade. Instituto de Letras da UFF, Niterói (trad.).

Whitehead, A., Russell, B., 1910. The Principia Mathematica. Cambridge University Press, Cambridge.

Whorf, B., 1956. Language, thought, and reality. In: Carroll, J. (Ed.), Selected Writings of Benjamin Lee Whorf. MIT Press.

Further reading

Cattani, C., 2010a. Fractal patterns in prime numbers distribution. In: Taniar, A., et al. (Eds.), Computational Science and its Applications. ICCSA, Springer-Verlag, Berlin, Heidelberg, pp. 164–176. LNCS 6017, Part 2.

Cattani, C., 2010b. Fractals and hidden symmetries in DNA. In: Mathematical Problems in Engineering. vol. 2010, pp. 1–31.

Cattani, C., 2011. On the existence of wavelet symmetries in archaea DNA. In: Computational and Mathematical Methods in Medicine. vol. 2011, pp. 1–21.

Cattani, C., 2012. Complexity and symmetries in DNA sequences. In: Elloumi, M., Zomaya, A.Y. (Eds.), Handbook of Biological Discover. Wiley Series in Bioinformatics, John Wiley& Sons, pp. 700–742 (Chapter 2).

Cattani, C., 2013. Wavelet algorithms for DNA analysis. In: Elloumi, M., Zomaya, A. (Eds.), Algorithms in Computational Molecular Biology: Techniques, Approaches and Applications. Wiley Series in Bioinformatics, John Wiley& Sons, pp. 799–842.

Cattani, C., Ciancio, A., 2016. On the fractal distribution of primes and prime-indexed primes by the binary image analysis. In: Physisca A: Statistical Mechanics and Its Applications. 460, pp. 222–229.

Cattani, C., Pierro, G., 2011. Complexity on acute myeloid leukemia mRNA transcript variant. In: Mathematical Problems in Engineering. vol. 2011, pp. 1–16.

Cattani, C., Pierro, G., 2013. On the fractal geometry of DNA by the binary image analysis. In: Bulletin of Mathematical Biology, pp. 1–27.

Cattani, C., Pierro, G., Altieri, G., 2011. Entropy and multi-fractality for the myeloma multiple TET 2 gene. In: Mathematical Problems in Engineering. vol. 2011. MPE, pp. 1–17.

CHAPTER ELEVEN

Conclusion

Le seul véritable voyage [...] ce ne serait pas d'aller vers de nouveaux paysages, mais d'avoir d'autres yeux [...].

(Marcel Proust, 1923).

In this book, we show new eyes ("noveaux yeux" according to Proust, 1923) on the concept of language, showing that the latter is strictly linked to different ways of objectifying the outside world by the human brain. We also show that language process consists of two essential elements: The element of causality (logical structure) that runs through intuition (axiomatic structure) and dominates it in a certain way, designating the meaning.

This comprehensive view encompasses a synchrony that connects several interdependent subsystems and reflects the periodicity of a dynamic system. The investigation of natural language from this point of view led us to observe how it organizes information taken from the context to build meaning, that is, uniting logical reasoning to the human body and the social context. This connection happens because the mind is relational and works according to a functional hierarchy to build the process of understanding. The criteria of "value" and "hierarchy" (relations) of the context are combined with rhythm, form, and movement in the appreciation of how meaning is constructed.

Artificial intelligence (AI) seeks to replicate qualities of natural language to map the learning of AI representation. Once "intelligence" is linked to the "way" how language constructs meaning, we find a point of overlap between natural language and machine language: A structured thread in the functioning of language that ensures coherence between reality and truth, the axiomatic-logical, which gives both an ethereal characteristic.

This book provides a generic formula that enables AI to perform specific tasks "in relation to" a specific context. The major contribution is in teaching AI to generalize the collection and execution of a set of more specific underlying factors, preventing the curse of dimensionality. Our universal model, therefore, specifies a generalized function (representational capacity) in the universal algorithm, which may be useful in specific cases.

The Natural Language for Artificial Intelligence
https://doi.org/10.1016/B978-0-12-824118-9.00008-4

As taught by Cassirer (1972, pp. 32–33), the language process takes place even within empirical research because the scientific way of constructing the representation of a phenomenon ends up describing the latter as a formal (logical) unit of consciousness. In this way the scientific branches tend to build a unity in the interpretation of the phenomena. This leads us to deduce that there is a structure governing the thought (Levitt, 1996) so that it does not fall into multiple private interpretations.

AI must be aware of the way in which science explores the axiomatic-logical characteristics of language—if it places value on the axiomatic characteristic, which allows the individual to represent the world in an individualized way; or if its value is focused on the logical characteristic, allowing the individual to represent the world in a process shared with his peers through the assumption incorporated in conventional language. The combination of the relationship between these characteristics of language varies widely according to the scientific branch in question, which, in turn, will influence the formation of meaning.

On the other hand, it is important that AI knows the general law that governs natural language. The universal language structure described in this book is not related to a collection of special states of language, but to something that is capable of harboring the indeterminate future of complex language. It is a universal structure owed to its potential, its characteristic of hosting the creation that is in the future. Being aware of how natural language behaves does not mean dimensioning or directing all its uses, which is impractical due to its complexity and the impossibility of describing all the specific circumstances of its use. All that is needed is just to apprehend the indications of "how" natural language takes one direction or another in the branches of science because in these cases it will present a constant that will act as a comparison model, making AI more successful. The calibration of artificial language to the way natural language behaves in different branches of science, considering the universal structure of the latter, means that we do not underestimate the process of construction of meanings, preventing the advent of ambiguity.

In summary, the beauty of this book is the fusion of natural sciences, humanities, and formal sciences, describing the vastness of these areas of knowledge from a few basic principles of natural intelligence that can be tested experimentally and replicated to AI. We ignore theoretical misconceptions and contradictions to dwell on opportunities for unification around a structure with ethereal characteristics that is repeated as the basis for infinite combinations.

References

Cassirer, E., 1972. La philosophie des formes symboliques. La pensée mythique. Editions Minuit, Paris.

Levitt, N., 1996. Mathematics as stepchild of contemporary culture. In: Gross, P., Levitt, N., Lewis, M. (Eds.), The Flight from Science and Reason. Annals of the New York Academy of Sciences.

Proust, M., 1923. A la recherch du temps perdu. La prisonnière, France.

Index

Note: Page numbers followed by *f* indicate figures.

Printed in the United States
by Baker & Taylor Publisher Services